REAL TIME STRATEGIC CHANGE

How to Involve an Entire Organization in Fast and Far-Reaching Change

ROBERT W. JACOBS

Berrett-Koehler Publishers
San Francisco

Berrett-Koehler Publishers, Inc.
155 Montgomery St.
San Francisco, CA 94104-4109
Tel: 415-288-0260   Fax: 415-362-2512

Ordering information
Individual sales. Berrett-Koehler publications are available through most bookstores. They can also be ordered direct from Berrett-Koehler at the address above.

Quantity sales. Special discounts are available on quantity purchases by corporations, associations, and others. For details, write to the "Special Sales Department" at the Berrett-Koehler address above.

Orders for college textbook/course adoption use. Please contact Berrett-Koehler Publishers at the address above.

Orders by U.S. trade bookstores and wholesalers. Please contact Publishers Group West, 4065 Hollis St., Box 8843, Emeryville, CA 94608; 510-658-3453; 1-800-788-3123.

Printed in the United States of America

Printed on acid-free and recycled paper that meets the strictest state and U.S. guidelines for recycled paper (50 percent recycled waste, including 10 percent postconsumer waste).

Library of Congress Cataloging-in-Publication Data
Jacobs, Robert W., 1963–
    Real time strategic change : how to involve an entire organization in fast and far-reaching change / Robert W. Jacobs
        p.   cm.
    Includes index.
    ISBN 1-881052-45-1 (hc : alk. paper)
    1. Organizational change—Management. 2. Management—Employee participation
I. Title
HD58.8.J336   1994
658.4´06—dc20   94-13444
                                                                             CIP

First Edition
99 98 97 96 95   10 9 8 7 6 5 4 3 2

Book designer: Detta Penna
Production: Penna Design and Production, San Carlos, CA
Copyeditor: Joyce Connelley

Cover designer: Cassandra Chu

For Cheryl, Alison, and Aaron

CONTENTS

PART III   GETTING STARTED IN YOUR OWN ORGANIZATION

PART IV   PUSHING THE BOUNDARIES OF REAL TIME STRATEGIC CHANGE

PREFACE

Too many organizational change efforts result in frustrated leaders, disillusioned workers, and few, if any positive, lasting changes. Fast-changing environments leave organizations struggling to institutionalize new strategies and ways of working, some of which end up being no longer relevant by the time they are implemented. Skeptics complain about "flavor of the month" change efforts—and understandably so—as they continue to see new programs and initiatives launched to do what others have failed to deliver. At some level, leaders and workers alike have learned to live with these sub-optimal results as no better choices seem available. And yet, something needs to be done.

I believe the vast majority of these efforts fall short for a very simple reason—the key people who are interested in and affected by these changes are not included in planning and implementing them. By involvement, I mean engaging these people in deep and profound ways, not just inviting them to a mass meeting to hear someone else tell them how they are going to be doing business differently in the future. Yet engaging the hundreds or even thousands of people who comprise some organizations at this deep and profound level seems like a pipe-dream to most people.

So instead, small groups of well-intentioned—and sometimes even well-supported—people apply themselves with firm resolve to addressing the issues they and their organizations face. Unfortunately, although these same people may bring about remarkable changes in how they do business, they alone cannot shift the future course of the entire organization. In fact, the more progress these small bands of believers make, the worse off the total organization is in the long run. This is because their decisions and actions support their own cause instead of the aims of the larger enterprise. The results are generally the same regardless of whether these small groups are comprised of the top leadership team, a group of front line workers, participants in a pilot project, or even a representative cross-section of the total organization.

This book directly challenges basic assumptions, often unstated, which have long governed these most common approaches to organizational change. I argue in the first chapter that these fundamental assumptions are responsible for the most troublesome and frustrating issues people have to deal with in bringing about change in their organizations. For the past decade, my colleagues and I at Dannemiller Tyson Associates, our clients, and a growing community of like-minded pioneers the world over have been rewriting the story described above. Our efforts have influenced all kinds of organizations that have been challenged to change in a wide variety of ways. Real time strategic change, an approach that involves an entire organization in fundamental, far-reaching and fast-paced change, is the result of our combined explorations and innovations.

The foundation for this approach involves interactive large group meetings, which enable people across entire organizations to collaborate in crafting their collective future. Change happens faster because the total organization is involved in deciding which changes are needed. At the same time, the actions people take on a daily basis throughout an organization are aligned with an overall strategy that they themselves have helped to create. This approach fundamentally redesigns the way organizations change, and it is equally applicable in small organizations numbering as few as a dozen individuals or in large ones representing thousands of people.

My Purposes in Writing This Book

My purposes in writing this book seem lofty to me, yet are ones for which I have great passion. My first passion is to see organizations change the way they change; to redefine what is considered normal, so that a decade from now real time strategic change has become a common way of doing business for all organizations. Second, I have written this book to help organizations, the people who work in them, and those who are served by them to more effectively and efficiently bring about change. Whether your organization needs to achieve faster cycle times, cutting-edge innovation, total quality, entry into new markets, a more empowering and rewarding work environment, expanded or reduced core competencies, growth, product diversity, or any number of other outcomes, real time strategic change supports you in making these changes faster and better than you may currently imagine possible. My third and final purpose in writing this book is to clearly describe the real time strategic change technology and the overall change process in which it is embedded so that you can apply it in your own organization. I wrote this book as a practical, step-by-step roadmap through an entire real time strategic change process. It is complete with conceptual frameworks, tools and techniques, roles key actors need to play, criteria by which custom applications can be developed and the principle-based practices and processes which form the foundation of this approach. You'll find within these pages a comprehensive description of a proven technology for achieving real time strategic change.

Who I Wrote This Book For and How It Can Be Used

In a broad sense, the audiences for this book are people who find "business as usual" approaches to organizational change too slow, ineffective, or otherwise less than satisfying in the results they deliver. Specifically then, this book is written for four kinds of people:

- Organization leaders and members who want and/or need to significantly accelerate the pace and effectiveness with which changes are implemented in their organizations;

- Both internal and external consultants responsible for supporting various change initiatives;

- Experts in the fields of organization strategy, culture, total quality management, work design, and re-engineering; and

- More broadly, for those whose focus is on social, political, economic, or community issues of change and development.

The book's design lends itself to three different, yet complementary uses. The first of these is as an overview or broad-based survey course in this powerful approach to change. Using it this way, you should be able to identify whether real time strategic change makes sense for you and your organization. If after taking the survey course, you and others in your organization decide to pursue a path of real time strategic change, this book can also serve as a reference guide through each stage of your change effort. Finally, I hope that you will use this book as a basis for creating your own innovations and applications of real time strategic change.

Another word about the book's design. You will be joined on your journey through these pages by a whole host of companions who have first-hand experience with real time strategic change efforts. They represent a wide variety of organizations, levels and roles. Their quotes, liberally spread throughout the book, and represented by oversized beginning quotation marks, provide a "behind the scenes" look at the realities, challenges and opportunities you will face by choosing this path. The wide range of levels and roles represented by these people is purposeful: whole system change efforts involve everyone in an organization and each individual's perspective contributes to building a richer composite view of reality.

The first type of quote represents tips and advice, insights, and the personal experiences people have had regarding particular aspects of an entire real time strategic change process. Woven within the text, they provide a kind of color commentary on the topic discussed. I characterize the second type of quote as individual perspectives on the entire process. Presented between a number of chapters in the book, these individual perspectives offer opportunities to pause and reflect on what it would mean for you and others to apply the technology in your organization. The third and final type of quote appears in the form of case studies which you'll find in Chapter 9. These stories are presented by key players in their own words, and take you inside five real time strategic change efforts. You will see how the technology was customized to meet unique needs and what results were achieved. Treat the case studies as conversation starters; a place for you and others to begin an inquiry into the potential that real time strategic change may hold for your organization.

How It's Organized

The book is organized into three parts. *Part I, Redesigning the Way Organizations Change,* explains why organizations need a better way of changing (Chapter 1); what real time strategic change is and the powerful results organizations can expect to achieve by applying it (Chapter 2); and a question and answer section based on the most common initial inquiries people have about real time strategic change (Chapter 3).

Part II, Moving Further Into the Future, Faster, introduces the conceptual frameworks, principles, and processes underlying this approach to organizational change. This part of the book answers the questions, "What is the real time strategic change technology?" and "How and why does it work?" Chapters 4, 5, and 6 immerse you in an example three day real time strategic change event as a "virtual" participant. These three chapters combine the actual meeting process, individual perspectives and underlying theories into a multi-dimensional experience, which forms the basis for the remainder of the book. In Chapter 7 I discuss the key dimensions of the technology and the magic behind it. Chapter 8 concludes Part II by laying out a step-by-step roadmap through a real time strategic change process. Although each application of the technology is unique, this chapter provides a context for how it fits within the larger framework of an organization's overall change effort.

Part III, Getting Started in Your Own Organization, shifts gears from providing general methods and models to customizing the technology to meet your organization's particular needs. Chapter 9 is devoted to the five stories of real time strategic change described above, while Chapter 10 outlines a series of questions which you can use to explore how you might apply this unique and powerful approach. Chapter 11 takes you through a planning process for real time strategic change events, while key roles in the actual events are covered in Chapter 12. Finally, in Chapter 13 I offer a menu of ways in which organizations have institutionalized their real time strategic change efforts. It also includes examples of initiatives designed specifically to support the institutionalization of those new ways of doing business—both critical components in all real time strategic change efforts.

Part IV, Pushing the Boundaries of Real Time Strategic Change looks to the future. Chapter 14 sheds light on three paths that point the way toward realizing the full potential from this powerful approach. The first path is one of application, the second outlines the contributions of innovation, and the third speaks to the need for collaboration. Finally, the appendix provides a detailed day-by-day design for the example real time strategic change event described in Chapters 4, 5, and 6. Although real events are not as neat and tidy as this version might suggest, it offers you a backstage pass to the theater where these large group gatherings unfold.

A Closing Comment

In closing, I invite you to join me on a journey into an exciting world you may not have believed possible. A world that already exists in which entire organizations come together for a common cause; one in which fast-paced and far-reaching change is the norm; one in which your organization's collective knowledge, skills, and creativity are brought to bear on creating your collective future; and one in which people's hearts, minds, and spirits are engaged in productive and positive ways, both for themselves and their organizations. This is the world of real time strategic change. May the journey begin. . .

Chelsea, Michigan
April, 1994
                                                    Robert W. Jacobs

ACKNOWLEDGMENTS

Significant contributions from a whole host of colleagues, clients, friends and family made this book possible. Each of these people helped me navigate my way over, under, and through what was at times for me, some rough and challenging terrain.

Kathleen Dannemiller is one of the inventors of the unique and powerful approach to organizational change described in this book. Along with her late partner Chuck Tyson, fellow external consultants Al Davenport, Bruce Gibb, and Jeff Walsh, and Ford Motor Company internal consultant Nancy Badore, Kathie began changing the way organizations change more than a decade ago. A good deal of what I have come to believe about organizations and how they can change most effectively has been influenced by the work of this talented and innovative team. In addition, many of the models and concepts that form the foundation of real time strategic change are the result of Kathie's work through the years. The practical, user-friendly methods and frameworks you'll find throughout the book reflect her bias for tried and true common sense instead of unnecessarily complicated models and theories.

Ian Peters, my friend and colleague, was a source of great insight, company, and humor along the way. Having applied the principles and practices of real time strategic change in various community and corporate settings, Ian's personal experiences proved to be a good barometer for measuring the clarity and utility of what I thought I had to say. In addition, since he makes his home in California, I was able to regularly engage him in late night explorations and dialogues long after those closer to home had called it a day. Irene Sanders, another friend and colleague, has been part of my writing this book from the get-go. Her consistently positive perspective and belief in what I was up to strengthened my own resolve and her reviews and comments on various sections strengthened the book immeasurably.

I also thank the clients and colleagues whose stories, perspectives, and opinions are interspersed with my own throughout the book. The insight they offer is grounded in their experiences on the front lines of organizational change efforts, thereby adding a healthy dose of reality to the pages that follow. The thinking and ideas I've included have been culled not just from those quoted, but from the experiences of many others who are part of the growing community of people successfully applying the concepts and practices of real time strategic change. CEO's, front line workers, program and process managers, and internal consultants alike have all collaborated in this past decade's worth of work. The essence of their lessons and learnings are captured in what you'll be reading, even though their names do not appear in print.

I feel fortunate to have *Berrett-Koehler* appear on the cover of this book for many reasons. Steve Piersanti and the rest of the people at Berrett-Koehler Publishers are writing a new chapter in the history of the publishing industry and I am delighted to be able to play a role in their unfolding story. My involvement was welcomed and encouraged in every aspect of the editing, production and marketing of this book—a rare and powerful example of partnership in publishing circles. In addition, Steve's editorial comments and suggestions challenged me to deliver the best book I was capable of writing. He also provided me with the space and time I needed to make it happen.

I extend a sincere set of thank-you's to the entire staff at Berrett-Koehler. Pat Anderson, Valerie Barth, Mark Carstens, Robin Donovan, Valerie McOuat, Liz Paulus, John Sax, Kristen Scheel, Elizabeth Swenson, and Steven Zink brought a spirit of collaboration, commitment, and enthusiasm to all of our work together. Detta Penna's flexibility, creativity, and good humor made the production phase of this project smooth and author-friendly, while Joyce Connelley's copyediting resulted in a cleaner, clearer (a fair bit shorter), and more readable text. Thanks as well to Cassandra Chu for her great work on the cover design. I also want to acknowledge Kathy Lee, who did the proofreading, Pat Rogondino, who gave form to the illustrations, and Earline Hefferlin who compiled the index.

Jill Janov, Sue McKibbin and Jerry Want served as reviewers for my first complete draft of the book. Many of their suggestions and comments are represented in this final version. Most important, their feedback led me to undertake a major revision and expansion in the book's scope and direction. Their feedback, coupled with several conversations with Steve Piersanti, led me to start painting on a much larger canvas.

Many others provided me with various forms of encouragement, ideas, support and interest along the way, and to them I offer my appreciation: my fellow colleagues at Dannemiller Tyson Associates including Randy Albert, Roland Loup, Stas' Kazmierski, and Tony Putman; Lynn Moore, Tammy Weller and Kathy Forier from our office management staff; Geoff Bellman; Peter Block; Becky DeStefano; Danite Fried; the gang at Barry Bagel's Place in Ann Arbor, Michigan; Elizabeth Geiser; my parents, Marvin and Marilyn Jacobs; Myron Kellner-Rogers; the late Ron Lippitt; Marv Weisbord; and Meg Wheatley.

My family has been a source of great support throughout this odyssey. Their patience, interest and words of encouragement were and continue to be a great gift for me. At one point as I wrestled with how to position the book in the first few chapters, I had a conversation with my ten-year-old daughter Alison. After listening to my dilemma she offered her counsel: "Write what you believe and other people will believe it, too. Anything else will just be a lot of hoopla." To Ali's (and my) credit, a hoopla-less book exists today. My two-year-old son Aaron's contribution was also significant: with a playful grin he regularly invited himself into my study as I was writing, reminding me of the world beyond "The Book."

I am convinced that my best friend, soul mate, life partner, and wife is one of the few people on the planet who could reframe the amount of time I spent writing this book as an opportunity to deepen and expand our relationship in a number of dimensions. The stability she provided for our family and for me personally during the past year has been nothing short of miraculous. In addition, Cheryl also served as the first reviewer for many portions of the book, its overall layout and flow, and my earliest musings about its possibilities.

A Special Acknowledgment

Frank McKeown, a colleague and friend of mine, has made a substantial contribution to many parts of this book. I have collaborated with Frank for the past three years, consulting on a variety of challenging and successful real time strategic change efforts. As I was writing this book, he continually challenged my implicit and explicit assumptions, added new perspectives, and also offered fresh material for inclusion. His input has greatly enhanced the conceptual rigor and clarity of the text, as well as its depth and completeness. Frank's perspective, drawn from a diverse background in the natural sciences, business world, and social sciences, has fueled his understanding and application of the principles of real time strategic change and uniquely positioned him to contribute to this book. I am grateful for his support and the value he added to this endeavor.

PART ONE

REDESIGNING THE WAY ORGANIZATIONS CHANGE

CHAPTER 1

WHY COMMON APPROACHES TO ORGANIZATIONAL CHANGE FALL SHORT

Most people consider fundamental, far-reaching and fast-paced organizational change to be a contradiction in terms, and basically impossible to make happen. Their past experience in a variety of change efforts reinforces this belief. Yet fundamental, far-reaching and fast-paced change is something that most organizations would benefit from and many need to achieve.

The factors driving this need are changing market forces, increasing customer demands for quality and service, the introduction of new technologies, and people's desire for a greater say in shaping their own and their organization's daily operations and future direction. "Business as usual" is no longer a viable response. Large multinational corporations and small local volunteer organizations alike are being forced to rethink basic assumptions governing their strategies, the way they organize themselves, their work processes and support systems, workforce composition and competencies, and their culture. Said another way, an organization's capacity to change is a key factor in its short and longer term success. The most successful organizations of the future will be those that are capable of rapidly and effectively bringing about fundamental, lasting, system-wide changes.

Despite the best efforts of boards of directors, leaders, managers, and workers, organizations are failing to effectively respond to these clarion calls for change. Why, with such clear demands, do most organizations and the people in them—from leaders to front line workers and everybody in between—find themselves frustrated, still searching for concepts to guide and practices to implement really effective change? The problem is that most troublesome issues plaguing organizational change initiatives are inherent in their design. They occur because of the way in which these initiatives are commonly planned and implemented.

A look at how a typical change effort occurs sheds light on why these issues are largely unavoidable, even when the best plans are implemented flawlessly. The following scenario could occur in a wide variety of organizations raising diverse sets of issues and located anywhere around the world.

> A small, select group of people regularly meet for a period of several weeks or even months, carefully crafting plans for a new and better future for their organization. They may be a strategy development or planning and policy unit, a top leadership group, a steering committee or task force. Informed by surveys, studies, and analyses, plus additional data collected from others both inside and outside of their organization, this team of highly committed and respected people forges new ground. Others, especially senior managers and maybe the board of directors, get periodic progress reports from this group and offer comments regarding the focus and direction of their work. However, in large part, the initial journey into the future is their own.

> After documenting the strategy or plan, including recommendations for change that need to be made and securing senior management approval, the implementation phase begins. The plan and recommended changes are rolled out to the entire organization. The case for change is clearly communicated, necessary actions spelled out, questions asked and answered and buy-in, agreement, or compliance sought. Numerous informational meetings may be held to allay people's concerns about the impending changes and to inform them of the new ways in which they will need to do business in the future. For some in the audience, resistance to the plan remains high; others agree with the recommendations and begin implementing them back on the job. Overall, enthusiasm for the plan exists, at best, in pockets. The organization moves into the future with some needed changes being made and others, unfortunately, being left on the drawing board. After an initial flurry of activity, eventually things pretty much return to business as usual.

The exercises illustrated in this scenario may have been a moderate success in many people's eyes. But the result was not nearly enough considering the depth and breadth of change required for the organization to thrive in the future, let alone recouping the investment in the change effort itself. Rather than proposing minor modifications to this existing paradigm of organization change, such as adding a few more key people to one of these working groups or including a little more time to really hammer home and clarify expectations in the rollout phase, I am advocating a fundamental redesign of the way organizations change. The result of this fundamental redesign is real time strategic change, an approach that involves an entire organization in fundamental, far-reaching and fast-paced change. Let's visit our scenario once again, but this time let's explore it as if it were a real time strategic change effort.

> Hundreds of people come together at the same place and time to address substantive organizational issues and to create their collective future. Creativity and synergy are unleashed as system-wide strategies and decisions are set in motion. These strategies and decisions are informed and considered, based on a shared view of the challenges and opportunities facing the organization, its customers' expectations, and internal capabilities. Planning and implementation merge together as collaborative working agreements are established across levels and functions resulting in common purpose, shared goals, and renewed commitment to their organization's future, which they themselves are creating.

> People practice new ways of doing business in real time in this and in other similar large group gatherings. They leave these interactive, organization-wide events behaving differently, making different choices about how they work together and where they focus their time and energy. Change happens faster because the total organization is the "in group" that decides which changes are needed and how they can best be made. Over the long term, using this approach increases the individuals' capacity for strategic thinking so that each person is better able to respond on a daily basis—no matter where he or she works in the organization—to other changes as

they continue to emerge over time. An entire organization moves together into its future, aligned in a common strategic direction. Each person commits to how he or she can and will contribute to doing business in new ways, both during the large group meetings, immediately afterward, and on into the future.

This sounds like a tall order, and it is. But not impossible. In fact, the better part of the rest of this book outlines this innovative approach to change that my colleagues and I have developed, refined, and extended during the past decade. The result of these efforts is a set of principle-based processes and practices that are constantly being renewed and applied in different contexts. This concept of real time strategic change has been put into practice and successfully applied in diverse settings ranging from businesses, to industry, service, health care, education, government, other non-profits, and in community development. It has proven equally useful within the United States and in joint ventures between U.S. and Pacific Rim companies, as well as in Eastern and Western Europe, the Middle East, and the Far East. In addition, this way of thinking has been used to significantly accelerate the implementation of major system change efforts involving organization strategy, total quality management, work design, reengineering, cultural diversity, and community-based initiatives focused on social, political, and economic issues. Because these initiatives rarely occur in isolation from each other, we have achieved powerful synergies in many organizations through their appropriate combinations.

The two scenarios of organizational change described represent entirely different mindsets and yield substantially different results. Most organizations have tried for years to implement organization-wide changes through numerous variations on the first scenario. These small scale methods take longer, cost more—in opportunities lost, as well as in money spent—and are ultimately less effective than the large scale approach described in this book. I also believe that the design of the change effort described in the first scenario inherently contributes to why many improvement initiatives produce less than they promise and result in more "business as usual" instead of delivering what's really needed—fast and far-reaching, system-wide change.

Life cycles of products, technology, services and processes continue to get shorter. Despite people's best efforts, it is clear that many organizations are falling behind the power curve of change that exists worldwide. We may feel capable of supporting, managing, and leading change efforts in small teams of ten or even twenty people; however, many organizations are comprised of hundreds or even hundreds of thousands of people. This sheer size and the scope of the changes required leave those committed to leading positive, directed change efforts quietly resigned to the limitations of approaches they currently possess. The need to build clarity, commitment, and collaboration across an entire organization is a critical component of any change effort. However, most people's experiences suggest that meeting this need is more wishful thinking than a deliverable result. Unfortunately, many change efforts confirm this suspicion by falling out as too little too late, being too limited or incremental in scope, or by categorically being referred to as outright failures by their architects, implementers, and those ultimately affected by the proposed changes.

Four Common Approaches to Organization Change

Over the years I have listened to people from all levels and in all kinds of organizations vent their frustrations about how "the system" normally operates and how difficult (or even impossible) it has proven to bring about change in the status quo. In reflecting on what I've seen in many different organizations, I categorize these less than satisfying experiences into four common approaches.

Top-Down Strategies

The first of these generic approaches is what could be referred to as a top-down strategy in which an organization's leadership team decides which changes need to be made. In most organizations using this approach, brief large group meetings are held in which leaders explain why new ways of doing business are needed and what will be required from people in the organization to successfully bring about this particular set of changes. Other less participation minded organizations following a top-down philosophy issue substantive business changes through the publication and distribution of strategic plans, task force reports and executive memos. In top-down organizations, the desired changes are rarely crystal clear to everyone, even those prepared to listen; the commitment and collaboration required for effective implementation are also often missing. Likewise, a key to putting those changes into practice—people feeling personal ownership for making them successful—is lacking because most of the people who need to do things differently have neither been consulted nor involved in the process of deciding which changes need to be made.

Bottom-Up Strategies

Bottom-up strategies are another avenue for organizations to follow in bringing about change. In these scenarios, individual teams of front-line workers are accountable for making changes in the way they themselves do business. Borne out of the empowerment movement of the 1980s, teams using this approach largely end up working independently of each other, crafting innovative solutions to their own most pressing problems. This approach usually results in a satisfying, short-run experience with major improvements being made and good results achieved by many of the individual teams; however, the gains for one team are often at the expense of another and the long-term headaches for the entire enterprise usually remain. In most cases, either a lack of overall strategic direction and/or adequate system-wide coordination between these internally-focused teams overshadows any incremental progress that is achieved. Commitment is much higher with this approach than a top-down strategy. However, lacking an overall context and without collaboration across the entire system, success is limited to good solutions to only those problems which exist exclusively within separate functions, areas, or levels—a small part of the universe of issues confronting most organizations.

Representative Cross-Section Strategies

A third generic approach to change involves recruiting representative cross-sections of the actual people ultimately affected by proposed changes to help decide which changes are necessary and how they can most effectively be implemented. This collection of people is often convened by consultants and has become known by names such as task forces, working groups, diagonal slice groups, subcommittees, parallel organizations, and by other special names in different organizations with different cultures. These groups gain an extensive understanding of the overall context of the change effort, develop a deep and genuine commitment to their cause, and provide a model of collaboration with representatives from other parts of the organization that they have long held in disdain. Coordination issues for the entire enterprise get worked through in these cross-section groups as members are encouraged to keep a big picture perspective throughout the process. However, these results are likely enjoyed by only the few people most directly involved in the task force's work. The problem with this approach is that many other people throughout the rest of the organization are never meaningfully involved in the process, don't understand the changes themselves or why they are needed. Furthermore, they don't view the cross-section group as representative since it's been so long since they have been around the real work that they've lost touch with reality. Because of these dynamics, most people's ownership of and commitment to their organization's change efforts are understandably lacking.

Pilot Strategies

A fourth common method is to identify a specific part of the total organization as the flagship or leader for change. Sometimes referred to as pilots, these change efforts benefit from having a well-defined task, the attention and support of organization leaders, and the allocation of resources required to ensure success. The people within the part of the organization selected to participate in the pilot project are involved closely in the planning and implementation of change. The results of their efforts are often showcased throughout the entire organization. However, even when measurable improvements have been achieved and communicated, it proves difficult to transfer these new ways of doing business to other parts of the organization. The "not invented here" syndrome gets in the way of other groups adopting what appear to be reasonable recommendations and suggestions for improvement. Some so-called "resisters" may believe they have even better ideas than those developed by the pilot group, whereas others may resent not being chosen to participate; still others maintain that their circumstances are unique, they are nothing like the pilot group's, and that none of the solutions are applicable to them. As people in the pilot area continue to make progress toward a future they find exciting and rewarding (sometimes even accompanied by a potentially more lucrative pay scale than other groups enjoy), the gulf separating them from the rest of the organization continues to expand. Infighting, coordination issues at hand-off points between the old and new parts of the organization, and sometimes even sabotage lead to a less effective change effort overall.

Typical Results From Common Approaches to Change Efforts

One or more of the following results typically occurs when applying these above approaches to major organizational change efforts. When taken together, they conspire to render even the best-laid plans and initiatives ineffective.

Less Informed and Ultimately, Less Effective Change Efforts

Each person has a unique view of their organization's reality—what's working, what's not working, what are the pressing external issues, and what changes they believe need to be made to ensure its future success. A small group of people working together, even when combining their individual perspectives, never sees a complete picture of an organization's reality. Leadership teams are distanced from day-to-day issues on the front lines. Workers do not have access to broad-based strategic information. People in different functions, departments, sections, and work groups suffer from gaps in knowledge regarding each other's challenges and opportunities. Small groups face three potential traps in the methods they most commonly employ to support organizational change initiatives. The first and potentially most dangerous option is for the group to ignore the fact that their views represent only a partial window on the world of their organization. Less information in many endeavors leads to greater risk. This maxim holds true for organizational change efforts as well. Not involving more people in planning changes reinforces people's beliefs that their narrow, fragmented views of reality are accurate and complete—a potentially costly and disastrous assumption.

A second option is to make assumptions regarding the thoughts and ideas of those not able to participate. This choice reflects a more considered path than the first, because people realize they need more information than they themselves possess. However, as more and more of these assumptions are made, each based on the previous set of assumptions, errors in judgment grow exponentially and the collective view of reality becomes less reliable.

A third path is for the team to expand its information base through interviews, surveys, or by actually having other members of the organization, content experts, or representatives from benchmarked organizations join them for certain parts of the process. Although including additional information as part of their thinking makes for stronger recommendations, this reaching out is often a one-time affair in an ongoing process. The small group is still charged with the ultimate interpretation of these learnings and how they apply to their organization's unique challenges and opportunities. This leaves many potential responses not considered simply because less people exploring possibilities and their subsequent implications leads to less informed decisions.

Issues arising from having only a narrow or fragmented information base are not confined to the planning phase of a change effort—they also show up during implementation as well. Though real consensus is not a common phenomenon in most organizations, I have discovered that there is one issue on which every organization agrees. Poor communication is always mentioned near the top of the "hit list" of organization problems. However, a more substantive issue underlies the lack of communication. Without good information, people can't make informed decisions. Another repeating cycle emerges . . .

Some leaders don't trust their people to make wise decisions regarding implementation efforts so they keep these decisions to themselves. Other more progressive leaders give their people a chance to make these decisions, but don't have the means or systems to provide them with the information and understanding required to make informed decisions on an ongoing basis. Pushing decisions down to lower levels in an organization while keeping strategic information privy to only the top levels is a sure-fire way to cripple any change effort. There are enlightened leaders who realize that not only are their people ill-equipped to make strategic decisions regarding implementation, but that they themselves do not have all the information they need to make the right decisions at their level. In all these cases, leaders, workers, and ultimately customers lose. Let me be quick to point out, however, that this is not a new dilemma for organizations, as illustrated by the following statement Thomas Jefferson made on September 28, 1820.

"I know of no safe depository of the ultimate powers of the society but the people themselves, and if we think them not enlightened enough to exercise their control with a wholesome discretion, the remedy is not to take it from them, but to inform their discretion."

This answer of informing discretion has been clear for the past 170-odd years. What has been missing in most organizations, is the means to bring it about.

A Few People Try to Convince Many That Change Is Needed

Everyone who has taken part in any change effort recognizes the importance of securing buy-in from key players who can make or break the initiative. In real terms, buy-in translates into commitment to and actions supportive of, intended changes. Succeeding on this issue is a tough challenge because most members of organizations have seen what they describe as "flavor of the month" change efforts unveiled in their organizations for years, with few measurable results achieved for the organization or themselves.

In so doing, we have all colluded in creating organizations filled with appropriately cautious, skeptical people. An inevitable trap evolves in this scenario: everybody waits for somebody else to make needed changes before they sign up for the latest program. They think, "This way I'll be sure it's the real thing so I won't get suckered in like I did the last time!" Still others who are more experienced lie low, hoard resources, reinforce the status quo in every way they can and assume an attitude of "We can wait this one out, too." In these organizations, change becomes something to avoid, instead of something to embrace. In either case, substantial progress can't be achieved until those leading the change effort successfully sign these other two groups of people up for the cause. In terms of the larger organization, these dynamics create an unproductive standoff resulting in no winners, only losers.

A Partial Responsibility Mindset

By breaking change efforts into their component parts either by function, level, process, or through involving only a small, representative cross-section of the organization, few people end up feeling and being responsible for the total organization's change effort. Therefore, more loose ends occur, hand offs often slip through the cracks, and insufficient time and energy is devoted to ensuring adequate integration across multiple portions of the change effort. The end result: changes will not be effectively implemented. The status quo prevails once again.

However, organizations do not stop paying the costs of this partial responsibility mindset when change efforts begin to falter. Evidence of this can be seen in how blame is attributed for failed or failing change efforts. Those involved in planning changes claim they have done their part well only to have those in charge of implementation drop the ball. Implementation teams argue that their shortcomings can be traced directly to poor planning. In other cases the debate is focused hierarchically, with people blaming the lack of success on poor leadership, uncommitted middle management, or a resistant workforce. Still other organizations prefer to pin blame on particular departments, such as marketing, engineering, finance, or any number of other culprits. Sometimes specific work groups, historical precedents, cultural folklore, or even a sole individual are cited as responsible for the failed change effort.

In each approach, cause is attributed as if there were a single problem that could be isolated. This mentality suggests that if we could find the one broken part of the organization and fix it, all would be well. The complicating factor in this scenario is that each "part" believes it is some other "part" that is broken. Nobody takes ownership for their own contribution to the problem. Any sense of teamwork or collaboration falls by the wayside as people run for cover, preparing their own "not guilty" pleas and "closing arguments" for their blame of others.

In these situations, "we-they" infighting takes precedence over making change efforts successful. Perhaps it is safer to wage internal intellectual battles that assess primary and secondary responsibility for lack of progress than to risk moving together as an organization into an uncertain world of change. Certainly the outcome of the former option is more predictable. However, changes in how organizations do business are required. Arguing about who or what is to blame for why they have not been made does little to affect an organization's future in positive ways.

Change Occurs Sequentially

This issue poses a particularly significant challenge in larger organizations which are often unwieldy institutions, sometimes with several identifiable businesses with nothing obvious in common, and comprised of thousands of individuals. Many people believe committed change efforts and innovative breakthroughs occur best in smaller teams—they're easier to communicate with, manage, and support. However, successfully bringing about change in a large organization requires that a great many individuals and small teams change in similar ways at the same time.

Through the years, consultants and management specialists of all types have compounded this problem by identifying work groups with a maximum size of 15–25 people as the targets for most change initiatives, education, development, or training. From a broader perspective, successfully creating these highly effective, small teams ensures failure of change efforts at the macro level. No single small group has all the data required to make informed decisions on the part of the whole organization. Therefore each decision made in a small group meeting increases the likelihood that people are maximizing the results achieved by their part of the organization, but intrinsically sub-optimizes the performance of the entire enterprise.

Whether they reside at the top, middle, bottom, or in a representative cross-section of an organization, people in these pockets often get discouraged when the whole system is not supportive of *their* change efforts. Sometimes these very committed, small groups end up working at cross-purposes to each other. In any case, resulting frustrations decrease momentum and people in these pockets of change end up feeling like they're always against the odds—which in reality, they are.

Change Is Perceived as a Disruption to "Real Work"

Despite the numerous books; articles in management journals, business newspapers, and magazines; videos; training courses; and how-to manuals devoted to the topic of change, many people still believe that change is negative and that it happens in their organization only between times when they're doing their real work. It is an additional task or responsibility called for only in particular situations or circumstances—a disruption to stability, to the status quo. Even people who recognize and believe that uncertainty and ambiguity are now a constant part of their organizational lives separate the notion of change from their day-to-day work. However, real work is not something to get back to after you have finished changing in some way. These days, change is an integral part of people's real work in organizations.

A small percentage of people thrive on change, and even sometimes create or contribute to it out of an innate preference or even sense of adventure. But for the vast majority, challenging long-held assumptions and shifting well-honed patterns of behavior proves to be a difficult and uncomfortable undertaking. Because of the unpredictable nature of change, people generally view it as a necessary evil, or worse yet, something to survive. Productivity and quality levels often drop when new ways of doing business are introduced into an organization mainly because people are focusing a lot of their time and energy on coping and dealing with their reactions to change, not on the organization's "real work." Conversely those periods designated for "real work" (i.e., not for changing) may lead to short-term successes in productivity and quality, but ongoing improvement efforts suffer for a lack of attention and focus. In either case, these artificial barriers between change and real work lead to less effectiveness and poorer overall results than if their inseparability was embraced and dealt with directly.

The Pace of Change Is Too Slow

Even when change efforts appear to be making progress, new ways of doing business just are not happening fast enough. Consultants, or other outsiders, may highlight progress achieved, but it either seems trivial in scope or even nonexistent to those who live in the organization on a daily basis. Too many potentially effective change efforts lose momentum and commitment because nobody on the inside notices successful changes that have been made in small pockets of the organization. Perhaps most sobering, if people inside the system do not notice that change is occurring, important stakeholders on the outside such as customers and suppliers are likely not to notice either.

In this scenario, momentum becomes an organizational aspiration rather than a catalyst to further change efforts. People's commitment wanes as progress becomes difficult to discern. In a world of increasingly fast-paced change, slow-paced responses only serve to dig organizations into a deeper hole. The worst case scenario takes one of two forms. In one all-too-familiar example, changes stack up on people's plates before they can effectively digest previous helpings. In another even more disconcerting scenario, new strategies are institutionalized so slowly that they lose their relevance even before they have been fully implemented. Rapid and continuing shifts in an organization's environment coupled with the methods described in these four common approaches to change practically ensures that organizations and the people in them remain one step behind the times.

Substantial Change in Part or Modest Change in an Entire Organization

Opting for one of the four common approaches to change described earlier often means choosing between substantial changes being made in part of an organization or limited changes being made across the board. Small group methods are most effective when applied to a target group of up to around twenty people, and when the implications are minimal for the rest of the organization. Although some change efforts may be highly successful on the local level, they often fail to contribute much to the success of the rest of the organization because of a lack of surrounding support. Interdependencies between functions, layers, departments, and work teams should be high for optimal performance, whether people acknowledge this or not. The effectiveness of small-scale approaches is inversely proportional to the number of people ultimately affected by any changes being made: the more people affected, the less useful these means are in effecting lasting change.

On the other hand, as people in an organization become further removed from being able to influence changes that affect them, their understanding of, commitment to, and ownership of these changes decreases commensurately. What results from this is more modest change, dispersed across a wider area. Examples of this dynamic can be seen when senior executives announce key strategic changes to their entire organization through memos or formal briefings, or even "town hall" meetings. Even when common understanding is gained through these approaches— and that is a rare occurrence—substantial organization-wide changes seldom ensue. Simply put, information sharing and common understanding do not automatically translate into ownership and commitment to making change happen.

The compromise stated in the title of this section is explicit. There is no way around it. Common approaches to change force an "either-or" choice, with neither option being desirable. Although mindsets and methods that enable substantial change to be made across an entire organization are much sought after, they still prove elusive.

From "Business as Usual" to Real Time Strategic Change

Organizations need a better way of changing, a means for involving large percentages of their people in making the shift from a "business as usual" scenario to one of real time strategic change. In a real time strategic change scenario, all members of the organization are meaningfully involved in deciding upon and responsible for delivering the organization's results. Interactive large group events form the foundation of this approach. At its essence, real time strategic change is about a new way of understanding organizations, how they operate, the role individual people can play in making a difference in their organizational lives, and how collectively they can get ahead of the "power curve" of change facing organizations of all sorts worldwide.

It is a bold undertaking to bring together hundreds of people at the same place and time with diverse knowledge and experience bases, sometimes competing needs, and each with single pieces of a large and complex jigsaw puzzle we call reality. (My colleagues and I have succeeded with groups as large as 2,200 people.) Having them leave aligned with each other and as a total organization, motivated, and empowered is a powerful result.

CHAPTER 2

THE POWER AND POSSIBILITIES OF REAL TIME STRATEGIC CHANGE

Real time strategic change defines an overall process, accompanying technology, and the type of results organizations achieve by engaging in the process and applying the technology. First as an overall process, it outlines a complete approach to the business of change, including the specific phases involved and the various roles required. Second as a technology, it provides a method—a set of principle-based practices and processes—that is employed in different ways at different phases of a change effort. Third and finally, real time strategic change defines the results achieved—fundamental, far-reaching and fast-paced change.

Several years ago, my colleagues and I came to call the methods underlying this unique approach a technology. According to Webster's dictionary, technology is defined as systematic knowledge gained through experience. This definition accurately captures the essence of this work. We have effectively deployed this systematic knowledge gained through experience around different parts of the world and in a wide variety of organizations. Over time, even we have been surprised by the flexibility, rigor, robustness, and power of the technology. Specific roles, methods, and models exist for leaders, consultants, people planning these sessions, and those responsible for myriad logistical details that are part and parcel of bringing together large groups of people for interactive meetings. Strategic options to further support change are unlimited, while unique applications of the technology enable organizations to customize its use to meet their particular needs.

Although the words "real," "time," "strategic," and "change" are

20

commonly used in many different contexts, they have particular meanings in this book. First then, let me define the concepts of real time and strategic change as used throughout these pages.

What Is Real Time?

In this book, I use the term "real time" to refer to the simultaneous planning and implementation of individual, group, and organization-wide changes. The approach described in this book brings this concept into an organization's everyday life. Participants in large group gatherings experience, experiment with, refine, and institutionalize these new ways of doing business in the events themselves and continue to do so over time as they respond to an ever-changing environment. Individuals, work teams, functional groups, and the organization as a whole practice new ways of doing business as people begin communicating, making decisions, and collaborating in productive and satisfying ways. People leave interactive, organization-wide events clear about why change is needed, committed to creating a successful future for themselves and their organization, and aligned with the organization's overall strategic direction.

Another aspect of "real time" emphasizes the importance of current reality as a main driver throughout the process. Real current issues and all their accompanying messy interconnections are the basis of this work. No artificial barriers are constructed so that problems get "cut down to size"—a popular organizational remedy to complexity that results in ineffective, piecemeal solutions to systemic problems. Second, everyone who needs to make changes happen is involved in the large group gatherings, not just a small representative group. Third and finally, real, lasting changes can be implemented throughout an entire organization. This approach stands in stark contrast to one in which the planning of change is done by a small, select group of people. If ever implemented, these changes crafted by small groups have half-lives most likely measured in months rather than years. "Real time" means working through real issues with the real people affected by them, and getting real results.

What Is Strategic Change?

I refer to "strategic change" throughout this book to mean an informed, participative process resulting in new ways of doing business that position an entire organization for success, now and into the future. Three questions help to clarify this definition: Who needs to be informed? On what particular topics do they need information? And in what ways do they need to participate in the process? First of all, there needs to be a critical mass of people in an organization actively involved in a real time strategic change process. I offer no mathematical computation or formula for the number of people required in any one organization to achieve critical mass. Instead, think of critical mass as being enough of the right people in your organization to "turn the tide" in the way you do business currently. The number and type of people may vary widely by organization and circumstance. The key is to make sure the right number and type of people are involved in your organization. To emphasize the tremendous variation in defining "critical mass," we have achieved significant results working with groups comprising less than 1 percent of a very large system and with others that represented 100 percent of smaller operations (Some suggested criteria about who to involve and when to involve them in a real time strategic change process are in Chapter 10).

The work of this group must be informed on two fronts in order for it to qualify as "strategic change." First, a common understanding needs to be built, based on the current realities of the organization's external environment. Such issues may include customer and supplier needs, competitors' strategies, industry trends, market challenges and opportunities, societal values, legislation, or any number of other issues that may be relevant. Second, current, real, and important internal issues and potential implications of the changes being explored serve as a contrast to this external scan. This internal-external balance of perspectives ensures that informed, considered decisions are made regarding changes in how an organization does business.

Participation in this definition translates to people's active, significant involvement in substantive dialogues. The result of these dialogues is an innovative response to important, organization-wide issues. This process of thinking together leads to more individual perspectives being shared, a more holistic view of the organization's collective reality and ultimately, a more informed and effective change effort overall.

New ways of doing business introduce fundamental changes into the way an organization and the people in it operate on a daily basis. "Business as usual" is not an acceptable outcome from a strategic change process. New and effective ways of doing business are required—be they based on changes to an organization's goals, systems, structures, work processes, values, mission, or culture. Using the definition I have proposed, the adoption of almost any new philosophy or practice would qualify as strategic change. These might include total quality, world class timing, self-managed work teams, and the development of knowledge and skill bases required for people to competently do business in new ways.

Any definition of "strategic change" also needs to account for the impact that the changes will have on the entire organization. In so doing, you position it for success, now and into the future. A successful change in one part of an organization rarely translates into successful change for the entire organization. Numerous improvement initiatives fail precisely because only a part of the organization is positioned for success as a result of the changes being made. Systems thinking teaches us that organizations are comprised of highly interconnected and interdependent parts. Anyone who has tried to just make a small change in one function or work practice has felt shock waves reverberate throughout the rest of the organization as representatives from supposedly unaffected areas issue cease and desist orders. The greatest potential for grief, as well as the greatest opportunity for success, resides at the interface between different functions, processes or levels. A significant advantage afforded by the technology described in this book is that vast numbers of people from different parts of the same organization can work together to assess, plan for, and respond to the inevitable system-wide impact of major change initiatives.

How "entire organization" is defined in a real time strategic change effort represents a key choice point in the process. The issues that need to be worked and the changes that need to be made are the criteria by which this decision is made. Sometimes separating sub-systems that are part of larger organizations, such as individual divisions or different businesses, provides the greatest opportunity for leverage and impact. In cases where one division is another's internal customer, an integrated change process may make the most sense. In yet other situations, the total organization, even those numbering tens or hundreds of thousands of people, provides the focus for the change effort. It is important to remember, however, that this definition of what constitutes the entire organization can change over time as new information is gathered and the impact of early initiatives is assessed.

"Success" in this definition is determined by each organization, based on the unique set of challenges and opportunities it faces. Quantitative criteria such as cost, quality, or time may be used as measures of success. Others may include observable behavior changes, feedback from customers, suppliers and other key stakeholders, and the subjective experiences of people working in the organization. In addition, organizations must be "positioned" to achieve these results immediately and on into the future. Both the real time strategic change process and the technology support people in making fast-paced changes that have an immediate impact, while the common database of strategic information they develop and keep current prepares them to effectively respond in real time to changes in the future.

Typical Results from Real Time Strategic Change Efforts

With these definitions in place, let's focus on the type of results achieved from the innovative, interactive large group events that form the foundation of the real time strategic change approach. Just as the issues outlined in the first chapter are part of the inherent design of many common approaches to change, the results I describe below are part of the inherent design of all real time strategic change efforts.

More Informed and Ultimately, More Effective Change Efforts

Real time strategic change processes focus on three questions as a basis for achieving this result: Who is involved in developing these broad, whole-picture views? What perspectives are included? And how do these views, once integrated, become the basis of information used to support people in making changes?

First of all, at least a critical mass of, if not all, the people in an entire organization are involved in developing these views. These include all its key internal and external stakeholders. This widespread involvement serves three purposes:

1. A data-rich, complex, clear, composite picture of the organization's reality can be constructed by integrating the many perspectives represented.

2. Shared insights that emerge from this more informed view pave the way for establishing internal and external partnerships that previously would have made no sense when these stakeholders operated solely out of their limited perspectives.

3. All key stakeholders understand, accept, and can start to use these broad, whole-picture views in deciding how they want and need to do business in the future.

Second, the real time strategic change approach inherently demands inclusion of many different perspectives. For example, during typical events, people's views are expanded beyond their traditional boundaries. Whether it is physicians and medical record keepers, finance staff and marketing personnel, or production workers and research and development scientists who integrate their unique views, a holistic snapshot of their organization is created. Also, people at different levels see different, but equally relevant aspects of an organization's reality. The real time strategic change approach enables senior executives, middle managers, and front line workers to pool their collective perspectives resulting in a more complete picture as these vertical (level) points of view are integrated with horizontal (functional) perspectives. At another level, key external stakeholders such as customers, suppliers, benchmarked organizations, experts from the industry or field and other relevant external stakeholders have their say in piecing together a complex puzzle called reality. Finally, these multiple perspectives are shared and combined against the backdrop of an organization's past, present, and preferred future, ensuring that decisions and actions taken are based on reality, not restricted by its partial presence or fragmentation.

Third, these perspectives form the basis of information used to support people in making changes, because they establish a common database that results in a shared understanding and reference point for the entire organization. From the foundation of this albeit complex platform arises the capability to distill a congruent and clear direction. This leads to the development of considered, congruent plans across the organization, within each of its units, for each individual, and with key stakeholder groups. As people begin doing business in new ways, the real time strategic change process established provides a system-wide forum within which these new ways can be explored, agreed upon, integrated, and initiated. Further, this process allows the continual sharing, updating, and renewal of the common database both to support ongoing implementation and also to identify the initiatives needed for an organization to remain relevant and responsive to the realities of dynamic and uncertain internal and external environments.

A Critical Mass of People Making Changes That They All Believe Are Needed

Social scientists have told us for years that the level of buy-in, commitment, and ownership people have for change efforts (or anything else for that matter) is directly related to their level of involvement. When people become involved, their level of interest increases, which in turn, results in greater involvement. This cycle ultimately leads to their having a big stake in what gets said and what gets done. Widespread involvement of people from all parts of an organization is a basic premise of the real time strategic change approach. People come to believe in the changes they are making because they have been key players in the process of deciding which changes need to be made and how they can best be made. Separate strategies and methods do not have to be developed to garner support for change. People's involvement in the process through substantial participation in real time strategic change events is the strategy and method that meets this need.

By gaining people's buy-in, commitment to, and ownership of the process, the time, money, energy, and other resources usually allocated to securing people's support can instead be brought to bear directly on the task at hand. It also means that more people care sooner that proposed changes are implemented successfully.

A Total Organization Mindset

The real time strategic change approach helps break down barriers constructed by the parochial win-lose mindsets and behaviors that have built up for years in organizations. Through large group events and subsequent implementation of change initiatives, people from all parts of an organization learn to see, appreciate and consider systemic implications of their individual and team decisions and actions. Changes are planned and implemented as a total organization using the jointly developed strategy as a guiding light, further strengthening people's awareness of and commitment to the organization's success. Almost every aspect of the change process serves as a live, practical course in systems thinking. Individuals, functional groups, process and project teams gain an understanding of the larger context in which they are operating and of the unique contribution they need to make to support the success of the entire organization. People become committed to collaborating in order to achieve common goals that best serve the total organization and its customers, not just their own functions or work groups. Redesigning reward and communication systems, in particular, helps to reinforce changes in behavior over time, further strengthening the impetus for change. Cross-functional working agreements become commonplace instead of being seen as isolated incidents. Institutionalizing this process of learning to see a bigger picture of the organizational universe that people can and must impact also provides significant support for people to do business in new ways.

Simultaneous Change

This result becomes possible because people from different functions, levels, and locations in an organization come together at the same time and place to plan and implement changes that they themselves have helped shape. The real time strategic change technology provides a path to greater coordination and integration of numerous change initiatives across an entire organization, while also ensuring that individual efforts are aligned and consistent with the organization's overall strategic direction. This is not to say that all change happens at once. Rather, there is a readiness developed in an organization that facilitates the implementation of multiple, simultaneous changes, while promoting the further evolution of those changes that have longer timelines.

The benefit of having changes occur simultaneously throughout an organization is the achievement of leverage and synergy. The more people in an organization making aligned changes at the same time, the more direct and indirect leverage is gained for achieving desired results. Archimedes, the Greek philosopher, described the concept of leverage when he said, "Give me a lever long enough, and single-handed I can move the world." Further, mutually supportive decisions and actions have a multiple or synergistic effect. It accomplishes this by giving each person and each unit in an organization a lever on the organization's overall strategy. With hundreds of people simultaneously implementing new ways of doing business and consciously prioritizing their daily actions and decisions based on the same strategy you can develop a powerful stimulus for improvement and for achieving the results desired. Although some of these efforts may seem inconsequential on their own, collectively they result in a tremendously positive impact on an organization.

Change Is Perceived as an Integral Component of "Real Work"

No matter how it is perceived or responded to, change itself is a constant and driving force in all organizations. As a result, changing the way you do business on a regular basis has become an integral component and significant focus of the business that organizations actually do. Said another way, organizations now often devote significant time, energy, and resources to continually responding to and promoting change as part of their daily operations. Stop for a moment and consider your own organization as an example. The odds are that you have been engaged in at least one major initiative requiring substantial change and impacting a good portion of your people during the past year.

We all regularly rate how effectively our organizations do business by using commonly accepted measures such as financial return on investment, equity and capital; supplier, customer, and employee satisfaction levels; and cycle times of everything from product development and inventory turns to responses to customer requests or complaints. However, given a steady diet of change as the current norm, these critical measures used to assess how effectively organizations do business, have become directly dependent on how effectively organizations change the way they are doing business.

In a real time strategic change effort, people are equipped with the information required to make informed decisions about how they need to do business to succeed in the future, and are empowered to make these decisions on an ongoing basis. In this approach, change becomes a positive opportunity for personal influence, even in extremely large organizations. This is in contrast with traditional approaches where change is usually code for "someone else has a good idea for me to implement." Given the broader perspective to which people have access in a real time strategic change effort, change becomes an entirely different and more useful version of "business as usual." Overall strategic direction and initial plans can be formulated effectively in these large group gatherings; however, actual change efforts succeed or fail in the day-to-day decisions and actions that follow them. A key reason real time strategic change efforts succeed is that people learn to view change as an integral component of their "real work," a part of their jobs that enables them to positively influence their own and their organization's future.

Fast-Paced, Real Time Change

Common knowledge suggests that change occurs in two discrete phases: the first is the planning stage, and the second is the implementation stage. Traditionally, a lot of time, energy, and resources put towards innovation in organizations is allocated to the planning side of the ledger. All too often, implementation efforts are treated as mechanical. Even the most brilliant plans sometimes yield disappointing results. Russ Ackoff, a professor at the Wharton School of Business, likens planning in organizations to ". . . a ritual rain dance which is performed at the end of the dry season to which any rain that follows is attributed"(Ackoff, 1977). He adds that this rain dancing has no effect on the weather, though it may have therapeutic effects on the dancers.

Organizations that use time as a competitive advantage in their product development, manufacturing, and distribution channels reap rewards ranging from lower inventory costs and higher quality (work must be done right the first time), to new market introductions that are more responsive to continuously changing customer demands. However, these changes can only happen as fast as they are implemented. In other words, the *implementation* of strategic change is the normal bottleneck, with the slow adoption of new ideas and changes being the limiting factor in the achievement of successful results.

The real time strategic change process described in this book creates an entirely new paradigm in which the cycle time between planning and implementation can be dramatically reduced, making it possible to accelerate the pace of change throughout an organization. Hundreds of people meeting to align their thoughts and plans with an agreed-upon strategic direction—and then beginning to implement these plans immediately—makes change happen faster. No time is lost moving from one work group to another in "spreading the word." No meaning of the message is lost through memos or by holding countless small group meetings with different people interpreting the strategy based on their individual perceptions. Using the real time strategic change technology ensures that the same message is sent, received, interpreted, and acted on by a critical mass of people in an organization at the same time.

Further momentum is gained by the power of numbers, with hundreds or even thousands of people supporting each other's change efforts through congruent thought and action. Change not only becomes socially acceptable, it becomes culturally desirable as people see an improved image of their collective future emerging. People make decisions in these large group sessions based on the realities facing their organization, and a bias for action ensures that these decisions rapidly translate into new ways of doing business. Rather than working at cross-purposes to each other, which makes progress difficult and slow, people collaborate across levels, functions, programs, and processes in support of their own and each other's change efforts. All of these factors provide a jump start for implementation efforts, thereby accelerating the pace of change.

Substantial Changes Across an Entire Organization

Rather than having to choose between either substantial changes made in limited parts of an organization or modest changes made across an entire organization, the real time strategic change approach makes it possible for substantial changes to be made across an entire organization. Successfully implementing substantial changes across an entire organization is the result of three key factors inherently designed into this approach.

First, people in real time strategic change efforts have had significant involvement in planning and implementing changes at the level of overall organizational strategic direction, in their particular team or unit, and in their individual work. This results in ownership of the entire change effort at all levels and collectively, a lot of concerted change happening in all parts of the organization. This involvement also creates an opportunity for members to envision a future they prefer for themselves and their organization and to have a hand in making it happen. Second, people are able to develop a deep understanding of the organization's issues and why change is needed, enabling them to make wise choices regarding which changes need to be made, when, how, and by whom. Third and finally, people make solid commitments to doing business in new ways. Ideas for innovative business practices emerge from the synergy generated during large group events. Given the opportunity to integrate their thinking, people from different disciplines gain valuable insights which trigger creative changes in how work gets done on a daily basis.

Suboptimal either-or choices do not have to made when operating out of this new mindset. Because the real time strategic change technology makes it possible to bring together so many people at one time and in one place, substantial change can be made across entire organizations.

Comparing Common and Real Time
Strategic Change Approaches

Table 1 summarizes the key distinctions between the results inherent in the common approaches described in Chapter 1 and the results inherent in the real time strategic change process discussed in this chapter. A side-by-side comparison highlights their fundamental differences and the potential value added by engaging your organization in real time strategic change.

Aspects of Organizational Change Efforts	Common Change Approaches and Results	Real Time Strategic Change Approach and Results
The kind of information available to people involved	A small group's narrow, fragmented views of reality form the basis of information they use to plan changes that others will be charged with implementing in the rest of the organization	A large group's broad, whole picture views of reality form the basis of information everyone uses to plan and implement change across the entire organization
How buy-in, commitment and ownership is gained	Through a campaign waged by a small group of people promoting their strategies, plans and recommendations to the rest of the organization's total change effort	As a natural by-product of involving people in the process of change
The scope of people's buy-in, commitment and ownership	People feel and are responsible for only their part of the organization's total change effort	People feel and are responsible for the total organization's total change effort
How change occurs	Sequentially, initiated in different parts of an organization at different times	Simultanteously, initiated in the whole organization at the same time
People's perspectives of change	Change is viewed as a disruption to people doing their "real work"	Changes is viewed as an integral component of people's "real work"
The pace of change and nature of change	Change occurs at a slow pace and in pockets of an organization; planning and implementation are distinct phases	Change occurs at a fast pace and in real time throughout an organization; planning and implementation are inseparable
The kind of changes made	Either substantial changes are made in part of an organization or limited changes are made across an entire organization	Substantial changes are made across an entire organization

CHAPTER 3

COMMONLY-ASKED QUESTIONS ABOUT REAL TIME STRATEGIC CHANGE

This section of the book answers a handful of the most commonly asked questions people have about this powerful approach. These questions, culled from experiences of working in a wide variety of organizations, represent a composite list of initial inquiries people typically make as they explore applying the technology in their own organization. There are two responses to each question. The initial responses represent first-hand accounts by leaders; these are supplemented with my own perspective in the plain text which follows.

When Would You Use the Real Time Strategic Change Approach?

" There are a lot of bright people ready to articulate ideas to make METRO or any organization better at what it does," says Dan Linville, president of Amalgamated Transit Union Local 587, who was involved with a culture change process at METRO, an agency responsible for the Seattle, Washington area's water pollution control and public transit needs. He describes his perspective of potential payoffs from using this approach to bring about change: "Getting all these people together at one place and at one time gives you a lot better shot at finding new solutions to old problems."

Making any organization better at what it does and finding new solutions to old problems is a broad but reasonable goal for an initial round of sorting through appropriate applications for the real time strategic change approach. Because this approach is founded on a set of principle-based processes and practices, it is highly flexible in application, and can be used to support a wide variety of change initiatives. It is equally adept when a strategy must be developed by hundreds of people from a "clean sheet" or when the strategy has been set by leaders and the large group's task is focused solely on developing plans for implementation.

So now we are left with the question, when is it not appropriate? The first situation in which this approach would be inappropriate is where minor or incremental changes are the goal. Given the time, money, and energy required to support a real time strategic change effort, incremental changes would probably not yield a big enough payoff to warrant the required investment.

A second case would be if an organization's leaders were not fully committed to creating an empowered, interdependent, organization-wide team. For some leaders, the most difficult organizational changes are in their own patterns of behavior. This process is designed every step of the way to unleash an organization's collective knowledge, skills, and creativity. If a leader were uncomfortable with pushing decision making down and raising people's influence in their organization, this approach would prove to be absolutely disastrous.

A third condition that would argue against applying this approach would be one in which the necessary commitment cannot be secured from other key stakeholders, be they union representatives, senior managers, or informal leaders in the organization. It is possible to move forward without buy-in from these important players, but the work proves harder and the risk of failure is greater. Dealing directly with these issues on the front end of the change effort makes for a cleaner, clearer initiative with much better odds of success.

A fourth scenario that raises a red flag is when the required resources are not committed up front by an organization's leaders. Even if substantial changes are required and an organization's leaders believe in creating an empowered, interdependent, organization-wide team, a real time strategic change effort is set up for failure by cutting corners and trying to get by with minimal investment.

How Can Organizational Leaders Support a Successful Real Time Strategic Change Effort?

❝ Whoever is the leader in this type of change process better be very visible to the troops and involved in the planning," advises Geoff Garside, general manager of Marriott's Hong Kong hotel, who used the technology to support a total quality management initiative. "You can't blend into the background and expect things to happen on their own. You've got to keep active and react quickly if you see things headed in the wrong direction in the large group events. Otherwise, things can just fizzle out on you because you're busy waiting for someone else to provide leadership. If you're not willing to personally involve yourself in leading this effort, you're better off saving your money and not wasting your time. You've got to be prepared to put your time and energy in, if you're going to be asking people in your organization to do the same."

The leadership role in a real time strategic change effort is not something that can be delegated to someone else and checked in on occasionally. Treating the application of this technology like another in a long line of projects on an organizational "to do" list minimizes its potential impact and a leader's ability to make the most of the time, money, and energy invested in the process. Because things move so quickly and are highly responsive to emerging data, key decisions are made on a continuing basis. Not being involved in these decisions is not being a leader of a real time strategic change effort. In addition to defining the scope of work for the change effort (normal leadership work in any change process), leaders also need to be a part of designing the overall process, or at least defining a context for it. Each organization's particular circumstances call for a unique application of the technology. Deciding how many people will ultimately be involved in the large group sessions, what their composition should be, and the actual agendas for these meetings may sound like details leaders usually wouldn't want to be bothered with. However, in applying the real time strategic change technology, these details have wide-ranging, strategic implications that warrant attention.

In the large group events that form the foundation of the real time strategic change technology, leaders join other participants in various working groups, and are as involved and accessible as anybody else in the room. Although leaders generally give a "view from their perspective" (illustrated in the three day agenda in Chapter 4) they take part fully in all other work as a member of the large group. Being accessible through question and answer sessions, in working groups, and during breaks and lunches provides leaders with an opportunity to communicate with people throughout their organization. Most people in large organizations have been burned at one time or another by past promises of change, and are wary about trying their luck again. Ensuring that leaders are personally involved in the key decisions guiding the organization's change effort and accessible throughout the process are key investments required for success.

How Can Others Support a Successful Real Time Strategic Change Effort?

❝ If you're aligned properly and focused on the same objectives, you can react to changes in the marketplace much faster," says Ken Kentch, hospital health plan administrator at Kaiser-Permanente's Santa Clara, California hospital that used this approach in designing a new facility and work processes. He discusses the advantages gained by having a strong, aligned organization-wide team: "People are clear on their individual roles and the organization is clear on its collective role. Bottom line, you get a lot more accomplished when you're all on the same page."

Along with the roles leaders need to play, people are also typically interested in how the rest of the members of an organization contribute to the success of a real time strategic change initiative. People throughout an organization add value in three distinct ways when applying this approach. The first of these involves building the common database of strategic information which forms the basis for an organization's overall strategy, and subsequently, the decisions and actions taken in line with that strategy. As mentioned earlier, the most complete picture of reality includes the most perspectives, and the large group events provide an excellent forum for these dialogues. A second equally critical role organization members play in this process is in crafting strategy, whether it's for the overall organization or for their individual work group. Thirdly, the skills and knowledge developed in this process provide people with the capabilities required to analyze emerging issues and opportunities, synthesize new data, and continue making real time strategic changes in how they do business in the future.

In addition, two smaller, select groups support the real time strategic change process: the design and logistics teams. In collaboration with consultants experienced in the technology, design team members are charged with determining the purpose and agenda for their organization's events. Logistics teams are responsible for all of the behind-the-scenes support that make these large group meetings a seamless experience for participants. Design team members are selected to represent a microcosm of the group coming to the event (in this way they are able to get their "finger on the pulse" of what will and won't work for the larger group); logistics teams are often staffed by internal consultants, trainers, and other support people. Although these two teams are discussed in several sections of the book, Chapter 11 details the planning process followed by design teams, while Chapter 12 includes an overall picture of the roles played by logistics teams.

How Many People Can be Involved in a Single Event?

❝ At first we considered designing our events for 500 people at a time with each session being held on three consecutive Saturdays," reports Gil Rodriguez, a bargaining committeeman at Ford's Dearborn, Michigan Assembly plant and the key union representative behind the design of the largest real time strategic change event we've held to date. He shares his perspectives on how many people can be involved in a single event: "With that approach it would have taken us four to four-and-a-half months for everyone in the plant to participate. As soon as someone put out the idea of having it at

Cobo Hall in downtown Detroit and having all 2,200 people come together for three consecutive days, we all said, 'Why not?' If there's any way for you to involve your entire organization in this process at once, do it. The positive impact you gain will far outweigh the extra time and energy you have to put into planning it that way."

The real time strategic change technology can be used to advantage in small organizations numbering as few as a dozen individuals or in very large organizations counting thousands of people as members. The size and scope of the large group events appear to be limited only by our own courage and that of our clients'. We began ten years ago working with sixty managers at a time at Ford Motor Company. Now 500 person real time strategic change events are commonplace.

As referenced in the quote, we supported Ford Motor Company's production launch of its thirtieth anniversary 1994 Mustang car. To do that, we brought together all 2,200 employees from the Dearborn Assembly Plant for a three day interactive working session. Although more complex than any real time strategic change event we'd ever held, the results were remarkably similar to those achieved in working with much smaller groups. Because 800 people had been the largest group we had ever previously pulled together for one of these events, we opted to stage this session in four separate rooms (with approximately 550 people in each room). In addition, all 2,200 participants joined together for certain parts of the process in a large auditorium. Because we used separate rooms, we designed the agendas in such a way that presenters could rotate to ensure that all participants heard the same messages from these key stakeholders. This added complexity meant that the flow of the design and target times became absolutely critical. One missed milestone would result in logistical nightmares for everyone. We also made use of closed circuit television for several simultaneous presentations to the total group.

Multiple large group events held close together in time have also proven to be an effective means for large organizations in achieving fast and far-reaching change. Chapter 10 includes criteria and questions you can use to help think through your organization's answer to the question of the size and scope of a real time strategic change event: how can you best achieve the critical mass needed to bring about change in your organization?

What Resources Are Required For a Real Time Strategic Change Effort?

❝ A lot of people ask me, 'How can we afford to spend so much money on these large group meetings when things are so tough financially?'" relates Bob Reilly, general manager of Ford Motor Company's glass division. "My answer to them is that when you're in trouble is when you most need to make these kind of investments. You're going to spend a lot of money with this kind of approach . . . just in time off work you're going to have a pretty steep bill. And you're going to have to have faith that it's a good investment, because there are no guarantees. But if you're lukewarm about it, go study it some more. We had observers in from three different companies watching our events. If you're not ready to get behind this approach right away, go see for yourselves what's possible. It needs to make sense for your business, but don't let the up-front investment get in your way of making a good business decision. It may cost you more not to do this in the long run."

Creating a profound impact on an organization's change efforts carries with it a significant resource investment. Specific dollar figures depend on the scope and magnitude of the change effort and the organization's size. But do not be deceived: the real time strategic change technology typically involves taking hundreds of people out of their normal jobs in an organization for two to three days at a time. In fact, one smaller organization actually opted to close up shop entirely to hold their event. Extensive pre-planning and thorough follow-up support are required. Time off the job is needed for teams to plan the large group event, gather data, and manage the numerous logistics issues associated with bringing together hundreds of people at the same time and place for an interactive working session. Arrangements have to be made regarding facilities, lunches for participants, and materials. Cost figures—people, time, and money—are substantial and need to be included in any "go-no go" decision dialogue. However, because of the large scale nature of this approach, direct and opportunity costs per person are much lower than comparable figures for multiple small scale consulting and training initiatives ultimately involving the same number of people. We also believe the returns are much better than those achieved by more traditional approaches, which makes real time strategic change a more than justifiable investment in the right circumstances.

What Kind of Follow-Up Is Required After Large Group Events?

❝ Follow-up is crucial, too." highlights John Devine, chairman of First Nationwide Bank. He stresses the importance of committing to the change effort over the long haul: " You open Pandora's box with these large group sessions by raising people's expectations, accountability, and responsibility all at the same time. Once you do that, it's awfully difficult to get people back in the box again. None of this is a quick fix by any means, and if you get started with it, you had better be prepared to continue working on it for awhile."

Although the real time strategic change approach makes the future happen faster, it is not a one-shot miracle cure for whatever ails an organization or the people who work in it. The process creates significant pressure for demonstrable change and people leave these events with high expectations that change will continue to unfold and be supported throughout their organization over time. People take charge of making changes happen at lower levels in organizations in the early going, but if they find that they are alone in doing business in new ways, these initial successes will be wasted.

What specific follow-up or support is needed depends on the types of changes to be made, an organization's circumstances, and the strategies and plans it decides to implement. In some situations, additional large group gatherings may be necessary. These might focus on certain aspects of the change effort. They may also include people at other levels or from other parts of an organization. They may also serve as training sessions to develop people's knowledge and skill bases required to do business in new ways. A wide variety of spin-off initiatives consistent with the changes agreed upon in large group events often emerge over time, further solidifying new practices and processes throughout an organization. Support over the longer haul could take the form of gradually pushing responsibility down to lower levels; building teamwork; or developing and implementing systems, structures, or new work processes consistent with an organization's new strategic direction. What is important to note here is that the final evaluation after a large group event is merely a checkpoint in your change process, not the finish line. If you are not committed for the longer haul, do not get started with this approach. The expectations you raise, and how far they fall when they go unmet, will leave you worse off than if you had never done anything in the first place.

What Kind of Control Is There in This Process and Who Has It?

❝ I've changed how I manage quite considerably through my involvement with this approach," says Martin Raff, a regional director in the United Kingdom's Employment Service. He noted that he's had to change his own style of management in order to take advantage of the real time strategic change approach: "The key changes have really been about sharing power and letting go. Even as a senior line manager, I felt I had to be responsible for pushing forward my agenda at all levels. It was incredibly demanding on me, but I didn't have any mechanisms that would meet my needs and objectives any other way. By getting the overall strategy into everybody's minds, I've found it easier to trust people to take things forward with the same objectives, maybe in different ways than I would have done, but taken it forward just the same. At the end of the day, I've found this approach more effective and less demanding of me."

"Trusting the process" is often one of the greatest investments required from participants in a real time strategic change process. Most people in organizations are accustomed to a certain level of personal control over their work and the results they achieve. Predictability, certainty, and having everything go according to plan becomes a goal, even if an unconscious one. Control is exercised by deciding who is going to do what in the plan, and then monitoring things to make sure that they happen in the prescribed manner.

In place of control by a few, participation and involvement of many is highly valued in real time strategic change efforts. This demands the building of a common understanding throughout an organization by free and open sharing of strategic information, as well as allowing decisions to be made by those most affected. There is no place in this formula for establishing and reinforcing a small group's privilege and power. Controlling information and making decisions for others runs counter to the basic premises of real time strategic change. In fact it most often leads not only to uninformed decisions being made, but also to people who lack motivation and a belief that they can make a difference in their organizational lives.

A real time strategic change effort follows an organization's natural dynamics. At first glance, to some people it may appear that little control exists. Plans change on a regular basis and flexibility is the norm. This image stands in stark contrast to the predictability normally associated with good control measures. However a great deal of control exists within this approach, but it is a different kind of control than what most people are used to. It is *control of the process,* not control of the content or specific outcomes. This new kind of control, experienced often for the first time by people involved in a real time strategic change process, becomes a model for at least one of the new ways of doing business.

Large group events are tightly orchestrated and flexibly implemented to provide the most freedom and to maximize the group's chances for success. By ensuring that all participants have ready access to a common database of strategic information and that they are aligned with the organization's strategy, letting go a little becomes easier. This oxymoron suggests a twist on the definition of control. Bob Waterman once described this shift in *The Renewal Factor* by suggesting the answer is to "Give up control, in the narrow sense, to get control, in a broader sense" (Waterman, 1987).

How Does an Organization's Strategy Fit Into a Real Time Strategic Change Effort?

❝ The thing about this process," points out Mike Mackie, senior vice-president for Marriott's Hotels, Resorts, and Suites, "is that it's a blessing and a curse. People walk out of these meetings on board and committed to making certain changes in the organization. That's a blessing assuming you're making the right changes. The curse comes if you're implementing the wrong strategy . . . and you've got hundreds or thousands of people in your organization basing their decisions on it every day. That can prove to be a very healthy wake-up call in a lot of ways!"

To succeed, you must make sure you've developed one of many possible "right" strategies. All strategic decisions take on added importance because of the power generated by having an entire organization acting in concert. Major positive results can be achieved in a shorter cycle time using the large scale technology, but flawed decisions, implemented in real time across an entire organization are sure to sink your ship sooner.

The technology makes it possible for the thinking of all key stakeholders to be considered when formulating the overall strategy. This provides an instantaneous quality control checkpoint. Strategy can be set by an organization's leaders, drafted by them and revised by the rest of the organization, or actually emerge during the large group event itself. The approach and processes used are designed to ensure a "right" strategy is the one you are implementing. The real time strategic change technology can be used to determine a "right" strategy and add significant value to your change effort. As noted earlier, if the choice of methods for selecting a strategy involve only a small group, the chances of developing a "wrong" strategy increase significantly.

What Impact Does a Leadership Team Have on the Process?

❝ As part of our large group events, we spent a lot of time in our organization developing values that we'd live by," explains Bill Buchanan, county manager in Sedgwick County, Kansas. "One of our values had to do with two-way communication and listening to people from all levels in the organization. We had been discussing merging departments. After considerable work had been done examining that possibility, I called in the department head who had not yet been consulted. She said, 'I thought the value of communication was important to you and this organization. If you valued communication, you would have asked me what I thought about this instead of telling me.' She nailed me. To understand the power of her statement, you have to understand our organization and its history. I threw my hands up as if to surrender and said, 'You got me. Now let's start over with this plan.' That changed the dynamics of not only the meeting, but also how others perceived we were going to do business from then on. I can tell you, too, that story got out in the County rumor mill pretty quickly. It earned us a lot of points from people who doubted whether we were serious about doing business differently. This was my learning. Other leaders in the county could tell you theirs, too. You all need to be on board if the process is going to work, and you can bet that people will test you every step of the way."

The real time strategic change approach both requires and creates a strong, aligned leadership team in an organization. The top team's involvement in designing the overall change process provides an excellent team building opportunity on high stakes and very visible issues. Top teams typically continue to gain confidence, clarity, and commitment as change efforts unfold. However, it is important to note that this new way of doing business puts a large spotlight on an organization's leadership team by magnifying their values and behaviors. They are on stage in a literal sense during the event and figuratively over time in the organization.

Even people who deeply want to believe that things can be different will watch for any crack in the leadership team's commitment or alignment with the new way of doing business to ensure they do not get fooled into supporting a superficial change process. How questions are answered, and even what leaders do during breaks in the large group events are scrutinized. Harsh or evasive responses to questions and even eating lunch with each other send the clear message that "business is as usual." Although minor issues in the scheme of things, during times of change these minor issues become symbolic acts to which people attach great meaning. A strong, aligned leadership team that sends messages consistent with new ways of doing business becomes a model of collaboration and commitment to common goals for the entire organization.

In addition, the real time strategic change technology creates a unique platform for a leadership team to educate people on the challenges they see facing the organization. It is also an opportunity to learn from their people and to integrate that new thinking into their own. Another is being authentic with each other, and even more powerfully, with the large group where honesty, vulnerability, and declared lack of knowledge go a long way toward building trust, confidence, and commitment. Leaders who do not know all the answers may be concerned that they will be seen by their people as weak or ineffective. But this supposed weakness is actually a fundamental assumption in this approach to organizational change. It is one of the basic premises underlying why large groups need to be brought together in the first place. Although a strong, aligned leadership team cannot bring about significant organizational change by themselves, their support, commitment, and collaboration are vital to the success of a real time strategic change effort.

What Other Benefits Does This Approach Offer?

❝ Unexpectedly, you find leaders emerging as part of this process," reports Anne Linsdau, a group director of human resources for Allied–Signal, who points out another likely return from the investment made in a real time strategic change effort saying, "It's marvelous to see people at different levels taking on more responsibility, and having the information they need to make a difference. It's a win-win solution because it enhances the self-worth of the individual, and there's value for the company because more people are tapping into their potential and can assist us in making things happen."

Although specific benefits possible depend on an organization's particular situation, several typical advantages of the real time strategic change approach merit mention. Often people are surprised to discover colleagues, previously wallowing in a sea of pessimism deep down in the formal hierarchy, being enthusiastic and optimistic about the opportunities they now see. People who want to make a difference discover many avenues for supporting a real time strategic change effort, such as committing themselves to do their part in implementing changes. They may also provide leadership back in their unit or section by involving and informing those who could not attend the event in the deliberation and outcomes, or they may join a cross-functional process improvement team to work on long-standing rivalries, competitive issues, or poor "handoffs" between departments.

New leaders also emerge in this process near the top of the organization chart. Some senior executives see the change effort as an open invitation to be the kind of leader they always wanted to be but felt would not be rewarded in the organization. Others recognize that their old ways will no longer be appropriate nor accepted by their colleagues, or those above and below them, and either decide to try to change their ways or to leave the organization, making way for new leaders to be discovered.

Although what I have described so far in this chapter could be called hard business results, there is another softer side that the real time strategic change approach effectively addresses. This approach does not force you to choose between hard and soft results. In fact, each becomes a path to the other as hard business measures are achieved in ways that promote individual dignity, meaning, and community in organizations.

Rarely do people have the opportunity to participate in dialogues regarding substantive organization-wide issues, or to personally influence strategic business decisions and outcomes. Often, initiatives designed with the best of intentions, including developing greater dignity for people, miss their mark and come under fire because of their exclusive, directive style of implementation. Conversely, knowing how our part fits with the whole, to see that valued, and to recognize that what we do day-to-day makes a difference to the customer, both the one in the next section and the paying customer at the end of the line, can be a great source of meaning and satisfaction in our work lives. Having a say in how we do business and where our organization is headed also adds depth and quality to our organizational experience. Developing organizations that are safer, more secure communities fosters feelings of belonging, commitment, and a common bond that far transcends the "punch the clock" mentality that still persists in too many organizations today.

The Choice For You and Your Organization

Real time strategic change represents a fundamental rethinking and redesign of the way organizations change. You may be interested in changing the way your organization does business in order to move ahead of competitors, face up to potential threats and challenges, more fully satisfy your customers' needs, or respond to calls for greater involvement from your own members. This technology has proven itself to be a rigorous, flexible tool for aligning large numbers of people with common goals and for stimulating collaborative action to achieve desired results. As you continue reading, I invite you to explore more deeply the question of whether this approach is a good fit for your organization. How effectively can it help you meet your particular needs and challenges? Can you create the capacity to implement all the phases of work required and provide the necessary ongoing support over the longer haul? My hope is that the remainder of this book will serve to inform your discretion and that the choices for you and your organization become clearer the farther on you read.

❖ A SENIOR EXECUTIVE'S PERSPECTIVE

Mike Mackie has worked for Marriott for 23 years and has at one time or another held every position in the international hotel chain except housekeeper. Currently, he is the senior vice president of operations for Marriott's Hotels, Resorts, and Suites division responsible for all food and beverage, rooms, engineering, retail services, procurements, and capital expenditures for architecture and construction. Schooled as a physics major, he has always had a self-described scientific bent and therefore learned to challenge the logic behind things before accepting their utility. Mike says he expects to have good reasons for why things work the way they do and in the following passage, he shares his perspective on why he thinks the real time strategic change technology works.

"One of the reasons I think this process works is that with hundreds of people in the room you get a different sense of what the elephant looks like than you do with nine blind men looking at it. By that I mean, you just don't get the same perspective traveling around putting the picture together piece by piece, which is how we normally did business (at Marriott). As only one person, you have trouble collecting all the pieces of the picture, let alone knowing how they fit together. The whole picture only starts to emerge when you bring all the pieces together at the same time and you begin to move them around with 500 people's help. My grandfather told me when I was first leaving for school that I shouldn't be going to learn as much as I could about as many different things as possible, but that genius comes from putting things together in different ways. Although we always seemed to agree on the problems we had in this company, we put solutions together in the same old way: each person would have their own solution to the problem and the other four people in the room would disagree. These large group sessions allowed us to put things together in different ways—my grandfather's definition of success.

"Another reason this approach works is that there's a clear intent to get some solid work done . . . to align your organization both conceptually and in some very specific areas. For most organizations anytime you gather together more than 100 people for an event, there's great opportunity for things to go awry. So the big events are always tightly controlled with motivational speakers or presentations. But that's no way to get real work done. You can't roll up your sleeves and get to the business issues when all you do is listen to other people talk. Too many organizations, I'm afraid, just send out "memos of change" when they need to radically transform the way they do business. The problem with this approach is that memos can't ever provide enough information to the people getting them, or enough feedback to the people sending them, to be a useful means for getting real work done.

"We've used this large group approach in hotels all over the world to support the implementation of our Total Quality Management (TQM) efforts and the single biggest thing I've seen come out of it at all levels is that people expect to be involved in major decisions that get made in the company. There's still a role for leadership in setting direction, but you'll hear a loud hue and cry and people will hold you to account if you just go off and try to run the show by yourself. So why should you bother with it? Does it sound like too much time and hassle?

"My belief is that you're going to make better decisions by involving these people, and you'll end up with longer lasting changes if you build commitment and support for them in your organization. You definitely need some kind of effort like this, even if it's a little different approach. This is a different way to do things and will require you to take some unusual steps. Thinking about the time and energy that goes into designing these meetings with a whole group of people from different places and levels in the organization is just one of these examples. But for us, that was a helpful step. We spent too much time "doing" in Deming's Plan-Do-Check-Act (PDCA) cycle in this organization, so stepping back a little to plan was a good model for us.

"Finally I'd like to say that I think there's been a basic shift in business thinking during the past few years that this approach is right in line with. We used to think that the best organizations were of one mind . . . one way to do things. Now I think it's much more about being multi-minded . . . getting a lot of points of view and feelings on the table and coalesced. I believe every person deserves the right to individual respect for their perspective and that we need to have the same regard for the thoughts, beliefs, and understandings of a dishwasher that we do for the general manager of the hotel where he or she is working. We're past the time where people will blindly follow leaders, no matter how good the leaders are. This approach gets ideas out on the table, whether you're dealing with twenty people or 500 people. It's the way we need to manage in the future. I really think we all need to move toward what I call a willing suspension of independence, and you're only able to do it if you can get your point of view out for others to hear. People won't commit to being on a team that doesn't fit their values. Just issuing a corporate directive isn't enough anymore if it will do harm to the environment or communities people live in.

"The common belief in organizations is that speed is served better in making changes by including fewer people in the decision making process. The fact of the matter is that no decisions are good decisions if they're not understood or implemented in the real world. My experience is that these large group sessions help you do both."

PART TWO

MOVING FURTHER INTO THE FUTURE, FASTER

Introduction

The purpose of the second part of this book is to answer the question: how is it possible to keep hundreds of people working interactively together for several days, and achieve meaningful results for their organization and themselves?

Chapters 4, 5 and 6 walk you through an example three day real time strategic change event. In doing so we explore each module on the agenda from three distinct perspectives, or "windows." These are:

1. The "Process Window," which outlines the elements or components of the agenda. This includes descriptions of specific tasks participants perform, and techniques for making these large group meetings productive and engaging.

2. The "People Window," which captures the personal experiences of those who have used this technology, shedding

light on the power and the possibilities this approach may hold for your organization. This perspective includes comments, cautions, and tips and advice from people who have played a variety of roles in real time strategic change events in their own organizations.

3. The "Principles Window," which highlights the underlying beliefs and concepts behind these large group events and the overall change process in which they are embedded. These principles have a holographic quality to them in that they all apply to each module of an individual event or phase of an organization's change effort. However, I relate each principle to a specific module in the next three chapters to best illustrate its direct application.

The example event is based on four assumptions:

- A leadership team has decided that its organization needs a new strategic direction based on drivers for change either from inside or outside their own organization;

- A draft strategy has been developed by a leadership team prior to the event;

- The leadership group is open to feedback on the strategy by participants, and to revising it based on this feedback; and

- The participants in this event comprise the entire organization, or a critical mass of people from a larger organization.

Chapter 7 describes the working model behind the real time strategic change technology. Finally, Chapter 8 guides you through the phases of work involved in a real time strategic change effort.

CHAPTER 4

DAY 1: BUILDING A COMMON DATABASE OF STRATEGIC INFORMATION

Your Journey Begins

The Process Window

Imagine this: you enter a large room. It could be the Grand Ballroom of a local hotel, a conference center, sports arena, or even a high school cafeteria during summer break (and we have held events in all these locations!). It is teeming with 600 people. A podium and microphone are situated along one wall of the room. As many as eighty round tables fill the room, and small groups of friends and colleagues are clustered between them. Break tables are set with coffee and a light breakfast spread. Flip charts stand at attention around the perimeter of the room—more of them than you may have ever seen in the same place at the same time in your life. Packets of materials including the event's purpose and agenda await you at your table, which is populated with people you may never have met before, even though you have worked together in the same organization for years. This, you learn, is your "max-mix" table (short for "maximum mix"), a diverse collection of individuals from different levels and functions throughout your organization with unique perspectives and experiences you will increasingly come to understand and appreciate as the event progresses. There is one piece of paper face up on the table at your seat. This is what you see:

Real Time Strategic Change Event

PURPOSE: To work together as leaders of this organization to:
- Build a common picture of where we are right now,
- Explore and agree on where we must be in the future if we are to be successful, and
- Make commitments to each other on what we need to do differently, individually and collectively, to get there.

AGENDA
Day 1

8:00 AM	Coffee, etc.
8:30	Welcome and Purpose
	Agenda and Logistics
	Telling Our Stories
	View from the Leadership Perspective
	Organization Diagnosis
	Lunch
	Content Expert Input
	View from the Customer's Perspective
5:00 PM	Evaluation/Close/Debrief

Day 2

8:00 AM	Coffee, etc.
8:30	Feedback on Evaluations/Agenda for the Day
	Change Possibilities Panel
	Valentines
	Organizational Norms
	Organization Strategy: Revisit
	Feedback on Strategy by Participants
5:00 PM	Evaluation/Close/Debrief
	Leadership Turnaround on Strategy

Day 3

8:00 AM	Coffee, etc.
8:30	Feedback on Evaluations/Agenda for the Day
	Response from the Leadership Group: Finalized Strategy
	Preferred Futuring
	System-Wide Action Planning
	Back Home Teamwork
	Back Home Planning
5:00 PM	Wrap-Up/Evaluation/Close

Surrounded by hundreds of people, seated with total strangers and faced with an agenda that is foreign to you, your journey begins.

The People Window

❝ At the beginning after walking in and being told where to sit I said, 'I knew I wasn't going to like this . . . it's too structured,' " recalls Dick Aiken, an international representative with the American Flint Glass Workers' Union describing his first real time strategic change event: " But when I got to meet the other people at my max-mix table I found out something very interesting. Basically, they had the same feelings as I did about the company and the changes we needed to make. A closeness developed among us almost immediately which surprised me because I really had little or no relationship with these people when I'd walked in at the beginning of the day."

The Principle Window

Principle: **No two events or change efforts are ever the same.** The particular design for this three day event focuses on strategy development and implementation. Of the dozens of change efforts and more than 200 of these large group events my colleagues and I have designed and facilitated during the past ten years, I cannot remember any that took exactly the same twists and turns as the following one. Different organizations face unique challenges and need to take advantage of particular opportunities. We continue to invent new applications, modules, and techniques to fit the specific needs of each organization with which we work. We have held a five day event for a joint venture steel mill, and two day events for a nationwide bank fighting its way out of a downward spiral of annual losses. We have effectively applied the technology to training people and implementing a total quality management initiative throughout a 100,000-person hotel chain, and in implementing redesigned business processes in a 150-person machine shop. The purposes and activities within each of these events were different, but the events themselves all shared the common principles that are described in these next three chapters.

Agenda Items: Welcome and Purpose/ Agenda and Logistics

The Process Window

The leader of your organization opens the session with the Welcome and Purpose, sending a clear message to you and everyone else in the room that this is an important event and that opportunities will be available for each person to make a difference. You hear your leader describe the purpose of the event in his or her own words, explaining that you all must play a leadership role in the future if the company is to be successful. Leadership is no longer the sole responsibility and privilege of those people at the top of the organization's hierarchy. This meeting, in simplest terms, is about charting a new course for your organization's future that is exciting, successful, and requires significant changes to be implemented throughout the whole organization at one time, aligning everyone with a jointly agreed-upon direction. Next, your leader introduces the consulting team which will be facilitating the event.

One of the consultants steps up to the podium and reviews the Agenda and Logistics. This serves to reduce the mystery of the next three days and to build a common language around strategy by introducing a simple, common-sense model for strategy development and implementation. The consultant explains the importance of developing a broad-based, common understanding of the needs of your company's key stakeholders—the people and/or organizations who have a stake in your outcomes. The agenda begins to make more sense as you recognize the separate items early on as representing these key stakeholders. The logic of the event comes into focus as the model is reviewed. The consultant concludes with some logistics items, emphasizing the need to take care of your personal needs during the next three days so that you can do your best work. Most of the basic logistics like phones and breaks are covered, but you get a slight hint of things to come as the consultant concludes, "If you need to use the restroom, do it. Don't wait for a break because you can't listen or think strategically when your bladder is full. If you need to stand up and stretch your muscles, go to the back of the room so you can still listen. Because what we're doing is building a common database, your voice is important, so don't use going to the bath-room as an excuse to escape the work or to use the phone!"

The People Window

❝ When you first sit down at these tables with people you hardly know, you're wondering 'How in the world does learning occur with 400 people in the same room?' " says Anita Dias. Anita has been in charge of coordinating the system-wide cultural change effort in METRO, the government agency responsible for water pollution control and public transportation in Seattle, Washington. She describes what goes through many people's minds as the event begins: "Those of us who attended large universities and had fresh-man lectures with five or six hundred people in them have some idea of what to expect at the beginning of these meetings. You're sure somebody's going to talk at you for three days. Listening to the agenda and knowing that it's your meeting helps some. Very early on you get some clues that you're going to have more of a say about your future than you normally had in the past. In the begin-ning, a lot of people are still skeptical but I guess that's understand-able. Hundreds of people seated at max-mix tables is a pretty different way to run a meeting for most organizations."

The Principle Window

Principle: **Empowerment is a constant focus in all that we do.** Change happens in organizations when people make change happen. I am convinced that people most effectively make change happen when they think and feel they are empowered individually and collectively to create a future for themselves that is different from their past. This principle of empowerment is illustrated in three ways during these first two modules in the agenda. First, the leader's welcoming comments highlight an invi-tation to all participants to play a leadership role—in this event and out-side of it—in shaping the future direction of the enterprise. These large group events provide a unique opportunity for individuals to exert substantial influence regarding the organization's overall strategy, relation-ships they have with other functions or colleagues, and even in how they choose to spend their time on a daily basis.

Second, the consultant clearly walks through the purpose and agenda of the entire event and of each activity within it. Basic conceptual models are presented to illustrate the logic and underlying philosophy behind the meeting plan. This sharing of information not only demonstrates a new way of doing business, but also makes it clear that participants will not be asked to passively jump through hoops for the leader's or consul-tant's benefit. Armed with the thinking that went into developing the meeting design, participants are better able to assess whether they are on the right track throughout the process. (We regularly check this out with non-scientific random samples at breaks and lunches, in addition to the formal evaluations participants complete at the end of each day.) By clearly explaining the logic behind what we are doing, participants can begin experiencing the future they are creating for themselves within the actual real time strategic change event itself.

Third and finally, regarding these first two modules, participants receive clear messages from the leader and consultant that the event is largely in their hands. Participants are empowered to and need to take care of their own needs throughout the three days. In addition, each of their voices is a critical component in building a common database of information from which organization-wide decisions will be made. Together they will make strategic decisions that will impact the organi-zation, perhaps for years to come.

Agenda Item: Telling Our Stories

The Process Window

Having heard the Welcome and Purpose from your leader and the Agenda and Logistics items from the consultant, you and your table mates begin the first module entitled "Telling Our Stories." Each person at your "max-mix" table has an opportunity to meet the rest of the group members by sharing his or her proudest and most frustrating experiences in the orga-nization during the past year. You also describe what you see as your organization's most significant challenges and opportunities in the coming year. Finally you clarify your expectations for the three days, increasing your ownership of the event as you begin to build relationships with people across traditional organizational boundaries. As a small group, you take the first step in creating a common database for the organization with your own input at the core. For some people at your table, this is their first experience of really listening to each other across functional lines. You clearly hear the pain and possibilities interwoven in the stories as they unfold.

After everyone has had a chance to speak, your group summarizes the common themes and significant differences in your stories, and the common key expectations for the event. You post your table's flip chart summary sheet on the wall of the room next to those of the other tables. During the break, you read through several of the other table's summaries while listening to others describe how amazed they are at the consistency in the messages. People want to leave the event clear about the future direction for the organization and the roles they can play in transforming this vision into reality.

The People Window

❝ From my experience in these sessions, these introductions level the playing field," explains Hila Richardson, an assistant vice president of long term care at New York City's Health and Hospitals Corporation. "You're ten people sitting around the table for several days. After hearing about each person's story, you have to start seeing these people as people. You listen to them differently . . . appreciate their point of views more. At this stage everybody's feeling a little uneasy about being in this new situation, and for most people, they feel less inhibited after meeting the rest of the people at their table."

The Principle Window

Principle: **Ensure a consistent flow of information by continuously shifting from the individual to the small group to the whole group and back again.** Throughout the real time strategic change process it is critical that each person feels heard, and that each has contributed to the common database of information the organization is building. Individuals influence the small group in which they are working which in turn contributes to the larger group's perspective. Likewise, the reverse is true in that the whole group contributes to shaping each small group's thinking, which in turn, influences each individual. Throughout these interactive sessions, this iterative process of shifting from the individual to the small group and then on to the large group transforms the individual knowledge bases people enter with on Day 1 into a pool of organization wisdom on Day 3. This process comes to represent a living metaphor of the changes taking place in the organization.

It is important to note, however, that each individual has a different contribution to make depending on the role each plays. In the Telling Our Stories module, for example, participants educate each other on their experiences in the organization and their expectations regarding the three day event. In the View from the Leadership Perspective module which follows, the leader (or leadership team) of the organization is uniquely capable of providing a "big picture" view of the organization.

Agenda Item: View from the Leadership Perspective

The Process Window

You rejoin your max-mix table after the break. A second consultant who will be facilitating various parts of the event relates that the purpose of the View from the Leadership Perspective is to build a common picture for all participants of the world your leaders see. You expect to sit through a standard "State of the Company" speech with plenty of slides, but the short, informal presentation sends a different message—one that paints an honest picture of your organization. The different members of your max-mix table group listen to the issues laid out during the presentation. Some of these they know a good deal about, while others they are less clear on. Finally, your leaders share their proposed strategy for your organization's future. This strategy, once revised and adapted by the large group, will serve as a focal point for your organization's time, energy, and resources during the next few years.

The speakers sit down after only twenty minutes of talking. The consultant asks you and your table mates to discuss what you heard, your reactions, and to identify any questions you have. You are urged to focus on questions of understanding only—to make sure you see the world the leadership team sees, not whether you agree with their view. You cannot learn by holding only to your own paradigm, but must allow in other viewpoints in order to find common ground. Your table group has an animated dialogue about the leaders' presentations. You find as a group that the questions you generate are more considered and multi-dimensional than any one of you would have been likely to develop on your own.

Then an open forum question and answer session begins. The consultant rotates around the room randomly calling on tables, making sure that a table's question is answered to the group's satisfaction before moving on. The anonymous "table questions" (each table designates a question asker) seem clearer and more direct, and there are fewer personal axes ground than in any other "State of the Company" question and answer session you can recall. In fact, the consultant even cuts off a few long-winded participants in mid-sentence, reminding them they will have their chance to share their perspectives later. The session ends with people feeling wiser about the big picture and more than ready to get their own perspectives on the table.

The People Window

❝ What I found most useful about the open forum question and answer process," spells out Bob Reilly, general manager of Ford Motor Company's glass division, "is that I got a chance to tell everybody without any filtering, how I aspire to run our business and what the current conditions are of our business. I was able to look people in the eye, and I think that helps personalize our management team. We're no longer a faceless bureaucratic group in Dearborn making all the decisions. Second, I personally believe in being as open and straightforward in sharing information as possible. This approach enabled me to demonstrate that value. People can say, 'We can trust him because he's telling us the truth, even if we don't like what he's telling us.' We've got to be willing to put our problems out on the table, and being able to ask anonymous table questions legitimizes another level of honesty, even early in the meetings. There really are no undiscussables."

The Principle Window

Principle: **Encourage participation through interactive designs and processes.** Many ways exist to create a common database of strategic information in organizations: memos, reports, e-mail, and speeches, to name just a few. However, organizational alignment is not achieved merely by opening people's heads and dumping strategic information in. When shifting cultures and rekindling a belief in people of an exciting future they can create for themselves, I believe there is a need for face-to-face dialogue. And with so many people attending any large group event, the challenge of ensuring an interactive process becomes more difficult.

Interactive event designs serve two purposes. First, they generate higher quality plans that address strategic organizational issues. And, second, they build increased commitment in people to implement those plans. Creating opportunities for people from across an entire organization to interact, not just with their leaders but also with each other, leads to creative "out of the box" thinking. New ways of doing business are a natural by-product of the process. Getting everyone involved in decision making increases people's ownership of changes that they themselves will be responsible for implementing. They are not being "done to" by somebody else, but rather they are meaningful contributors to the plans for change and the process of their implementation.

The real time strategic change technology matches the interactive nature of the events with an appropriate risk level for participants: the further into the event they progress, the more we ask of them. For instance, the open forum question and answer session with the leaders in this module follows the relatively safe max-mix table group discussions in Telling Our Stories. Given that even the most open and welcoming leaders can be intimidating by title alone, questions that are asked by individual participants are clearly identified as table group questions. On more than one occasion we have had to remind leaders—both union and management—of this fact. This message is repeated throughout the event as table members rotate responsibility for facilitating and managing their own group working process based on clear instructions and role definitions for each task that we provide. Occasionally some tables may need a little help getting back on track, but by and large the vast majority of tables become high performing teams. The next module asks participants to take a bigger risk by adding their perspectives to the growing database of strategic information.

Agenda Item: Organization Diagnosis

The Process Window

The next step on your journey, the Organization Diagnosis, involves adding each of your 600 perspectives to those just shared by your leaders. Your max-mix group reviews a list of organization-wide processes like communication, decision making, and rewards and recognition from a list and chooses one for your group to assess. These processes affect all the people at your table in one way or another. Then your table group brainstorms all the things you are glad, sad, and mad about concerning that process during the past year, venting issues that are not normally discussed. No outside expert is telling you what is right and wrong in your organization—each of the 600 people in the room serves as their own best expert.

Although your table group assesses only one process, you have the opportunity to comment on all of the others. For each process you are asked to vote during lunch for your two gladdest "glads," two saddest "sads," and two maddest "mads" from among all perceptions generated by groups working in each topic area.

After you have finished your voting and lunch, you settle back into your max-mix table and listen to reports on the high vote getters within each process. You realize you are not alone. As each report is followed by applause, you begin to feel the earliest rumblings of a critical mass of people committed to making changes in the organization and how it operates. There exists a good deal more agreement across functions and levels than you ever believed possible. You roll your sleeves up, prepared to tackle these problems one at a time, only to hear one of the consultants say, "We are purposely not going to let you solve the 'sads' or 'mads.' After all of the stakeholders have shared their input, we will work together on ways to do things differently in the future. This information we've just generated is an important part of the common database we are in the process of building—but it is only a part. We need to add a few more pieces to the jigsaw puzzle before we move into the future."

Looking down at your agenda, you recognize there are two more perspectives to hear from even in this first day: the content expert and your customers.

The People Window

❝ It's really quite unusual for people, at least in our organization, to find out that what they think actually matters," explains Julie Beedon who is a quality support consultant in the United Kingdom's Employment Service. She has applied this technology in a number of venues throughout her region, and sees several advantages to using the Organization Diagnosis module. "Our perspective is valid no matter where we are in the hierarchy. After doing the 'glads,' 'sads,' and 'mads' people can say 'Right, now that we've got all that out, we can put it behind us and move on.' Another advantage of this part of the agenda is that people can be a little surprised with others' perspectives at their table, thinking, 'Well, I'd never have thought of looking at this situation like that before.' Finally, I'd have to add that once people begin to see value in different perspectives at their table group, you can then do that on a bigger scale. Someone they'd never have listened to in the larger group, they can now hear better. It's a lot of data at once, but I think that helps start to open people's thinking beyond what it was when they walked in the room . . . and that's always helpful."

The Principle Window

Principle: **Integrating diverse perspectives leads to discovering common ground.** By virtue of the breadth and depth of information generated during these large group events, integration becomes a necessity. On a broad scale this integration occurs at several levels throughout the meeting:

1. Participants need to integrate diverse and sometimes competing stakeholder needs to create a holistic picture of the organization and its environment. Understanding this picture leads to innovative, win-win solutions to complex problems.

2. Plans and commitments made during the event must be integrated into actual work done outside of the event. That is, the stakeholder input must be synthesized, analyzed and, as Peter Drucker said (1974), the plans must "degenerate into work" or they are merely words on paper, not actions taken in the real world.

3. The organization as a whole must also become more integrated through the change process. Functional barriers are known by different names depending on the organization (e.g., chimneys and missile silos). However, by any name, they get in the way of work being done by the whole system in an efficient and effective manner. Real time strategic change events address this issue through the use of direct feedback such as Valentines which are described on Day 2 (see Chapter 5), and indirectly through the use of the max-mix working groups.

The integration of diverse perspectives occurs on three levels in this Organization Diagnosis module. First, participants integrate their thinking in their max-mix table group during the initial brainstorm. Different, sometimes even contradictory, views are all recorded on the same flip chart page during this activity. (One person's "glad" is sometimes another person's "mad.") Integration at this level means acknowledging each person's different realities regardless of whether agreement exists or not.

A second level of integration occurs during the "post and vote" process. Individual participants integrate the volumes of information generated by the tables working on various organizational processes, and identify individual priorities by voting on which they most relate to and agree with. In this step, people absorb a total group perspective of the multiple processes being analyzed and begin to see the interconnections between them.

Finally, we achieve a level of total group integration on all the processes through the report outs on the highest vote getting "glads," "sads," and "mads." Here, integration takes the form of pulling together a whole group view of how the organization operates on a day-to-day basis, most likely the first time this picture has ever been assembled from so many diverse perspectives.

One foundation of the real time strategic change process is creating a common knowledge base of strategic information for the whole group. Following the principle of integrating diverse perspectives ensures the continued use of this pool of information to discover the common ground that exists across levels, functions, and even sub-cultures in an organization.

Agenda Item: Content Expert Input

The Process Window

Having added your personal perspective of the company's internal processes in the Organization Diagnosis, you and your max-mix table now look to the external environment in the Content Expert Input module. Perhaps you hear a presentation on trends affecting your organization including global, economic, or political issues or technological trends specific to your industry or its marketplace. Maybe an expert on total quality, re-engineering, or systems thinking makes a presentation to the total group followed by an open forum question and answer session.

It is possible that your organization has the necessary knowledge base in the particular content area you are addressing and that an outside speaker is unnecessary. In this case, sharing and pooling the collective wisdom in the total group may be your best option. Whatever the particular content of this module, most people complete it feeling that they have expanded their point of view and that they can make more informed choices regarding your organization's future.

The People Window

❝ I believe this kind of input broadens people's horizons," begins Anne Linsdau, a group director of human resources at Allied–Signal, who has had extensive experience applying this module in worldwide executive conferences. "When you go outside to an expert, it serves as a reality check for people because so many of us 'insiders' are so focused on our tasks that we don't get much outside interpretation. When we've used leading academics in the fields of strategy and systems thinking,
people got a lot of 'a-has' because they'd never looked at the world the way these experts did. We've also used an automotive industry expert who described the future he saw unfolding for our industry. A lot of people were surprised by what he had to say. They wanted him to say that they were living in a safe little world but his message was that the future of our business is anything but safe or little. In that case, we used this approach to shake up our system."

The Principle Window

Principle: **Promote learning by adopting a participant-focused mindset.** Throughout the real time strategic change process we explore each module, activity, and choice point by adopting a participant-focused mindset. Three core beliefs guide our thinking in making these decisions. The first of these is that we work hard to ensure there are *no negative learnings*. "Teacher tell" lectures in which the person speaking up front is the only one who knows the answer have no place in this process. The purpose of building the common database on the front-end of these large group events is to ensure that everyone in the room knows as much as possible before we begin making decisions regarding the organization's future and plans to achieve it. The only tests in this process with right or wrong answers are the tests the people in the room put themselves to in bringing about significant change in their organization in a small window of time. What leaders know, they tell their people—good news and bad alike—adult to adult.

A second belief we apply throughout the process is that we *manage the energy in the group* by making sure the process is varied, that people don't have to sit and listen for long stretches, and that people take responsibility for managing their own energy. Participants work in several different kinds of teams throughout the three days. Some tasks are best worked on in functional groups, while others are better suited to a max-mix configuration in which each table group represents a microcosm of the entire organization. In addition, the max-mix tables are created in such a way that nobody is seated at the same table with their immediate boss, which encourages the free flow of dialogue required in these events.

Finally, and most importantly, the goal of this process is for people to feel *empowered*. Participants are responsible for their own table group's facilitation, flip chart recording, and report outs to the whole group. Specific instructions supplied by a consultant legitimize these roles, which rotate throughout the event so that each has a chance to support the table group. Consistent with this concept of empowerment, we have effectively used the real time strategic change technology in organizations with high illiteracy rates by creating opportunities for max-mix table mates to team together on certain modules that require reading or writing skills. All aspects of these meetings are structured to create an environment in which participants can significantly influence their own destiny—both during the events and back in their work places when they return.

You can see this principle at play in the Content Expert Input module through how three design questions are answered:

1. What does the large group need to be more knowledgeable about in order to make informed choices regarding strategy?

2. Who are the most appropriate people to provide this information?

3. How should this material be presented so that participants are able to understand and apply it in their decision making throughout the remainder of the event and beyond?

Taken together, these three questions ensure that participants have no negative learnings, stay engaged, and feel empowered throughout this particular module.

Agenda Item: View from the Customer's Perspective

The Process Window

You return from the afternoon break for the View from the Customers' Perspective, something people in your max-mix table group have been looking forward to since the agenda was reviewed at the beginning of the day. At this point in the process, customers join the meeting, make brief presentations, and answer questions. Ordinarily, dialogues with customers are problem-focused, but in this case three of your organization's key customers speak about the challenges they and their people are facing in their own environment and what they will need from your organization in order to help them be successful in the future. This approach shifts the focus of the dialogue from one of assigning blame for past mistakes to one of working together to create a better future for both the customer and your own organization. During the question and answer period, customers commonly receive applause for telling it like it is. "Undiscussables" are explored openly in search of a real understanding of their issues. You hear that your customers want you to succeed. In fact, they need you to succeed for their own well-being. They are usually very impressed by the commitment your company has made to investing in its people and in hearing from customers first-hand. They readily pledge to work with you as partners in the future. This module often concludes with a standing ovation for the customers. You can sense a few more people getting on the bandwagon of making needed changes in the organization.

The People Window

❝ You can see a light bulb going off in people's heads as they hear the real customers talking," says John Devine, chairman of First Nationwide Bank. "It's not just some senior person spouting off from your own organization about why things need to change.

You've got a range of expectations, backgrounds, and thought processes in these large groups, but everybody sits up and takes notice listening to the customers. You're getting insight into your business that you didn't have before about how your customers see you. And you're getting that information into a lot of people's heads at the same time. It's very insightful."

The Principle Window

Principle: **Reality is a key driver throughout the process.** A good deal of the power of the real time strategic change technology can be traced to a strong bias toward incorporating current reality into every facet of the process. We accomplish this by:

- Acknowledging an organization's hierarchy. We provide a forum for leaders to share their thinking and beliefs with workers, but do not allow the leader's voice to be the only one that is heard;

- Having interested and affected parties raise and work on real issues at the events. There are seldom simulations or games included in the process. Everything is based on reality from the Telling Our Stories assignment on the first morning to the Evaluation on the last afternoon. This means that data drives the event design, so it is typical for significant changes and redesign of the event's processes to take place in real time;

- Facilitating training, skill development, and learning in large group events. Learning good meeting techniques, how to give and receive feedback, and how to listen to each other in new ways in a team setting are all part of the real time strategic change technology.

We introduce reality into the View from the Customers' Perspective module by inviting real customers to join the event and share their perspectives with the whole group. Listening to leaders or people from your sales and marketing staff is not the same as hearing things directly from real customers. Leaders are often surprised by the significant energy generated by customer input in these events, saying, "I have been telling them the same things that the customer just did for the past six months but nobody seemed to hear what I was saying." For people in most organizations, these large group events represent the first direct non-problem-solving exposure they have had to the issues, concerns, and aspirations of their customers in an environment of open discussion and dialogue.

Depending on the particular purpose of the event we have used processes other than the open forum described above. For example, in one organization we brought in seventy customers so that each max-mix table could conduct their own "personal interview" with a customer. We have also had customers participate throughout the entire event as part of a max-mix table group. The method of bringing reality into the room varies—the objective always stays the same.

Agenda Item: Evaluation

The Process Window

The first day has been filled with new learnings, understandings, and insights from your leaders, from your max-mix table group and from your customers. One of the consultants asks you to complete one last task before leaving—to fill out an evaluation. These evaluations will be summarized across the whole group overnight by the consulting team and presented the next morning.

The leadership and design teams stay at the end of the day to read the evaluations and determine what, if any, mid-course corrections are required based on the reality of Day 1. The whole group has been building ownership in the process throughout this first day as they prepare for the next day's work. The work of Day 2—critical to ensuring your organization's success—will involve crafting a strategy for the future.

The People Window

❝ After reading the evaluations in one organization, the management team and design team really took on the role of defining the process for the following day," explains Rob de Wilde, an external consultant based in Amsterdam, The Netherlands who has used the real time strategic change process with his clients. Rob adds, "They were clear on what was needed out of the event and the evaluation comments were clear about what the rest of the group needed. Together, we made the changes we needed, and the management team assumed even more ownership of the event and change effort in the process."

The Principle Window

Principle: **Designs need to be flexible and responsive to the emerging needs of the whole group.** This principle is closely linked with the first principle, which states that no two events or change efforts are ever the same, and with the previous one, which states that reality is a key driver. The nature of the real time strategic change technology is that the large group is changing in real time during the event itself, and we need to make course corrections along the way. Sometimes we make these design changes after lengthy dialogues with the leaders and design team at the end of the day based on evaluation comments from the large group. We weigh trade offs of different options, using the purpose of the event and our collective intuition to guide our decisions.

In other situations we need to change course "on the fly" in the middle of the day. Reasons for this can range from a shift in the large group's energy to having the product from one activity that feeds into the next module be different from that which we expected. In some cases, even someone missing a plane and running late triggers the need for course corrections.

The design of each meeting is merely a means to an end. As the large group shifts its thinking and needs during the event, we shift the design accordingly. The Evaluation and subsequent Debrief provides us with a comprehensive picture of where participants are at the end of each day, making sure we keep our finger on the pulse of the whole group.

CHAPTER 5

DAY 2: DISCOVERING THE FUTURE IN DIVERSE PERSPECTIVES

```
Day 2
        8:00 AM   Coffee, etc.
        8:30      Feedback on Evaluations/Agenda for the Day
                  Change Possibilities Panel
                  Valentines
                  Organizational Norms
                  Organization Strategy: Revisit
                  Feedback on Strategy by Participants
        5:00 PM   Evaluation/Close/Debrief
                  Leadership Turnaround on Strategy
```

Agenda Item: Feedback on Evaluations/ Agenda for the Day

The Process Window

Day 2 begins in your max-mix group with one of the consultants giving feedback on the Evaluations, including exact words from a representative cross-section of them. Listening to the summary, you are able to compare your experience to others' and gauge where the total group left off yesterday. Even the negative comments are read out loud with the group's reaction showing how counter-cultural it can be to tell the truth in your organization. After the summary, the consultant briefly reviews the purpose of the event and the Day 2 Agenda.

The People Window

❝ I went into the event in my organization thinking I needed to change the people who reported to me," begins Norm Collins, vice president of Boeing's computer support group. "I left the event believing I needed to change myself . . . I was quite surprised when I learned from the evaluations after the first day of our session that my people were not comfortable asking me questions directly for fear of retribution. The questions they had wanted to ask me, but didn't feel free to, didn't even seem that profound. They were telling me that they were afraid, and for the first time then, maybe we had some kind of hope that we could really work together.

When I looked at my own patterns, I could see that I was just playing out the role of a company manager. In that role I always had to know all the answers because it wasn't okay to even look like you didn't know. I now ask myself, 'Why am I doing this? Am I justified in taking this position? Is it fair to the other people involved?' Just a few years ago, I'd have said, 'I don't care if they like it or not. That's the way it's going to be in my organization.' The next two days of that first event were different—people were more comfortable voicing their own opinion, even when it was different than mine. The last few years around here since then have been more of the same."

The Principle Window

Principle: **All activities add to the common database of information we are creating together.** Everything that takes place in these large group events in some way adds to each participant's knowledge and understanding of the organization's current situation. This common database ensures that everyone sees more of the big picture and develops a better appreciation of the whole organization, and its issues, opportunities, and interconnections. With this information in hand, people throughout the organization have a basis for making better decisions, and the change effort stands a much better chance of succeeding.

The power of this technology can be traced to sharing, combining, and ultimately acting on information as a total organization. For example, we treat the formal evaluation summary (and the data we get from informal conversations we have with participants during breaks and lunches) as part of the common database that is shared with the whole group. If we make changes in the agenda, it is important that participants know why these changes have been made and how their feedback played a role in those decisions. Timely, accurate information is a key to empowerment. Finally, feeding back evaluation summaries follows the principle of shifting information from individuals to the total group and back again.

Often, the evaluation summaries contain good information for both dominant and passive participants at the max-mix tables. Representative comments of people's experiences in these groups are read out loud ensuring that this feedback is known to all participants. A great deal of freedom and responsibility for self-management falls on the max-mix tables during these events. Evaluation summaries shape individual and group behavior during the events, and as shown in the story above, after them as well.

Agenda Item: Change Possibilities Panel

The Process Window

Next on the agenda is the Change Possibilities Panel, a cross-section of people from another organization a few steps ahead of your own in the process of change. You hear them describe the roles they've played, the issues they've wrestled with, and what they've learned through their experiences. They caution you not to hear any of what they say as advice. You and the other 600 people in the room need to figure out what's right for your organization. People at your max-mix table find a certain comfort in recognizing you are not the only organization faced with the sizable challenge of doing business in radically new ways. Even more heartening, though, is that people are becoming more energized as the open forum question and answer session draws to a close. The panel has stimulated new thinking in the entire large group. You hear people say, "If they can do it, so can we." You and others realize the work will not be easy, but promising paths for your future begin to take shape. By focusing on the customer, working as an organization-wide team, and doing business in ways that make the most sense, you and 600 others are doing the early survey work required to create your organization's roadmap for real time strategic change.

The People Window

❝ I think of it as taking 500 people on a benchmarking trip," says Lynn Brown, director of corporate human resources for Allied–Signal. She describes the value she sees in the Change Possibilities Panel. "You can get them externally focused on excellence models in other companies and doing it in the large group events gives you the opportunity to get lots of people learning, simultaneously. I've seen it stretch people's thinking, because the Q and A leads to lots of good dialogue—with the panel, and later in the event, with each other."

The Principle Window

Principle: **Throughout the process participants are treated as they really are—with complex sets of needs, wants, and issues.** The idea of change raises emotional issues, triggers turf battles, and uncovers competing needs and wants in the vast majority of people in organizations. Deep down, most of us can identify with wanting more control and security during times of upheaval in our lives. I once interviewed an assembly line worker in a large manufacturing plant who told me that although he was no longer effective in his job anymore he *still planned to continue the same unsuccessful approach in the future, because at least he knew how to do it that way!* Unfortunately, too often people choose predictable failure over the risk of change because they lack information or options.

The real time strategic change technology is about much more than disseminating strategic information to people. Participants need to be treated as people with complex sets of needs, wants, and issues. William Bridges (1986), a psychologist and organization consultant, has written extensively on the transition process people undergo after changes are made in their lives and the organizations in which they work. He describes three predictable stages in this process:

1. The Ending Phase, in which people need to let go of their old ways.

2. The Neutral Zone, in which people feel disoriented and as though things are falling apart.

3. A New Beginning, which is characterized by a vision for the future and people's energy and motivation to realize it.

The Change Possibilities Panel module supports participants in each stage of this transition process wherever they may be individually, or collectively. The panel acts as a model for the large group of people who are facing the challenges of changing a large and complex organization. By telling the whole truth to the group (the good, the bad, *and* the ugly), the panel serves as a mirror through which participants can see and confront their own fears and resistance about letting go of the old and moving through their neutral zone. However, at the same time, the Change Possibilities Panel module also affirms the quest for a new and successful beginning for the organization and its members. These dichotomies are just one example of how these large group gatherings address participants' complex needs, wants, and issues.

Agenda Item: Valentines
The Process Window

In this next step on your journey you have your first opportunity to apply what you learned from the Change Possibilities Panel. A member of the consulting team explains that the Valentines module focuses on breaking down barriers that exist between different parts of your organization. The key to this module is direct feedback. The goal is to change the perceptions people have of other functions so that they see each other as internal customers, rather than enemies. "This module is called Valentines," says the consultant, "because, when we truly care about someone, we send them the very best we can, which in this case is the truth."

You move to a breakout room with the rest of the people from your department or area (the first time you've met during the large group event). All of you begin to create Valentines—your wish list of changes you want other departments or areas to make. You achieve this by brainstorming responses to the statement: "These are the things we need you to do differently as part of your job in the future so that we can better meet our customers' needs." At the same time, all of the other departments or areas are generating similar requests for your group. Finally, you sign your department name on each Valentine so the recipient knows who sent it. After finishing your work you return from your breakout area and post your Valentines on the wall under the name of the appropriate department. The walls of the room are filled with requested changes— no department or area goes unnoticed in the process.

After lunch, the consultant gives the instructions for how you will respond to all of this feedback: "Okay, now we've handled the easy part—requesting the changes we want others to make. The next steps—receiving and responding to the feedback others have given us—is much more difficult. However, we know that if we keep doing what we're doing, we'll keep getting what we're getting, and that's not good enough for our customers or ourselves." The consultant then walks through a four-step process you will follow when you rejoin your department or area to read your Valentines:

1. *Read and Vent* about how the other functions do not understand what you do, how all the problems are really their fault, or even about what a bunch of jerks they are for sending the feedback to you in the first place.

2. *Read Again and Listen* to what the other groups are saying to you in the Valentines. Remember, it is *their* truth, regardless of whether you agree with them or not. If you find yourselves getting mad again, go back to the Read and Vent step.

3. *Summarize Your Feedback into Major Themes* of what the other departments or areas are telling you. What are the main messages? Which requests are repeated by the other groups and need to be acknowledged and responded to?

4. *Prepare a Non-Defensive Response to These Major Themes* consisting of what your group commits to do differently in the future so that everyone can be more successful in satisfying the organization's customers.

Just before you collect your group's Valentines, the consultant tells the group, "In most cases when we give someone feedback and they counter with a defensive response, we back off because we think, 'They never listen' or 'It's not worth it to pursue this any further.' Unfortunately for most of us, we hardly ever recognize that we're being defensive and that others back off from discussing certain topics with us as a result. This time, let's give them a gift—a second chance. If a group reports out anything even remotely defensive—like 'We'll try,' 'If you'd only . . .,' or 'You don't understand how much we have to do,'—we're all going to give them instant feedback in the form of gently hissing to let them know they are being defensive and let them try again."

After a quick practice round of hissing, you work through the four step process with your own department or area in a breakout room. You pass the Valentine sheets around and read them, vent your frustrations and note who sent which Valentines. During this, someone says, "We can't expect any of these other groups to change if we aren't willing to make some changes ourselves!" Someone else counters, "But if they don't change, then where are we? We'd be better off waiting to see what they do before we make any commitments." The debate continues as you read through the huge mound of Valentines. It is not easy for people to make the shift from blaming others to taking responsibility for your function's contribution to the problems plaguing the entire organization. Several times, your group is forced to return to the first step of reading and venting before you finally accept the challenge. With the prospect of the whole group hissing at your response, combined with a growing desire to chart a new course for the organization's future, you finally break through. It is at this point that the message becomes very clear. The only way to bring about significant change across the entire organization is for everybody—including you—to make it happen, to start *doing* things differently. So far, the one and one-half days of the event have focused on input. Now you see your first opportunity for action and commitment.

Although several groups get hissed during their report outs, you can feel a "sea change" all around you. Reports are punctuated by words you have seldom heard in any meeting in the organization in years. People on the front lines stand up in unison promising, "We will pack only quality parts, no more junk!" or "We commit to getting you that information you've requested and updating it weekly." Senior executives declare, "We commit to being more visible throughout the organization on a daily basis." Although these sound like small steps in the larger context of the entire change effort, a paradigm shift is unfolding in this critical mass of people in your organization. Your organizational world will never be the same again.

The People Window

❝ For our organization," explains Jerry Harrison, assistant county manager in Sedgwick County, Kansas, "the Valentines offered an opportunity to say things to each other that often wouldn't be said otherwise. They provide a basis of action for those not predisposed to act. The way it plays out it's not a 'gotcha.' Instead it's more like 'Let me help you so you can help me.' We set up a reporting mechanism after our events on the Valentines so we could monitor progress. People really didn't realize the impact they had on other departments, but when they kept getting the same messages from all over the county it became easier to see these themes and became harder to ignore them. It's such a massive amount of information at the same time and the messages are so clear that something clicks and you see the world differently. You shift from complaining to acting. You're not done by any stretch, but you're a lot farther along than you were when people first walked in the door."

The Principle Window

Principle: **A system-wide paradigm shift needs to occur at some point in the process in order for a real time strategic change effort to succeed.** A prerequisite for powerfully achieving the ultimate purpose of each real time strategic change process is to create a paradigm shift in a critical mass of people in an organization. A paradigm shift in these large group events means that hundreds of people experience a new reality in real time. A reality in which they feel in charge of their own destiny. Change happens system-wide because everyone decides it is time. Changes are made in how business gets done in the organization because everyone starts doing business differently. Once participants see a new world of possibilities, they can never not see it again. The reality of the organization's issues and challenges remains, but people's perceptions of reality change, leading to new behaviors, decisions, and attitudes throughout the rest of the large group event and on into the future.

These paradigm shifts are unmistakable when they occur in a group of several hundred people during a real time strategic change event. The energy level of the working groups is transformed. People are more lively, active, and excited. The noise level and pitch rise. People crowd around flip charts making sure their views are heard and integrated with others, where before they waited for someone to ask them for their input. Conversations shift from "what we can't do" to "what we must and will do." Participants take charge of the opportunities afforded them by the large group approach to effect system-wide changes in small windows of time. A lot of progress is typically made very quickly at this turning point.

The entire planning process leading up to the large group event is geared to designing an agenda that will take participants on a journey from where they are now to where they want and need to be to achieve success in the future. Real time course corrections are commonplace during the event itself as new dynamics emerge from the large group process. All of this planning, preparation and real time response is based on the overall goal of the process, which is to create a paradigm shift in the total group. Without these paradigm shifts, people have merely attended a good meeting. With them, entire organizations have developed and implemented new strategies in real time with astonishing results on many fronts at once.

Often, the Valentines module triggers such a paradigm shift in a critical mass of participants in these large group events. Although most of the information exchanged during this module is not new or surprising, the dynamics of simultaneously sending and receiving feedback between all functions and making it public leads to people really hearing it—perhaps for the first time ever. So many consistent requests from so many different sources makes it possible to start doing business in new ways in the large group event itself—an example of real time strategic change in practice.

Agenda Item: Organizational Norms

The Process Window

Following the Valentine report outs, you go on a break, then return once again to your max-mix table. During the break you heard people excited by the possibility that new internal relationships might develop. There was an obvious growing confidence evident in the hundreds of people around you. Their animated conversation pointed to a belief that you are all on the right track.

"Now that we've started practicing some new ways of doing business with each other on specific issues," explains one of the consultants, "our next step is to further solidify these agreements. We're going to do this by building a common picture of the ways in which we will have to act organization-wide in order to ensure the commitments we've just made don't end up as empty promises."

Organizational Norms, you learn, are those unwritten rules that lead us all to behave similarly in certain situations. Some of these norms are helpful in achieving certain performance measures and in ensuring that you live up to your Valentine commitments. Such a norm might be "the customer always comes first." However, others get in the way of smooth organizational functioning and will work to erode commitments made in the Valentines. An example of this type of norm might be "don't pass on bad news because we always shoot the messenger." You and your max-mix table group brainstorm all of the norms you can think of in your organization, all those unwritten rules that guide how we all act around here. One way to identify these rules is to respond to the question: "What would you tell a good friend who'd just joined your organization about how things *really work* around here?"

After you've listed several pages of these norms—including some "undiscussables"—you take a quick look at the lists generated by several other tables. You are impressed by the consistency of data across the entire organization. Seated back in your max-mix table, you work through each norm on your list identifying if it helps, hinders, or has no effect on organizational performance, and more specifically, whether it will help you make good on your Valentine promises.

Finally, the consultant asks each table to choose the one negative norm that *must change* if each functional group is to live up to the commitments it made. She also asks the group to rewrite it as a positive norm that will support efforts in the future. Your table group decides to take on a tough one. You change "never disagree with your boss in front of others" to "we're all part of one team. We owe each other and the organization the truth at all times."

When it's time to share your table's work with the whole group, you are introduced to a new concept called a room-wide callout. Representatives from each table stand up and tell the whole group the old norm that they believe must change, and introduce the new norm that needs to take its place. People are asked to applaud the new norms they agree to help implement. The enthusiasm of their applause is proportional to their level of agreement. The energy level rises in the room as participants from all levels and functions in the organization begin describing the type of organization they want to call their own.

The People Window

❝ For most organizations, I believe, norms are something that nobody checks on," suggests Imre Lovey, a management consultant working in Budapest, Hungary who has applied the real time strategic change technology in a number of eastern European organizations. He describes the value he's seen from large groups working through the Organizational Norms module. "Discussing them openly like this deepens people's understanding and awareness of what the organization's norms really are. Knowing what they are, and knowing what you want them to be is a good basis for change."

The Principle Window

Principle: **Creating community is a valuable component of all real time strategic change efforts.** Scott Peck (1987) opens his book *The Different Drum: Community Making and Peace* with two powerful yet somewhat disconcerting images of community:

"In and through community lies the salvation of the world.

"Nothing is more important. Yet it is virtually impossible to describe community meaningfully to someone who has never experienced it—and most of us have never had an experience of true community. The problem is analogous to an attempt to describe the taste of artichokes to someone who has never eaten one."

Later in the book, Peck describes one scheme for isolating and naming the most salient characteristics of a true community: inclusivity, commitment, and consensus; realism; contemplation; a safe place; a laboratory for personal disarmament; a group that can fight gracefully; a group of all leaders; and a spirit that can—at least temporarily—transport people out of the mundane world of ordinary preoccupations. These characteristics permeate the real time strategic change technology and are not typical in the vast majority of organizations.

Most of us spend an enormous amount of time in organizations of one type or another. The time we spend in these organizations should be reason enough to explore more deeply ways we could transform them into communities. But benefits from this transformation would extend into our relationships with our families, friends, and others as well.

The Organizational Norms module builds a sense of community in the large group by creating opportunities for people to surface deeply-held beliefs about the kind of organization to which they want to belong. We have used this design module from Hungary to Houston to Hong Kong. And we have arrived at startlingly similar results. It seems that people the world over yearn for the same things—honesty, openness, individual responsibility, and collaboration, to name just a few of the most common characteristics of the new norms that are generated. No legal contracts are signed by participants regarding these new norms, and observers at large group gatherings often ask how we get bosses or subordinates to follow them. Unwritten rules of behavior provide an extremely powerful leverage point for change, yet they are still only one piece of the complex jigsaw puzzle the whole group is in the process of assembling. People from all levels of the organization commit to following these new norms not because someone forces them to, but because they themselves had a hand in shaping them. Through this module and the larger context of the entire event, people's beliefs that their future can indeed be better are awakened. The isolation they have felt for years on the factory floor or in the executive offices need not continue. In fact, mirroring Peck's assessment of the world, "in and through community" lies the salvation of their organization.

Agenda Item: Organization Strategy Revisit/ Feedback on Draft Strategy by Participants

The Process Window

You notice another example of real time strategic change in the next two modules on the agenda, Organization Strategy Revisit/Feedback on Draft Strategy by Participants. One of the new norms that received the loudest support was: "We are all responsible for the success of the organization and seize opportunities to expand our individual and collective influence towards that result." In these two modules you have the opportunity to transform that new norm from words into action.

The leaders of your organization revisit their draft strategy presented yesterday and link it to what you have heard during the past two days. They clearly identify those parts of the strategy that are open to revisions from the large group and those that are not. They also explain why this is the case. The proposed strategy comes to life for you as you listen to your leaders walk through each part of it. Although you do not agree with the entire strategy as it now stands, you understand why your leaders are offering this proposal.

Now it is your opportunity to speak out. Your leaders have been honest with you. It is time to be honest with them, not give them a "yes, boss" salute. They need your best ideas and you are prepared to give them just that. Your max-mix table eagerly begins answering the three questions the consultant has asked you:

1. What do you agree with in the proposed strategy?

2. What do you disagree with and why?

3. What changes do you recommend to the draft strategy and what is your rationale for those changes?

You especially appreciate the diverse perspectives in your max-mix group during this assignment. Others at your table make strong arguments for changes you would never have recommended in your natural work group, or another like-minded collection of people.

The second day concludes with everyone having the opportunity to vote on all the recommended changes from the max-mix tables that they really agree with. You also fill out your Evaluation form back at your table and head for the door. Most people file out of the room physically drained from the two days of unaccustomed work they have just completed. Although tired from the pace of the two days, people's spirits and emotions are energized by being able to contribute to and influence their organization's strategy and direction—a profound and unique opportunity to make a difference in their organizational lives. You head home to get some rest, hopeful that tomorrow's work will be even more engaging and challenging than today's. Your leadership team will stay to revise the draft strategy based on the voting and their own beliefs

The People Window

❝ This turnaround makes a powerful statement to the organization that ownership and involvement are for real," explains Ian Peters, an organizational development consultant at Northrop. "First, leaders speak with authority and passion about the direction they believe is right. Asking for feedback, though, gives people a green light that says this is much more than what we've done before. People's input really matters, and this is one part of the event where ownership of the strategy is transferred from the leaders to everyone. The dialogue here gives an opportunity for any number of people to question the leaders' assumptions and to offer their own. Ultimately I believe this approach gets you a better strategy."

The Principle Window

Principle: **You can only influence as far as you can see.** Often, members of organizations are under-informed regarding organization-wide strategies and change initiatives. People on the front lines are asked to be "good soldiers" and to fall in line with corporate directives they know little or nothing about. Therefore they are never able to make sense of how they might contribute to the organization's overall success.

By and large, top managers have had no meaningful access to the wealth of knowledge and experience across different levels and functions within their organizations. Some leaders prefer to keep control of things; others don't know how to quickly or fully tap into this expertise. Middle managers have felt the pressure to make changes from the top, as well as the bottom of the organization, only to be left to sort through the sometimes conflicting needs and wants of these two groups.

Applying the principle "You can only influence as far as you can see" can be likened to turning on a bright light of information throughout your entire organization. The real time strategic change technology allows everyone in your organization to "see" further—across different functions and levels, across key internal and external issues facing the organization, and into the future. This creates an opportunity and sets a precedent for everyone to exert influence far beyond their traditional boundaries. With informed discretion based on a common understanding of "big picture" organizational issues, individuals can and do make a difference system-wide. This is true whether it takes the form of doing their jobs differently or doing an entirely new job triggered by what they have learned in the process.

Several years ago Jan Carlzon, President and CEO of Scandinavian Airlines System (SAS), coined the term "moments of truth" to describe each interaction a customer has with his organization (Carlzon, 1987). Managing these 50,000 daily interactions became the focal point for the remarkable turnaround the European airline enjoyed in the 1980s. This same concept of "moments of truth" can also apply to any decision made that supports or hinders the successful implementation of strategy. When people can see far enough, they will have the understanding they need to make informed choices regarding the development and implementation of new strategies. Giving people the freedom to make these choices, strategic change can and does happen in real time.

The modules, Organization Strategy: Revisit, and Feedback on Strategy by Participants, model the application of this principle by inviting all participants to see, understand, and own the total organization's strategy. In essence, each individual in the room has an opportunity to influence the future direction of the organization. This is an exciting, significant, and compelling act of empowerment. Similarly, participants begin to realize at this point that if they can exert influence within the traditional domain of others, they can exert this same level of influence on a day-to-day basis back in the workplace on a whole host of issues they previously felt were out of their control.

Agenda Items: Evaluations/ Leadership Turnaround on Strategy

The Process Window

Your organization's design team, consultants and leaders read through the participant Evaluations from Day 2, review the agenda for Day 3, and make any changes needed. After a short break for dinner, the leadership team reassembles for the next module, the Leadership Turnaround on Strategy. And do they have their work cut out for them! All four walls of the Grand Ballroom are covered with flip chart sheets, each filled with recommended changes to the draft strategy. Highlighted are those items that received the widest support across the large group. However, your leaders realize the work they are about to begin involves much more than merely tallying votes with a "majority wins" mentality. They are beginning a process of setting organization-wide strategy in real time, with input from 600 co-creators to help them.

Although these leaders usually work independently, the turnaround module requires them to put their minds together under the time pressures of the evening to revise the strategy for the entire organization. Working through their own consensus process, your leaders integrate participants' ideas into the final strategy they will present to the large group the following morning. By the time they complete their work, they agree that the final strategy is cleaner and clearer than the draft they originally presented. It positions your organization for success now and in the future. Your organization's leadership team is also cleaner and clearer with each other because they have benefited from the team building opportunity demanded by this module.

Representatives from the logistics team gather together a clean version of the final strategy to be typed and copied for distribution first thing in the morning. Finally your leaders agree on their respective roles in presenting the strategy and leave confident that they are no longer alone in trying to change the organization. During the past two days, 600 people have gotten on board to make needed changes in the organization. As your leaders leave the Grand Ballroom, they point out to each other the noticeable shifts in attitudes, inter-functional relationships, and strategic focus that have occurred in the real time strategic change event. People are seeing a new world of possibilities and they are claiming it for themselves and their organization.

The People Window

❝ After we presented our mission, values, and goals in the first of these events, I was amazed to see fifty max-mix tables generating suggestions and ideas for us," begins Dick Sandaas, executive director of METRO, the Seattle, Washington area agency in charge of water pollution control and public transportation. He has taken part in ten of these turnaround modules involving all 4,000 of his organization's employees. "All four walls of the room were plastered with recommendations. Our normal way of dealing with conflict in our directors' team was to shrug our shoulders and go along anyway. However, as we worked throughout the evening sorting through these recommendations, somebody would pick up on ideas that the rest of us had missed. We disagreed with each other openly, but really listened to what each other had to say. Although we did get impatient and frustrated at times, we knew we weren't going to go anywhere until we all went together. It was a struggle and we didn't get out until close to midnight. I was physically exhausted, but we knew we had to go back and face that group in the morning and we weren't about to tell them we just didn't get around to listening to everything they had to tell us. I still remember that first turnaround evening as a key factor in the development of our leadership team because we learned how to dissent with each other productively."

The Principle Window

Principle: **Formal leaders are different from and the same as everybody else in the organization.** A significant volume of writing has been produced during the past decade on the importance of leadership in organizations. Some have argued that good leaders possess certain qualities that set them apart, and that they must play roles different from other organization members during times of change. Still others make a case for leaders being the same as these other members. In effect, they are stating that we are all leaders—in different leadership roles at different times—if we decide to be. Within the context of the real time strategic change technology (and in reality) both of these perspectives are accurate.

For the most part, during these large group events formal leaders work in their max-mix table groups just like other participants. However in some situations, as in the case of the Leadership Turnaround on Strategy module described above, leaders are called on to play special roles. The design teams that plan the large group events and leadership teams work together to determine the most appropriate roles for leaders based on the current issues and needs of their particular organization.

For example, in one organization where increasing empowerment and reducing dependency were key issues, the leaders and design team decided the event would be most effective if the leaders never made any presentation in front of the large group. In another situation, the turnaround session, which focused on developing a core set of values for the organization, was presented as an open invitation. Everybody who wanted to and could participate in the turnaround did. Sixty-seven people stayed into the evening to draft the values statements. In some organizations the turnaround module has not been a good fit. Although a powerful tool, like all modules, it must make good sense given the purpose of the event, and in the broader context of the organization's culture.

Real time strategic change technology can and has been adapted for very different organizations with diverse needs. The roles leaders play throughout the process—whether or not they are the same as other participants—is a key choice point with significant implications not just for the leaders, but for the rest of the large group in terms of the messages that get sent. For example, when it is decided that participants need to hear about a given topic or issue, the message that gets sent by the further choice of a particular leader to deliver that message, as well as its context and timing, sometimes overshadows the content or tone of the delivery in terms of what is talked about and remembered. This powerful "event memory" can be positive or negative. Clear and explicit input to participants on the various roles leaders play throughout the whole process is another part of the common database that needs to be built during the event. Working through these choices with the design team before the event provides a basis for educating leaders about how people will react to different choices in the event itself. In this way, we inform the leaders so they (and we) can make wise choices.

❖ A FRONT LINE WORKER'S PERSPECTIVE

Peggy Wilson is a paramedic and captain in the emergency medical services department in Sedgwick County, Kansas. She describes her department's goal as delivering knowledgeable medical care with care and compassion. Paramedic crews do their work in what are known as pre-hospital settings, or uncontrolled environments, all over the county. Working in this department means you have to do a lot of thinking on your feet and sizing up situations quickly because people's lives and safety often depend on how well a team does its work. One of her jobs as captain is to act as liaison between the office staff and the technicians that work in the ambulances to ensure that technicians get the training, support, and supervision they need to do their jobs well.

"In order to service such a wide area," she begins, "our personnel are assigned to stations within a 1,009 square mile area. These assignments distance these personnel from co-workers and management, making effective communication difficult. Communication is a vital part to any organization that builds trust and fosters camaraderie and teamwork. To feel a part of the team and to achieve the organization's mission, they need this communication and feedback to stay apprised of changes as they progress.

"It is important that communication exist between all levels. This is where our events helped. I attended two of these large group events; one which included people from all departments across the county, and one which was only for people in my department. The county-wide event allowed each department to see how they contribute to the County's mission; to see the big picture. The smaller departmental event brought about strategies and goals to make our unit more effective, ultimately in conjunction with the County's mission, goals, and objectives.

"Although many were skeptical of these events in the beginning, they can see that progress is being made now. We're not through with what we have to do by a long stretch, but our voices are being heard and we're making progress. In both of these events, communication was the key. It might be easier to try and do things with smaller groups of just the top people, but then you'd be missing some important perspectives. Different perspectives provide people with a better understanding of each other and what we need to do our job better. Too often we get so involved in our own particular work assignment, we forget to consider others' perspectives, wants, and needs. Getting different groups together in these large group events lets you discover innovative solutions because all perspectives get shared at one time. Then you can start working together on common goals, rather than individually trying to make a difference.

"By working together on these goals, upper management is reminded of the daily challenges experienced by lower levels. In addition, the lower levels are exposed to the obstacles that upper management faces. This mutual understanding provides for a firmer foundation and working relationship. Without this, the organization will become ineffective. Finally, having this opportunity to share ideas makes you feel more included in the organization. Having your voice heard matters, no matter what level you're working at or what job you're doing. In turn, you are a more motivated and more productive employee."

CHAPTER 6

DAY 3: CREATING COMMITMENTS AND ACTION PLANS THAT MAKE A REAL DIFFERENCE

```
Day 3
        8:00 AM  Coffee, etc.
        8:30     Feedback on Evaluations/Agenda for the Day
                 Response from the Leadership Group: Finalized Strategy
                 Preferred Futuring
                 System-Wide Action Planning
                 Back Home Teamwork
                 Back Home Planning
        5:00 PM  Wrap-Up/Evaluation/Close
```

Agenda Items: Feedback on Evaluations/Agenda/ Response from the Leadership Group

The Process Window

You and others enter the Grand Ballroom for Day 3 of your event, eager to hear how your leaders have integrated the thinking of 600 with their own. You think this is no small task as you head towards your max-mix table. There you find the revised strategy document waiting for you. You scan through the changes made to yesterday's version, which are highlighted in bold type. One of the consultants finishes reviewing the Feedback on Evaluations and Agenda saying, "For those of you who've been saying, 'Let's get to the action planning,' this is your day. But before we do that, let's make sure we all understand and agree with the overall strategy for the future."

In the next module, Response from the Leadership Group: Finalized Strategy, you listen to your leaders describe the process they used to integrate the mountain of recommendations they received. One by one they cover each element of the strategy and what they heard people recommend for that particular element. Then they explain what changed based on the feedback and the rationale for not changing certain elements. The general feeling at the tables is that your voices have been heard in the process, even though the leaders did not make all of the changes recommended by the total group.

99

After the leaders have finished presenting the revised strategy, the consultant asks, "Well, how did they do?" The group of 600 is only too ready to bring the strategy alive. People applaud for a whole host of reasons. Some of the applause is acknowledging that the leaders worked overnight, some is for their courage in including you, yet another part is for each person's contributions to the final product. Deep down you suspect you are all also applauding a new organization—the organization to which you aspire to belong.

The People Window

❝ When we presented the final strategy, there was this great silence from the group," explains Janice Saunders, an area manager in the United Kingdom's Employment Service. "To the English eye, you could tell that it was a positive silence accompanied by lots of nods and ascents with affirming faces. This was a big deal to the people here. We got a lot of feedback afterwards from people saying, 'You really changed things,' and 'Those were my words in there. I didn't actually believe you would listen.' We underlined the actual changes we'd made, and giving people a chance to influence the strategy really seemed to convince them that we were serious about listening to what they had to say. And they had some very valuable things to say, which we included in our strategy."

The Principle Window

Principle: **Listen to see the world through the eyes of others.** As quoted earlier, Thomas Jefferson noted the importance of informing people's discretion in describing the effective organization of society at large. Consistent with Jefferson's counsel, informing people's discretion is a fundamental purpose underlying the real time strategic change technology. Creating a common database of strategic information throughout the total group is a prerequisite to informing people's discretion. Listening to see the world through the eyes of others ensures that people understand and can make decisions based on the common database developed.

Throughout a real time strategic change event we often remind participants to practice a different kind of listening than they might normally do. Traditionally, most of us have been trained to evaluate what people are saying as they talk: Do we agree or disagree with their views? Are they right or wrong? Are they interesting or boring? Or perhaps we have learned through the years to treat the periods when others are talking as preparation time for our responses. The open forums, small group dialogues, posting and voting, and a host of other techniques we use as part of the large group process make it easier for people to listen in new ways. Paradigm shifts do not occur by closing our minds to the thinking others bring to the party. We need to integrate other viewpoints and perspectives with our own by really listening and seeking to understand realities different from those we currently believe in order to see the world in more whole, broad and often less absolute ways. Subsequently, we act differently based on these insights. It is a simple principle with great power behind it, no less applicable to an organizational leader than to a front-line worker.

This principle can be clearly seen in the module, Response from the Leadership Group: Finalized Strategy. If the leaders do not or are not prepared to listen to what people in the organization are collectively telling them, then it will not work, plain and simple. Although few and far between, we have had occasions in which the leaders' revised strategy does not garner support. In those cases, we have had to put max-mix groups back into table discussions and move into what we call an "emergent design." This happens when the leaders have not listened well enough and as a result people did not buy into the final proposal.

However, I need to point out that neither "my way or the highway" nor blind obedience to others' wishes and desires are the answer. Organization leaders must believe in what they are presenting to the large group at the beginning of Day 3. The process we ask leaders to engage in during this module has been described as transformational leadership (Burns, 1978). Transformational leaders state where they stand and why, listen to feedback and ideas for change from those affected, integrate that feedback, and ultimately formulate a position in which both they and their people believe. At some level, this concept of transformational leadership is applied in each real time strategic change event. If people listen to see the world through the eyes of others—be it a leader, customer, or peers—they are then capable of establishing a position with which all key stakeholders will agree.

Agenda Item: Preferred Futuring

The Process Window

Now that there is widespread support for the organization's overall strategic direction, it is time to begin creating a future for yourselves. During the introduction to the Preferred Futuring module, you hear one of the consultants describe the history of this planning technique, which was developed by social scientist Ron Lippitt in the 1970s. Rather than getting into traditional problem solving activities regarding your new strategy, you each get a packet of 3″ x 5″ Post-it™ notes. For each portion of the strategy you have just agreed on, you brainstorm answers to the questions: "It is two years from today, and you are pleased and proud of the progress we've all made on this portion of our strategy. What do you see happening? What do you hear people saying? What do you feel tells you we are succeeding?"

You quickly begin writing down your ideas, each one on a new Post-it note, which you label with the portion of the strategy to which it corresponds. All of the ideas people have yearned to implement for years, and those that have been developed during the event, come pouring out of you and others at your table, sometimes faster than you can record them. People from the logistics team circulate around the room, picking up your notes and sticking them onto blank flip chart sheets posted under signs for the appropriate portion of the strategy. After a while, the walls are awash in a sea of notes. Here is visible evidence that long-untapped wisdom in the organization has been unleashed.

The People Window

❝ Everybody sees the world a little differently and the Preferred Futuring module lets people churn out ideas about things they really care about," says Gill Thompson, an internal consultant in the Boeing Company. "I like the freedom it gives people, and from my experience it really represents a transfer of ownership in the event. Up to that point, the design team, consultants, and leaders are pretty much in charge. When the preferred futuring works really well, people in the room know they've taken hold of something. As people first begin writing the Post-it notes though, there's an eerie silence in the room for more than a minute or two. Then slowly, you hear some murmuring as people start jotting down their ideas. By the end of the writing, people are milling around ready to sign up to work on some part of the strategy, and you literally have thousands of ideas on the walls.

"There's a power in the preferred futuring that is really quite something. I remember in one event I was facilitating that there was a senior manager near retirement age who had been neutral or indifferent through the entire process. As people were signing up to work on different parts of the strategy, I noticed that he was reading some of the ideas describing a preferred future for the division. He looked over at me and said, 'Boy, I sure wish I was going to be around for all this stuff in the future.' That was really a sign for me that we had engaged him."

The Principle Window

Principle: **Choose the future you prefer.** The vast majority of organizations attack all problems by trying to isolate them and solve them. Books, training courses, and consultants exhort techniques on how to take problems apart piece by piece in order to uncover the true cause of our grief. Done well, problem solving ensures you will not have your current problems pestering you anymore. However, not having your current problems is different from working out the future you would prefer, then taking steps to achieve it. Problem solving is least applicable when deliberating systemic issues like organizational strategy, realities and trends in the external environment, changing societal or customer needs and expectations, or creating a picture of a preferred future for an organization, section, or even a product.

Ron Lippitt, a pioneering social scientist and co-founder of NTL

Institute and the Institute for Social Research at the University of Michigan, invented an alternative approach to planning that challenges the long-dominant problem-solving mindset. In 1970, Lippitt, along with a team of graduate students, studied the effects an exclusive problem-oriented approach had on those who practiced it (Lippitt, 1983). His findings were startling:

1. As groups continued using a problem solving methodology, depression increased over time.

2. The longer groups worked on problems, the less responsibility they assumed for solving them. They tended to attribute causes of their problems to sources outside the control of the group.

3. The problem solving groups exhibited an increase in the frequency of words and phrases indicating feelings of impotence, futility, and frustration. Ultimately, the groups opted for short-term, symptom-oriented solutions that reduced present pain, instead of longer-term solutions that would move them toward a future they all preferred.

These findings led Lippitt and his team to begin experimenting with a new approach to planning, which later became known as preferred futuring. He described the process of preferred futuring as one in which "we examine the data of the past, the present, the events, trends and developments going on around us in our world, community, organization, and personal lives. Then we use these data to imagine and envision images of the future that we prefer, not limited by presently perceived frontiers, yet triggered by the realities of the present and emerging . . . situation" (Lippitt, 1983, p. 7).

In contrast to the groups Lippitt originally studied, those that follow a preferred futuring approach experience much different outcomes than when they solely used problem-solving methods. Specifically, groups demonstrate increased energy over time, take more ownership of their situation and responsibility for doing something to change it, and the solutions they create are innovative "whole new ways of doing business," not merely reductions of present pain. So it would seem that even where application of problem solving techniques is the way to go, it may be in some cases, that doing preferred futuring as well will produce an even bigger payoff.

Once we have established a common database of strategic information within the large group and agreed on an overall strategy, preferred futuring provides a powerful wellspring, an "image of potential" from which ideas generated in the upcoming System-Wide Action Planning module will flow. Seeing the future, in the context of the real time strategic change technology, is more akin to being there already because one of the features of this large group approach is that it makes the future happen faster.

Agenda Item: System-Wide Action Planning

The Process Window

You survey the walls covered with Post-it notes and sign-up sheets posted around the room. Then each of the people at your max-mix table (and the rest of the large group) sign up to work in one of the sub-groups on a specific portion of the strategy they have the most passion about. You move to your breakout area and meet with others who have signed up for the same topic, ready to work on your group's share of the ideas in this module.

The consultant introducing this module has challenged the entire group of 600 to be transformational leaders by integrating the best thinking contained in the Post-it notes with an action plan your sub-group believes in. It's a big task and you have only two hours to develop a recommended plan of action on your particular area of the strategy to propose to the rest of the large group. After introducing yourselves in this new group of people and choosing a facilitator and recorder, you immerse yourselves in the assignment.

You begin by sorting the dozens of ideas into several categories or themes that make sense. Your new group works efficiently and effectively together applying the teamwork learnings gained through participating in the max-mix groups, and because they are highly motivated to produce a good result. Next you develop a composite preferred future statement of your area of the strategy based on your own beliefs and the input you have received on the Post-it notes.

After completing an analysis of the situation your organization is in currently, you launch into a brainstorming session about what you need to do differently as an organization to "move the needle" on this part of the strategy. Finally, using your brainstormed ideas, you develop and agree on a specific, realistic plan of action for your part of the strategy (who, what, when, and how) that you will recommend to the total group of 600.

After completing this work, you receive instructions for posting your group's recommendations under the appropriate banner and for voting on all the action plans. This time, the voting instructions are a little different. You have twenty-five gold stars and twenty-five red dots at your disposal. Gold stars mean "Great idea! Let's go for it!" The red dots signal anything from "In a pig's eye!" to "You gotta be kidding!" A consultant explains, "We need to be honest with each other with both the stars and dots. No hidden agendas. We need to prioritize the best ideas for action in the future, regardless of which group came up with them." The good, the bad, and the ugly become easy to discern during the lunch and voting period as some recommendations are surrounded by stars, while others drown in a sea of red dots. Your leadership team reports out the results from the voting at the end of the lunch break. Your job is to make sure that the system-wide action plans become part of the whole group's common database of strategic information. In the last part of the event, you and your natural work group will transfer the common direction chosen during the past three days to your day-to-day operations back in the workplace.

The People Window

❝ Any kind of system-wide planning is important," explains Ken Kentch, hospital/health plan administrator of Kaiser-Permanente's Santa Clara, California facility. Having used the technology to involve a large group in designing patient-focused practices and work processes in his organization, Ken continues, "In our industry, we have become very autonomous, much like a university. That is, the various departments do not share common visions and strategies. If this is part of your problem, this kind of planning would work well for you."

The Principle Window

Principle: **Build the teams that are needed to bring about real time strategic change.** Building a wide variety of teams (e.g., natural work groups, cross-functional, self-select and total organization) is a natural by-product of engaging your organization in a real time strategic change process. Kathleen Dannemiller, my colleague and one of the inventors of this technology, created her "Arthritic Organization Theory" (1988) to explain why these multi-dimensional teams have been so tough to build in large, complex organizations. It finds its roots in the work of two major theorists from the late nineteenth and early twentieth centuries and in her own experience in consulting with Ford during the 1980s. The first of these theorists, Max Weber, who was known for his work in the French bureaucracy (1947), divided an organization horizontally into layers of responsibility with specified spans of control. Frederick Winslow Taylor (1915), the father of scientific management, drew lines vertically through the structure of organizations helping to launch a golden age of specialization in which tasks were divided into their simplest form. Structures consistent with these contributions have dominated organization designs for the better part of the past century.

The application of scientific management and the interchangeability of capital and labor led to huge gains in productivity and capacity in the first half of this century. The outcomes to be achieved by organizations and the environments they existed in were far more predictable than today despite wars and the Great Depression of the 1930s. However, more recently, the outcomes needed and external environments have changed radically in their nature, scope, and pace. Sophistication and globalization of trade, transport technologies, communications, and the advent of the post-industrial age of information technology together with much more intense competition and demanding customer expectations have forced us to rethink some basic assumptions about how our organizational structures serve our needs.

Just as weather changes affect arthritic conditions in people, environmental changes such as those above exacerbate issues related to "organizational arthritis." Existing structures prevalent in mature organizations have come to mirror a by-product of the natural process of aging in humans, leading to a rigidity of the joints. In organizations, this maturation process leads to a system less able to effectively communicate between levels and across departments, less able to function in a coordinated way, and less able to adapt to its changing environment. Many young organizations also suffer from this malady, as evidenced by their poor level of system-wide communication and low flexibility to fast-changing environments. In fact, this concept even accurately describes dynamics at play in modern organizations whose structures have been designed based on key processes they employ to do their work, as well as to their more traditional, functionally-based counterparts. "Arthritis" can be seen in any organization in which members reflect an attitude of "if I do my job and you do yours, the work will get done." These blockages occur across different levels, functions, and project or process-based teams, and they lead people to focus their time and energy on their narrow fiefdoms instead of on what's best for the entire organization.

We use the "Arthritic Theory" as a nuts and bolts way for people to understand overall organization dynamics and how representatives from other departments and levels with whom they are experiencing conflicts are not necessarily "born jerks." When systems and structures work against the sort of collaboration needed to achieve results for the whole organization, people get trapped in their "boxes," regardless of how the organization has been designed. The real time strategic change technology creates an opportunity for people to break down arthritic blockages and develop enduring ways of working together. It also encourages the development of new systems and more useful structures in order to achieve shared goals and create their preferred future.

Building these diverse teams throughout the entire process is an effective start to addressing an organization's long-standing arthritis. It also begins to produce three concrete results during the event and after participants return to their day-to-day business. First, the various teams that work together during the event produce higher quality results and generate more innovative solutions than they would working exclusively in their natural work groups. Second, participants manage their own group processes during the event (a skill they can and do transfer to their "back home" teams). Finally, a total system team is developed as representatives from departments and functions with long-standing conflicts begin to see a bigger picture of their total organization. With this expanded view, participants recognize shared frustrations, as well as their common goals. Ultimately this broader perspective enables people to begin acting as an organization-wide team.

Agenda Item: Back Home Teamwork

The Process Window

When you are seated in a breakout area with the people you work with everyday you fully appreciate the productivity and effectiveness you enjoyed with your max-mix group and the system-wide action planning group you just left. A lot of long-standing issues still exist in your natural work group and the only time you spent together these past three days was during the Valentines session on Day 2. However, the Back Home Teamwork module you are now beginning provides an opportunity to transfer learnings from your max-mix experience to your regular work group, as well as to make plans for how you need to work differently based on everything you now know and believe.

"First take a few minutes by yourself to reflect on your experiences during the past few days as you worked in different groups," explains one of the consultants. You are asked to share what you learned about good teamwork from your max-mix and system-wide action planning groups. You are also asked to share one thing you would like to change about how your back home group works together. You listen to the rest of the people in your group describe what they'd like to see changed about how you all work together. None of it is fancy or complex. The power though is that you are all agreeing on what needs to change about how you work together. The next assignment will give you an opportunity to make these changes in real time.

The People Window

❝ Even in only a few days, you find yourself making bonds with people from other departments," notes Geoff Garside, general manager of Marriott's Hong Kong hotel. He explains that there's a typical regret in returning to your back home group after spending several days with your max-mix table. "You know you have to return to all the problems you left in your own department when you go to do your back home planning, and quite frankly, the few days you spend away from the people you work with every day is quite refreshing. You get some new perspectives about problems you may have been causing others that you didn't even realize were occurring. I found stopping to talk about how you worked with your max-mix group and how you might be able to adapt some of those learnings for your back home team was quite beneficial."

The Principle Window

Principle: **Apply learnings gained in real time.** A real time strategic change event is a continually evolving process. As new data emerges, it is integrated into the design of the meeting. Each module builds on the one preceding it, incorporating all of the information accumulated to that point in time. Continuing to create and access this living database of strategic information serves two purposes: First, the quality of work done and decisions made by participants, leaders, and the logistics, design, and consulting teams are high because they are based on the most informed discretion possible. Second, participants get some experience thinking and acting in real time, a skill that will serve them well when they return to the workplace.

The Back Home Teamwork module is a direct application of this principle: learnings from working in max-mix and system-wide action planning groups are immediately transferred to natural work groups. Back home teams benefit from these lessons in the last assignment of the real time strategic change event (their back home planning session), as well as when they return to work after the event concludes.

Agenda Item: Back Home Planning

The Process Window

You have heard from your leaders, content experts, each other, and your customers. You have listened to the challenges faced by another organization bringing about significant change and the lessons and learnings they have gained through their experience. You have made agreements to work in new ways with other functions so that you can all best serve your customers. You have had a hand in shaping your company's overall strategy and in developing system-wide action plans to implement that new strategy. Now, it is time for the Back Home Planning assignment, which is designed to translate agreements, commitments, concepts, and intentions into action. You have worked throughout the three days integrating new learnings, ideas, and the image of a new future emerging, one that you prefer both for your organization and yourself.

It is important to connect the hopes and dreams borne out of this event with the back home realities you will be confronted with starting tomorrow back on the job. Your real time strategic change event has provided you with a powerful launching pad for change. Now it is time for you and the 600 other people in the room to take charge of implementing the strategy, to shift from hopes and dreams to commitments and action.

Meeting with the rest of your back home work group, you evaluate the impact of the last three days on your work, the commitments you have made to do things differently in the future to contribute to your organization's new strategic direction, and how you will bring the other people from your work area who weren't able to attend this event "on board." Your back home group's dialogue is focused and frank. You realize you have a unique opportunity to influence the future course of the entire organization.

Returning from your breakout area to the Grand Ballroom you listen to the final report outs from the other back home groups. The other group's plans are impressive, but you wonder whether they will actually follow through on their promises. However, you believe your back home group is committed and crystal clear that you're going to deliver on every commitment you have made.

Your leadership group reports out last, stepping up to some key issues that must be resolved in order for some of the changes to occur throughout the entire organization. As you listen to your leader tick off the top team's commitments, you realize just how crucial it is that each back home group follow through on their commitments. You viscerally come to understand the meaning of a fundamental principle underlying the real time strategic change technology: "If it is to be, it is up to me."

The People Window

❝ When we got to our Back Home Planning assignment," describes Leonard Carone, a laboratory supervisor in Ford Motor's Dearborn, Michigan Glass plant, "I got real mad right away. One guy said, 'They're eliminating our job,' but nobody ever said anything about that during the event. I was angry and said, 'Let's not hear what we want to hear! None of that was ever said out there on the floor.' After that we got back to the real world. Some other people backed me up, and right then and there we all faced the truthful realization that things needed to change back home. We needed to change the way we were working. A lot of people have seniority in our plant and they don't have a lot to lose in terms of job security. We've got an older, street-wise workforce in our plant, but I think we walked out of that room with more unity than some of those people would want to admit to."

The Principle Window

Principle: **If it is to be, it is up to me.** It is individual people whose actions change organizations and how they operate, even in corporations that count their people in hundreds of thousands. Waiting for top management to provide leadership, for front-line workers to fall in step or for middle managers to get committed just does not work. When the ultimate goal is strategic change, waiting around for someone else to do something first is a recipe for mediocrity. Organizations do not transform themselves; only individuals acting in concert can do so.

A prerequisite of any successful change effort is individual buy-in, ownership, and commitment. This principle guides the design, facilitation, and practice of the real time strategic change technology. Combined with the principles of building teams and creating community, the large group meeting dynamics strike a healthy balance between individual responsibility and collective support.

The Back Home Planning assignment drives home this principle by focusing participants on making commitments that capture their own best contributions to implementing changes, not what somebody else might or might not be doing to pitch in. The real time strategic change technology breathes new life into this age-old maxim as individual participants take charge of making changes in their own spheres of influence—now wider because of their involvement in the process itself. The collective critical mass of people ensures aligned changes are implemented system-wide.

Hundreds of people working together with a common database of strategic information at their disposal—each taking responsibility for their unique contribution to implementing the overall organization's strategy—can bring about significant changes for the better in even the most complex organizations. Having seen this technology applied in different parts of the world on a wide variety of issues during the past decade has more than confirmed this finding over and over again.

Agenda Items: Wrap-Up/Evaluation/Close

The Process Window

Your three day journey through a real time strategic change event draws to a close with the final module, Wrap-Up/Evaluation/Close. Your leader stands at the podium, summarizing and reflecting on the substantial progress made in the event and the significant work yet to be done back in the workplace. Although physically drained from the work of the past three days, people feel a personal sense of accomplishment about having been a part of a historic moment in your organization's life. You and the 600 other people in the room have moved further, faster than you ever could have imagined on the first morning as you listened to each person at your max-mix table tell their story. As your leader outlines the next steps coming out of this event for the whole group, you reflect on your max-mix table mates, all that you have learned, and all that you are going to be doing to successfully implement the new strategy you helped develop. After handing in your evaluation, you leave the event well prepared to make real time strategic change happen in your organization.

The People Window

❝ Powerful is the word that comes to mind when I think about the end of these events. What struck me at all the events I helped manage, was that people didn't want to leave after the event was over," recalls Barbara Cohn, a vice president with the Fund for the City of New York who was a key player in a real time strategic change effort in New York City's Public Hospital System. "It was late, they had worked long, intense days, yet they were lingering, exchanging more ideas and phone numbers and making work connections with people they'd just met. The big question on everyone's mind, though, is what lies ahead. People leave with a clear sense of direction, hope, and purpose. We know you have to support the next steps coming out of the event to achieve long-term results."

The Principle Window

Principle: **Always leave the group with unfinished business.** Traditionally speaking, the conclusion of any conference or training session sets off an alarm bell in the "Binder Preparation Department" of most organizations. Diplomas may be handed out and people say their good-byes. The real work, for all intents and purposes, is finished. Binders end up on people's shelves and changes often do not happen. It becomes another interesting, if not necessarily influential, meeting in the annals of your organization; business as usual.

A story that took place involving a handful of people in a Berlin coffeehouse more than sixty years ago helps us avoid these same pitfalls today with groups of several hundred people. Kurt Lewin, one of the earliest proponents of participation as a means for effecting lasting change, used to meet for hours with his students in a Berlin coffee shop for free flowing conversations of current research problems and curiosities (Marrow, 1969). On one such occasion, he noticed that the waiter recalled the exact total due and what everyone had ordered by tracking the entire bill in his head. About a half hour later, Lewin called the waiter over and asked him to repeat his memorization feat. Slightly perturbed at the request, the waiter explained that he could not remember the bill anymore because it had already been paid. Lewin was intrigued by the waiter's response and instantly formed a new theory: the waiter had erased his memory by completing the task. This informal experiment in a Berlin coffeehouse was pursued by one of Lewin's students, Bluma Zeigarnick, who proved experimentally that people tend to remember unfinished tasks better than completed ones—a dynamic now known as the Zeigarnick effect.

We build "Zeigarnick effects" into many aspects of real time strategic change events, evidenced by how each module leads into the one which follows it and the tight timeframes we set for group assignments, leaving more work to be completed back home. The large group events end not with emissaries being sent to compile binders, but rather with leaders and all participants focusing on the future, with actions that need to be taken, plans to be fleshed out, and the ensuing work that lies ahead for them. In this way, participants remember the commitments they've made through the discomfort of unfinished business and begin acting on them soon after they leave the event, if not before.

❖ A LOCAL UNION PRESIDENT'S PERSPECTIVE

Jim McNeil was recently re-elected to his second term as president of United Auto Worker's Local 600. Local 600 has approximately 17,000 members located at twenty-five different worksites. Jim has been a union representative for twenty years and has been involved in numerous organizational change initiatives during that time. In fact, several years ago he returned to school and earned a master's degree in organization development, which he says has helped him be more effective in his job as a local union president. In terms of the real time strategic change technology, he's been involved with it on two separate occasions: once in work at Ford's Rouge steel plant and more recently with a renewal effort at Ford's Dearborn, Michigan glass plant.

"From my perspective, the core of this approach is based on the principles of democracy and dignity in which workers have a voice in decisions that impact their jobs. The preamble of our union's charter speaks of not only improving our members' economic status, but of equal importance, that workers gain a greater measure of dignity, self-fulfillment, and self-worth in the workplace. It continues on to say that workers must have a voice in their own destiny and the right to participate in making decisions that affect their lives before such decisions are made. These large group events are consistent with our principles.

"Including union members in workplace decisions is an obvious step to take when you realize that these same hourly workers on the line run businesses, have families, and are active leaders in their communities when they're not in the plant. For some reason though, management wanted these people to turn it all off when they walked in the front door to the factory. For a lot of these people, the world went dark for the eight hours they were at work every day. In our view, the managing of the business is too important to be left to management alone. I've learned from my experience in the union that if you don't involve people, you don't get commitment.

"These events represent a very basic first step in a change process. But what you do after the events end is the key to your ultimate success. You must have a real in-depth commitment from the top on down. To attempt to change the culture of an organization is hard work, but this process gives people optimism and raises their expectations that they'll be listened to. You must make sure you set up the internal processes in your organization to support it because once you raise people's expectations you have to deliver.

"I think most organizational change efforts fail because they're really only lip service. To make this process work you need to deeply believe that by involving people in the decision-making process, the decisions you make will be better, people will be more committed to implementing them, and your results will be different. You'll be successful where others have failed. People these days recognize that the world is changing very rapidly and the only thing for sure is that there's going to be more change. Responding quickly is the only way to survive. If people are truly involved in this process and see the entire organization and how the work they do contributes to the organization's success, they will not be locked into specialist's mindsets. They will choose to be more flexible and able to adapt to changes you and I both know are coming.

"When organizations are run strictly like top-down hierarchies and you have no input, people are expected to salute the flag when it's hoisted. The only problem is that it really doesn't work that way. People are resistant to change and quick to recite all the reasons these new ways won't work. They shoot holes in them every time. Unfortunately, too often people have a greater stake in seeing these changes fail than in having them succeed.

"What I see happen in this process is that most people enter these events skeptical. They don't believe it's real. The first thing they hear is that things are going to be different because their voices are going to be heard, not just for the three days of the event but more importantly, back at the plant. People make commitments about specific behavior changes. Management answers workers when they ask, 'What are you going to do differently when I come to you when the quality is off or I have other problems?' Management must then deliver. Of course, some people leave the way they came in, but there are very few of these. Most people want to see things improve, they want to believe things will improve, and they leave optimistic that now there is an opportunity to do things differently.

"There's something special that occurs in these events, probably at different times in different events. You can feel it shift, too, from a mood of disbelief and distrust to one of 'this might be okay.' There's this certain magic moment where you win the group over and they say, 'Yeah, this is for real.' I have been struck by the power that occurs or is unleashed by this process. After ten years of threats that their plant would be closed or sold, a disheartened group of 200 people in the Rouge Steel plant were on fire at the end of their week-long event. I was somewhat in awe at how people could make such a dramatic shift from where they started to where they left. I was actually shocked because the process was so powerful that it could create such a change in individuals in a week.

"But it all comes down to what happens in the real world the next day, the next week, and the next month after an intervention. Most importantly, you need to lay the groundwork for next steps well ahead of time. These are not one-shot deals. You have to be committed to making changes in how you and everybody else in your organization operates every day. If you're not, this process is definitely not for you.

"I don't see many places where this approach couldn't be used. Anywhere you had a large group of people with a stake in an organization you could apply it. Where it won't work is where you have an organization that isn't deeply committed to making meaningful and significant organizational changes. And I know because I am a person who suffers directly when these things go in the tank. Management walks away, but I'm stuck holding the bag with my membership. My members look to me and depend on me to advise them wisely, and I'm very cautious and concerned about what programs I get behind. This is one approach I can recommend to you if you're serious and committed to dramatically changing the culture in your organization."

CHAPTER 7

THE WORKING
MODEL BEHIND
THE MAGIC

I think these events have a touch of magic in them," says Asma Ma'ani, director of human resources and training for the Marriott Hotel in Amman, Jordan. "I'm not sure exactly what it is, but I've seen participants leave these large group events in Cairo, Amman, and throughout Europe excited and motivated about having some influence over their destiny. Only very slight changes were required for the different cultures. I think people always wanted to participate. This process just gave them opportunities to do so they'd never had before."

The three-day event described in the previous chapters is an illustration of the real time strategic change technology. However, for some time I have been exploring why specific applications of the technology have proven effective in such diverse settings. How could large, bureaucratic organizations begin changing so significantly in such small windows of time? How could individuals, departments, even entire functions at war for years suddenly redirect their battle cries and begin forging partnerships for the future? How could these same people shackled by out-moded business practices transform their organizations and work processes, whether they were improving customer service in a Hong Kong hotel or building higher quality cars in Detroit? What could explain the many places, ways, and speed with which these system-wide changes unfolded in organizations deploying the technology? These changes seemed so numerous and diverse, yet aligned, that some set of forces had to be at work. What was the secret, I wondered, searching for the words, phrases or concepts that could explain what I already knew at a gut level.

I found some answers to these questions by reflecting on my own experiences working with this technology during the past ten years. Having designed and facilitated many of these interactive working sessions in different organizations, industries, and countries that addressed diverse issues, I recognized a simple yet powerful factor in what makes the real time strategic change technology work: the concept of simultaneity, or working on all fronts at once during these events. Simultaneity by definition is a natural process. More than one thing always happens at the same time in our lives. The daily routine in most organizations involves many people working many issues using many methods and making many changes. However, bringing all of these people together to work their diverse issues using a common database of strategic information and common set of methods results in significant and lasting organizational change. Ultimately, it also defines a new and better way for organizations to change. In essence, the working model behind the magic of the technology presumes that the right people working the right issues with access to the right information will make the right changes in their organization. This unique approach enables an organization and the people in it to deal with multiple dimensions of a change effort all at the same time. The working model I build throughout this chapter visually captures the patterned nature of these multiple dimensions and the effects they create.

A Common Database of Strategic Information

Creating a common database and achieving an understanding of strategic information throughout an entire organization is a powerful stimulus for change. People are motivated when they have a hand in crafting this common database. With the right information, people are capable of acting with well informed discretion, furthering their organization's goals, as well as their own. With hundreds and even thousands of people in an organization focused on achieving the same overall results, the concept of leverage takes on a whole new meaning. As new information surfaces and is added to the evolving database through these large group events, new insights emerge, attitudes change, and people's organizational worldviews are expanded. Combining individual interpretations to create a shared reality enables people to craft organizational strategies that provide direction for individual behavior while simultaneously fostering personal freedom. This potent combination of direction and freedom is a prerequisite for real time strategic change.

A simple, yet powerful change formula, which Dick Beckhard and Reuben Harris (1987) attribute to David Gleicher, guides the development of this common database of strategic information in the large group events. (See Figure 1.)

We revised the original elements of Gleicher's formula for ease of recognition and application in the large group settings as follows:

$$\text{Dissatisfaction} \times \text{Vision} \times \text{First Steps} > \text{Resistance to Change}$$

in which the product of dissatisfaction (D) with the present situation, a vision (V) or positive picture of what is possible in the future, and real, achievable first steps (F) people can take toward reaching the vision, must be greater than the resistance to change (R). If any one of these (D, V, or F) is zero or near zero, the product of the three will also be zero or near zero. Therefore natural, normal and ever-present resistance to change will not be overcome. Although this model is equally applicable to individual change, in an organization-wide effort a critical mass of people needs to share a common understanding and agreement on each of these three elements for change to occur.

Some organizations have a well-developed sense of dissatisfaction with the way things are that permeates the thinking and actions of their members, but no vision or first steps in place. In these situations people say, "We know what's wrong, but have no idea what better looks like (V), or how to get there (F)." These organizations are easy to spot if only for the long lines of frustrated people complaining and venting in the bathrooms, at the drinking fountains, and outside the break rooms about what's wrong. Over time, this complaining is replaced by apathy, low morale, and inertia.

Still other organizations have built solid agreement in a critical mass of people about their dissatisfaction and first steps, but have no clear, articulated vision to guide the organization's future direction. These organizations often fall into the trap of trying to solve their problems (address-

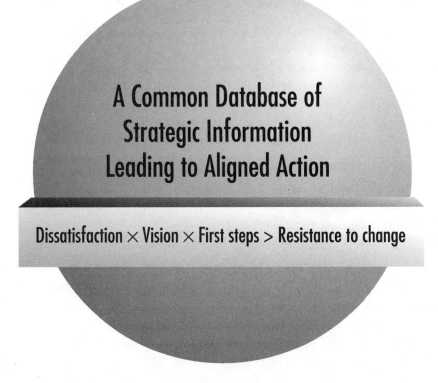

A Common Database of Strategic Information Leading to Aligned Action

Dissatisfaction × Vision × First steps > Resistance to change

Figure 1. The working model behind the magic of real time strategic change

ing D) by implementing each new management fad as the truth, the light, and the way. People who work in these organizations lament the "flavor of the month" mentality that drives their change efforts, with most folks hunkering down to wait out the latest and greatest change technique being tried out in their organization.

Perhaps the most frustrating scenario for anyone is to find themselves in an organization in which there exists a common and shared dissatisfaction with the status quo, an exciting vision of a future they want to call their own, but no collectively agreed-upon set of first steps in place that they can take to begin moving toward the future they prefer. This set of dynamics often leads to false starts, disjointed initiatives, infighting, and the emergence of informal leaders who can be, at best, only partially successful. Confidence in the hierarchy is quickly eroded and people try things in isolation bent on doing something—anything— instead of giving up altogether.

Organizations sometimes adopt a vision and a master plan, usually a top-down initiative, based on dissatisfaction as seen only from the top tier of management. Even in cases in which the vision and plan are relatively successfully sold down the line, the lack of shared dissatisfaction results in a narrow interpretation of the vision and actions, which are poorly aligned across the organization. This is because the driving force of dissatisfaction is seen from many different parochial perspectives which are never pooled or reconciled. Almost all action that ensues in this scenario is at cross-purposes because so many people know so little about the total organizational picture of reality.

Conversely, when a critical mass of people in an organization builds a common understanding and agreement across all three of these elements, a paradigm shift occurs. People acknowledge their current reality, but are not mired in it. They create an image of a preferred and possible future reality worth working towards in a collaborative effort. They also see a clear path of actions they can take immediately that will enable them to begin moving towards their vision. The frustration, isolation and inertia they had previously experienced is replaced with excitement, a sense of community and momentum for change. Although their external reality remains the same, their internal experience of that reality shifts dramatically and almost instantaneously.

❝ It's such a powerful model because it's so easy to understand." Ron Frederick, vice president of human resources for Thomson Information who has worked with the real time strategic change technology for more than five years in several divisions of his company, explains the value added through applying the Change Formula in the large group process. "You can begin to see light bulbs going off in people's heads as they identify the gaps between what is now and what it could be. After raising the level of dissatisfaction in the group you go to work on vision, which for me is like a diamond. There are many facets to a vision, and this process gives you an opportunity to look at the company's vision from many different perspectives. In a way, each individual articulates his or her own vision during these events and probably the most memorable thing for me is watching the level of empowerment build as groups work through this model. At the beginning of the event, people are usually resistant or indifferent. Midway through they're saying, 'We understand where the organization needs to go. What do you want us to do?' By the time they've worked through the entire Change Formula they're saying, 'We understand where the company is going, now it's up to us to decide what to do and do it.' "

We embed this same Change Formula in the foundation of each real time strategic change event to ensure that eventually a critical mass of the large group experiences a paradigm shift. Although the design of the meeting does not slavishly follow this formula (e.g., all modules having to do with visions must follow all modules that address dissatisfaction), it serves as a useful construct for designing the interactive events (see Chapter 11 for more discussion regarding the design process). Figure 2 illustrates how the Change Formula guided the design of the example real time strategic change event described in Chapters 4, 5, and 6 (adapted from Jusela, 1990).

Involving Many People

There are two main reasons for involving people in a change process:

1. They have information, experience, or expertise to offer that would increase the likelihood of success (i.e., better decisions get made about what to change and how to change).

2. By understanding, accepting, and owning their responsibility in implementing changes, they also increase the likelihood of success (i.e., what gets decided gets acted on).

These seem like self-evident truths. So why don't organizations follow these two simple criteria? Because once the number of people who qualify for inclusion gets above thirty or so, most of us don't have ways and

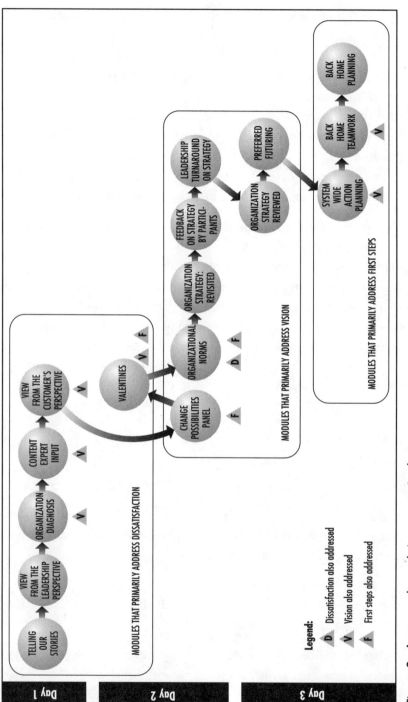

Figure 2. An example real time strategic change event

Figure 3. The working model behind the magic . . . involving many people

means of really effectively including them in a change effort. Therefore we consciously or unconsciously apply rules of exclusion, create a plan for change, then face the daunting task of selling it in what has likely already become an uphill battle.

The real time strategic change technology allows for many diverse perspectives to be brought to the table and for vast numbers of people to understand, accept and own their responsibility for implementing change. Figure 3 illustrates the kinds of people with different organizational roles (the inner band) and the wide variety of disciplines and content expertise (the outer band) from a typical manufacturing organization who could be involved in one of these large group events. These examples could just as easily be revised to represent the appropriate key players in service, government, health care, community-based and other types of organizations. My purpose in including this figure is to illustrate the breadth and depth of organizational involvement available through real time strategic change technology.

The aim of the real time strategic change technology is to bring together at least a critical mass of people from each stakeholder group in the same place at the same time—something that is seldom, if ever, done. Enough people need to be able to attend these events to successfully implement changes when they return to the workplace. We know from years of social science research that involving people in decisions that impact their work leads to increased commitment to and support of these decisions. Having your perspective represented by someone else is better than not having your voice heard at all. Actually being in the room and having a say in making these decisions is better yet. Currently the real time strategic change technology has proven capable of bringing together upwards of 2,200 people at one time and in one place for an interactive working session. This size would not constitute a critical mass for larger organizations dealing with systemic issues; however, the upper limit to effective inclusion of people in these meetings continues to increase. Furthermore, processes that include multiple real time strategic change events (discussed in Chapter 13) have been successfully applied in huge corporations. Chapter 14 also discusses possibilities for pushing the size and inclusion limits of the real time strategic change technology in the future. For example, it examines using innovations in communications technology for virtual co-location of simultaneous large scale meetings.

Several advantages arise from involving a critical mass of each of these diverse stakeholder groups in a real time strategic change event:

1. The common database that gets built is continually added to and updated so that the shared understanding in existence at any point in time is universal and does not suffer from either lag time in communications or obsolescence. Through the iterative process of working from the individual to the small group to the whole group and back again, everyone has the opportunity to get the same messages at the same time.

2. The integration of diverse perspectives elevates parochial viewpoints to a higher level where, when taken together, they constitute a new, different, and shared view of reality. We each bring our own filter with us

wherever we go, siphoning off data that does not fit our current paradigm or force-fitting everything within its framework. Working in a max-mix group with people from other functions and levels in the organization opens our thinking to ideas to which we would not normally be exposed. Piecing together the common database of strategic information in these events is akin to putting together a giant jigsaw puzzle. Each person's truth is truth—there are no right or wrong views. Integrating the diverse perspectives of all stakeholders ensures that the whole group sees "the whole truth," a more accurate picture of reality than any one person could develop alone.

3. People throughout the entire organization (and even those outside it, such as customers and suppliers) leave these events poised to bring about agreed upon changes. In essence by having more people making changes, you move further, faster.

❝ One of the most important messages it sent in our system was that we're doing business differently," explains Hila Richardson, assistant vice president of long-term care for New York City's Health and Hospitals Corporation. Hila was a key player in the organization's use of the technology to support implementation of a managed care strategy. She points to an additional advantage of involving many people in these large group events. "We used to only have small groups of people planning these massive changes for the whole corporation. Having hundreds of people from different levels and locations come together in one spot in lower Manhattan sets a different tone right away. People feel involved and that these changes will be pervasive enough to stick this time."

Working Many Issues

If we hold up the mirror to the organizations we work and live in, we see a complex set of interrelated issues staring back at us. Russ Ackoff, a pioneer and leading voice in the field of systems thinking, uses a technical term to define what we see in that mirror; he calls it a "mess" (Ackoff, 1977). In most organizations we attack these "messes" by breaking them down into what we believe are manageable chunks; it is a process in which we are well-schooled, and we see it applied everywhere. In fact, it has been the basis of most scientific endeavors to date. Also the task of addressing the whole mess feels overwhelming to take on, given so much to comprehend and deal with simultaneously. Normally, top leadership teams and front-line groups alike tend to define the individual issues in the mess and then parcel them out to separate sub-committees, task forces, and other working groups. These sub-groups are given clear mandates to tackle their specific piece of the pie, be it customer satisfaction, employee morale, or new manufacturing or distribution systems. This penchant for breaking down reality into bite-size pieces as the only way to deal with it has much more to do with our limited levels of tolerance for ambiguity and complexity and our high need for control than it does with selecting and using processes that effectively define not only the issues, but the interrelationships that exist in organizational reality.

The real time strategic change technology has embedded within it processes for systemic analysis and synthesis in which people work on capturing the nature of these interrelationships between the many relevant issues their organizations face, simultaneously. This is not to say that the real time strategic change technology does not allow for component parts of a complex whole to be addressed. It merely ensures that the systemic nature is dealt with as well. Figure 4 illustrates the wide range of issues addressed in the example real time strategic change event described in Chapters 4, 5, and 6.

Imagine axes on the circular model like spokes of a wheel forming links between issue pairs opposite each other. A first set of issues addressed simultaneously by the technology is contained along the planning-implementation axis. For years, planning and implementation have been viewed as distinct, separate, sequential phases. First we plan, then we implement. In fact until only recently, many larger organizations had a separate staff department in charge of planning and line management responsible for implementation.

Several problems emerge from this paradigm of separating planning and implementation:

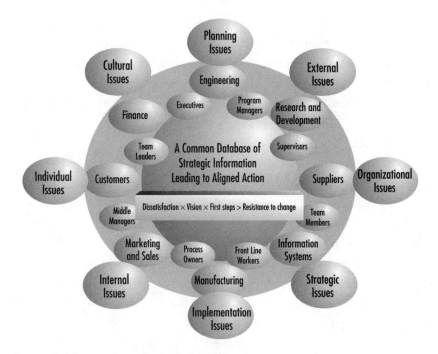

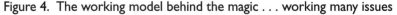

Figure 4. The working model behind the magic . . . working many issues

1. People in charge of implementing plans created for them by others do not "own," and may not even know that these plans exist.

2. Time lags between completing plans and implementing them result in missed opportunities in the marketplace. In other cases it may mean that plans are no longer relevant by the time they are implemented.

3. Plans created by people other than those who have to implement them, whether it be a group of planning experts or a representative cross-section of the organization, are based on limited information and suffer from inadequately dealing with the front-line issues at hand.

The real time strategic change technology focuses people's energy, thinking, and actions on planning and implementation issues at the same time. Particularly effective when widespread change must be implemented quickly, the technology creates opportunities for people to make some changes immediately, concurrent with the planning they are involved in.

For example, it is common for people to have meetings between newly created cross-functional teams within a real time strategic change event. These teams have not existed previously and may in fact be dealing with a purpose or issues that arose from deliberations at the meeting itself. New decisions and new behaviors take hold across entire organizations as people understand and own the plans they are charged with developing and implementing. In addition, plans are timely and address current challenges and opportunities facing the organization. Finally, these plans are based on a more complete picture of reality created from vested stakeholders' perspectives, rather than from a more narrow and objective view.

Another axis of the working model represents how the technology accounts for both internal and external organizational issues at the same time. "Inside looks" may take the form of sharing best practices across departments and facilities or may be diagnostic assessments of current organization-wide business processes. Another key aspect of this internal perspective is the establishment of collaborative relationships between functions and disciplines within the organization. Depending on the need, work on these relationships ranges from broad agreements between functions to detailed work flow and process changes within and between individual work groups.

This introspective analysis is balanced by a wide ranging external perspective garnered from numerous sources. For instance, leaders may share their view of the pressures facing the organization; or customers may join the large group events, sometimes as participants and sometimes as presenters (or both) to clearly spell out their expectations for products or services. Other external perspectives are gathered through the use of industry experts or case studies from other organizations. Design teams might also initiate task forces on specific issues in order to bring these important outside views into participants' thinking. Topics may range from people's experiences in changing the way they did business in another organization to the building of specific technical expertise. In some instances, where competitive pressures are a priority issue, participants can become their competitors to role play what they are doing and where they are headed, or even to formulate best guesses about how their competitors might view them, uncovering their own strategic vulnerabilities in the process.

A third axis of the model highlights the importance of addressing individual and organizational issues at the same time. In these interactive events, we continually shift between individual input, integrating the individual views into small group perspectives, and coalescing all this into an ever-growing organization-wide common database. We also continually shift in the other direction, from whole group data and decisions to smaller group implications to individual consequences, and then back again.

Roland Loup, a colleague of mine at Dannemiller Tyson Associates, believes that our real time strategic change technology implicitly addresses three basic individual human yearnings:

1. To have our voices heard.

2. To clearly be part of something larger than ourselves.

3. To be part of something successful.

The realization of these individual yearnings transforms into organizational learning as people begin to grasp the implications of their individual behavior and decisions on other members of the organization and those outside it (e.g. customers, suppliers, and communities). Each person engaged in the process has a right and responsibility to raise individual issues. Despite the seemingly daunting size of these events, participants in them normally feel free and are eager to share their truth.

The fourth axis in the model relates to the continuum between culture, or how we want to behave as an organization, and strategy, or what we hope to achieve and how. Both of these are considered at the same time when applying the real time strategic change technology. In the context of this book I define culture as the underlying shared values, beliefs, and assumptions that guide people's perceptions and behavior in an organization. With the real time strategic change technology, this culture begins to shift in the large group events via any number of counter-cultural experiences its members share. We begin the process through activities such as dialogues with leaders, customers, other functions and levels, as well as input sessions on organizational strategy. Empowerment and collaboration become more than just buzz words in the organization as system-wide decisions are arrived at based on newly agreed-upon assumptions and behaviors.

I broadly define strategy in this model as the focus for the change process, be it organization strategy development, such as mission, goals, and values; improving quality; redesign of work processes; building labor-management partnerships; leveraging diversity; or any number of other initiatives or combinations thereof. The real time strategic change technology is geared to addressing tough business issues and delivering tangible results. Each organization sets its own targets for change; the technology provides a powerful means for moving further, faster and changing an organization's way of doing business in the process.

Throughout the entire change process, and in the large group events in particular, these multiple issues are addressed. When taken together, this diverse set of issues provides another layer of foundation for the common database of strategic information built throughout real time strategic change events. In so doing, we enable participants to wrestle with the messy, complex issues and their interrelationships that must be part and parcel of any successful change effort.

❝ The low fruit on the trees can be found in your own area," points out Len Chuderewicz, president of USS-POSCO, a joint venture US–Korean steel company. He believes that only the simplest issues can get resolved within each individual area of his company. "Real big successes in resolving issues can only be done by getting planners, operators, accountants, and commercial people working together to fix specific processes. When you get people talking, it's amazing what you can accomplish. These events aren't an end-all to anything. They're a great jump-start to tackling a lot of issues, all at the same time."

Applying Many Methods

Another aspect of the working model behind the magic of the real time strategic change technology can be found within the various methods applied during the large group events. (See Figure 5 for examples of these different methods.)

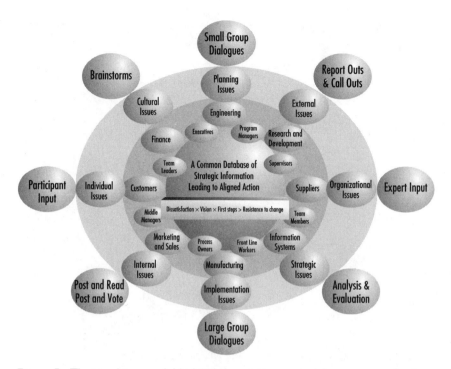

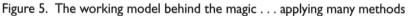

Figure 5. The working model behind the magic . . . applying many methods

Making use of a wide variety of methods or group processes in these events has several advantages:

1. People with different preferred learning styles are able to make valuable contributions because we employ several different modalities in the events, such as inductive and deductive thought processes, creative and analytical assignments, visual and auditory cues, and discussing and doing.

2. People remain attentive, engaged, and active throughout the process, even those not accustomed to sitting through lengthy meetings. Shifting among the numerous methods we employ during a several day event provides a lot of variety and enables people to do high quality work.

3. By continually changing the methods we use in the events, people focus primarily on the work being done, rather than on the process. Working to match the appropriate process methodology to people's nat-

ural desires throughout these events makes it possible for several hundred-person meetings to be efficient and effective. In so doing, the number of people in the room detracts minimally from the content.

The first axis of this working model of methods highlights dialogues that take place in small groups and those that occur in the whole group setting. Small group dialogues provide the best forum for individuals to listen and to be heard in some depth (e.g., Telling Our Stories and Organizational Norms) and for creating detailed plans (e.g., System-Wide Action Planning and Back Home Planning). Whole group dialogues, on the other hand, are tailored for broad, "big picture" learning opportunities, such as the open forums that are part of the Views from the Leadership and Customer Perspectives and the Change Possibilities Panel described in Chapters 4, 5, and 6.

Another axis of the working model describes the continuum between the free and open flow of ideas unleashed in a brainstorming session (e.g., Preferred Futuring) and the more rigorous examination, analysis, and evaluation that occurs in the Valentines module and in filling out Evaluations at the end of each day of the event.

The next axis highlights different ways in which we share information originally generated during small group work in the large group setting. Report outs and call outs are best applied when the information to be shared has already been integrated or prioritized (e.g., in the report out after voting on the System-Wide Action Planning), or to send a signal of increased importance or commitment. This is the case with the Organizational Norms module in the example design. In other situations the post and read and post and vote methods are more appropriate ways to share small group learnings or ideas with the total group. These include situations in which substantial amounts of small group data need to be seen by the total group (e.g., in the Valentines module) and when the large group needs to prioritize ideas generated in small groups, such as in the case of the System-Wide Action Planning module.

The fourth and final axis illustrates the continuum between the theory-based expert input (e.g., on total quality management tools) to the large group, and the input from individual participants (as in the

Organization Diagnosis or Preferred Futuring sessions). Occasionally during real time strategic change events, certain theories or models (e.g., the Change Formula, "Arthritic Theory" or even the tools and philosophies of Total Quality Management) are introduced during short talks. This input is interwoven with the work being done by participants in order to expand their awareness, or to learn tools and techniques necessary for the successful implementation of chosen strategies.

❝ Just getting the whole organization in a room and locking the doors would probably do a lot of good," muses Katherine Funk, manager of manufacturing and technical education at Corning. "But there's great variety in the activities and experiences people have as part of these events. You're invited to participate in a lot of different ways, and although the events are long, especially for some production workers who are used to more physical work, the different kinds of methods help keep people engaged and focused."

Making Many Changes

Finally, the great power and possibilities inherent in the real time strategic change technology can be found in the breadth and depth of organizational changes you can bring about through its application and the business results that can be created through the synergy among them. (See Figure 6 for examples of typical changes targeted by organizations who have applied the technology.)

These various changes occur for individuals, sub-groups (departments, sections, and work teams) and for the large group and organization as a whole. Different axes at this level of the model reflect the issues an organization chooses to work on. The critical point is that the real time strategic change technology is flexible and capable enough to address any or all of these diverse types of changes.

Along the first axis, the requisite paradigm shift during events leads to significant and lasting changes in people's attitudes. Participants leave these events with increased hope for, belief in, ownership of, and commitment to their organization and their roles in realizing its preferred

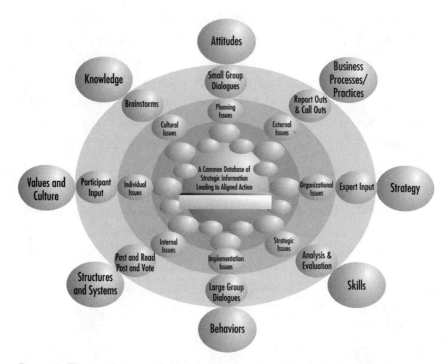

Figure 6. The working model behind the magic . . . making many changes

future. They possess a greater acceptance of individual responsibility, a willingness to make changes *and* an enhanced appreciation that they need to collaborate within and across functional boundaries to effectively make changes across the organization. The other end of this continuum addresses the need for behavioral change if the organization as a whole is to move into its preferred future. Behavioral changes can be seen in how people listen to each other in new ways—for understanding, not for evaluation—and in how people work together. "Walking the talk" of these new behaviors happens in real time in these events whether it be giving honest feedback in the Valentines module or working in cross-functional teams during the System-Wide Action Planning session. Over time, these same behaviors can be institutionalized back home in the workplace.

The second axis balances the need to develop both knowledge and skills. Participants individually and collectively expand their knowledge base as they learn more about their own organization's capabilities, the environment in which it operates, the relationships between their function and other functions, and even their role in the larger context of achieving results for the entire organization. All of this new knowledge supports people in making strategic decisions on a daily basis back on the job. They know the organization's overall strategic direction and align their individual decisions with it. People attending real time strategic change events also develop skills through their participation. The focus of the event dictates the skills they learn and enhance. For example, skills developed may include teamwork, dialogue, self-expression, creativity, facilitation, and listening from all the various forms, methods, and processes of working during these events. Other skills may include thinking strategically, using tools for total quality management or performing work design analysis. (See Chapter 9 for examples of these types of applications of the technology.)

A third axis addresses changes an organization may wish to make by placing strategy at one end of a hard/soft continuum, with values and culture at the other. Organization strategy is almost always shifted as part of a real time strategic change effort. Sometimes it is done explicitly, as in the example event described in Chapters 4, 5, and 6, and sometimes it occurs implicitly, as in large scale training initiatives focused on developing skill and knowledge bases required for people to do business in new ways. In the first case, participants have the opportunity to shape their organization's future direction by providing the leadership team with feedback on their draft strategy. In situations in which a top leadership team "locks in" the strategy and this turnaround technique is not utilized, implementation initiatives launched by the large group drive this shift in strategy throughout the entire organization. However, even the need for training people for their new roles and responsibilities can be traced to changes in organization strategy.

Changes in the soft end of this continuum, the values and culture of an organization, are addressed in a number of ways throughout a real time strategic change event. The Organizational Norms module raises everyone's awareness of the organization's current culture, while also providing a means for participants to begin building a picture of the culture they aspire to create for their future. When culture has been a key driver of the change effort, we have involved entire organizations in a process of developing a statement of values. This then becomes a guidepost for people's actions and decisions on a daily basis. Finally, the meeting process itself signals a shift in culture and values for many organizations. Broad-based participation and involvement in identifying, exploring, and addressing critical system-wide issues and opportunities represents a first step in doing business in new ways—one which occurs as an intrinsic aspect of all real time strategic change events.

The fourth and final axis in the working model describes the changes people make in business processes and practices, and the subsequent changes in organization structures and systems. New business practices emerge from these large group events through insights gained from external sources like the Change Possibilities Panel or benchmarking studies and internal sources like the cross-functional feedback exchanged during the Valentines module, or from a work redesign team. In organizations where work redesign is the focal point of the change effort, we address this issue directly with specific modules geared to analyzing current practices and developing new ways of doing business.

Often with the real time strategic change technology, people decide to form temporary structures to support their change efforts. For example, cross-functional teams formed during an event may continue to meet afterwards to make additional progress on system-wide issues. In some cases, the design team, a representative cross-section of all the people in the large group event, may sign up to coordinate all of the initiatives underway resulting from the event.

New strategies and business processes naturally lead to designing and implementing new, ongoing organization structures. For example, with new strategies or practices, some parts of an organization's structure may be either redundant or need creating; in other cases more subtle reconfiguring makes more sense. In addition, many organizations have used the real time strategic change technology to redesign systems ranging from information to performance appraisal, again in response to new strategies or processes. The wide cross-section of people able to be in attendance at these events ensures that all stakeholders' voices are heard in the process, and that implications inherent in changing fundamental structures and systems are raised, explored, and weighed before any decisions are made.

Finally, all of these changes ultimately lead to changes in business results. Lower costs, higher quality, and shorter cycle times have all been achieved by organizations employing the real time strategic change technology. Each organization defines the business results that matter most to them. The technology is a way to get further towards achieving those results, faster.

❝ We needed to change a lot of the ways we did business," explains Allen Gates, president of Kaiser Electronics, who has a long history applying the technology in several organizations. "For me the best gauges of our success have been the awards we've been winning from our customers and our improvement in some key operating measures. Not too long ago we had quality and delivery ratings of 50 percent—now those numbers are consistently in the 95 percent to 100 percent range. We've done a lot of follow-up to these large group events to make sure we don't lose any of the gains we've been able to make. We've found you really can't divide up the changes you need to make and work on them one at a time. Being able to bring together so many people to work all the changes at the same time has helped us deal a lot more realistically with the challenges facing our business."

A Proven Set of Principle-Based Processes and Practices

A real time strategic change effort may feel magical at some times and chaotic at others. However, all the proven strategies, tools, and techniques that comprise this technology are derived from a set of values, concepts, and principles drawn from theory and the experience gained from many applications. There is great variation to be found in the issues addressed, number and type of people involved, methods used, and changes made in organizations applying the technology. But the concept of simultaneity as described in this chapter is a critical component of all real time strategic change efforts. Innumerable options are available for large group event designs, enabling a customized fit of the technology to a particular organization's needs. Underlying this flexibility in design are the principles outlined in Chapters 4, 5, and 6. These principles comprise the foundation of all real time strategic change events. The actual work done in each stage of a real time strategic change process is described in Chapter 8. The example event previously described is only one stage of the entire change process. The remaining principle-based processes and practices that guide you through the overall design, preparation, and application take shape in Part III of the book, "Getting Started in Your Own Organization."

❝ Real time strategic change technology is an outstanding addition to the toolbox we use for manufacturing process improvement," says Dr. Anil Kharkar, a senior engineering associate at Corning. "Over the years, my co-workers and I have discovered a formula for continuous improvement of manufacturing processes. It consists of iterative sequential application of the three-phase strategy:

1. Improving operation consistency via good manufacturing discipline.

2. Achieving predictable performance by sound problem solving techniques.

3. Improving process capability via application of new technologies.

Substitute 'organization' or 'personal' for 'manufacturing' or 'process,' and substitute 'skills' for 'technologies' and you have a model for personal/organizational change.

"Effective implementation of the first phase in the strategy has been our toughest challenge," reveals Anil. "The problem is typically cultural, not technical. It requires a large number of people to think in the same direction. The real time strategic change process can produce that alignment in a very short time, and if followed up systematically with detailed actions, it has a tremendous potential of creating a cultural change with phenomenal speed."

❖ A HUMAN RESOURCES DIRECTOR'S PERSPECTIVE

Ed O'Brien, human resources director for Corning-Asahi Video Products Company, has worked at Corning for nearly thirty years. Although his college degree is in business, he admits to always having been a great student of the behavioral sciences. He enjoys searching for the answer to the question of what it takes to get people to change. He's held numerous human resources positions at Corning and his comments are derived from that broad base of experience.

"Earlier in my career as a human resources manager I had the chance to work with people on individual improvement and to drive change in an organization. Later, on special projects and as director of human resources for all of Corning, I began to focus more on an organizational perspective. In the late 1970s and early 1980s my main work in this company involved downsizing some businesses and divesting ourselves of others. Sometimes it meant closing plants. In 1987 I took over our corporate education and training group with the only direction coming from senior management: 'Make it have high impact in the corporation.' I set out to identify what high impact education and training was and what I found out was that although individual level learning is important and valuable, it actually constituted low impact for corporate education and training. Organizational level education is what drives fundamental change through a system, whether it's developing knowledge, skills, or abilities. It was in this context that I heard about these large group interactive workshops.

"At first I've got to tell you I was very skeptical. I came from a basic school of thought that said when Moses came down from Mount Sinai he had a third tablet of commandments which read, 'To have an effective interactive workshop, thou shalt have no more than twenty-five people in the room.' When we did some investigating with our own eyes and ears by observing this process in action in other organizations, we became convinced that it would work here in Corning—and it has.

"Looking back at a model we developed to distinguish high impact interventions driving fundamental organizational change from low impact interventions driving individual change, we discovered these events fall out on the right end of both scales. When you look at the rate an organization can change, the important factors that impact this are interaction, ownership, and giving people a better grasp of what's required to change and why. Working with twenty-five people at a time costs more than this approach ever will and worse yet, the time it takes is way too slow. More people than not choose to skip the interaction part of any change they're trying to make. They claim, 'My organization is too large. We've got to move on. We've got more changes to make, and besides, involving all those people is an expensive proposition.' I have found the dollar costs of this approach all very well justified over the long haul.

"We had a major reorganization in our domestic Consumers Products division a little while back. The division manager and staff cloistered themselves away and developed what they believed was the ideal organization. They really believed in it. They were planning the traditional company rollout of a reorganization—a two hour announcement event, with the senior staff staying for two more hours afterward for a further briefing. Organizations have done business that way for years and you get the traditional responses from that approach. People say, 'I'll lay back and see how it works before I sign up.' Others worry about how it'll affect their pay or whether they'll like the changes they'll have to make in their work. I asked the division manager and his staff, 'When you roll it out this way and say Follow me over the hill, why should they come? Why not try a different approach that involves bringing a large group of people together to work through how to make this reorganization different than any others in the past?' I think his only regret was that he didn't ultimately involve everybody in the division in the process.

"Plant managers, staff people and the sales organization all came together—350 in total—for several days. We built more ownership, car-ing, enthusiasm, and clarity than with any reorganization I've ever seen in this company. And it wasn't a flash in the pan. I honestly believe that this event and one that followed it a couple months later saved this organization at least one year's time in getting people supporting and operating effectively in this new direction.

"In the training area, we've changed a course called Impact, which has to do with reducing cycle time and reducing steps in any kind of process—production, sales, or engineering. In our old paradigm of having only twenty-five people at a time in these training events, we'd have people coming as individuals to this course. With the large scale approach at our disposal we effectively teach this course to a hundred people at a time and are able to move the company forward four times as fast. We also can bring in back home teams with real issues they can relate the training to, and end up passing on new skills and new business processes as part of the course.

"In terms of tips and advice, I'd have to ask you what your need is and what you're trying to accomplish. This is one of the greatest tools I've seen for energizing an entire organization fast and getting people focusing on real issues. It's the best time saver I know about for getting all of your people on board and moving in the same direction. You need to think through very clearly what you want to accomplish and design your process accordingly. Make sure you get the right people involved, even if that's a couple of hundred. I had my doubts when I first heard about this approach too, but I can tell you from personal experience that it works."

CHAPTER 8

A STEP-BY-STEP GUIDE TO REAL TIME STRATEGIC CHANGE

F or years now, organizational trainers and consultants of one sort or another have targeted groups of fifteen to twenty-five people as the focus of their work. Good ones think through the implications their interventions have on the rest of the system in which they are working; however, with such small groups of people coming on board at a time, systemic influence from this work is minimal and slow to spread. The exact opposite occurs in a change effort based on the real time strategic change technology: systemic implications stretch across entire organizations, occurring in rapid-fire fashion.

The large group events—and the work preceding and following them—add a level of complexity to the change process that, while necessary, can be very demanding. This necessity is based on the principle of dealing with all major issues simultaneously, in a true systems approach that addresses parts only in the context of the whole. Consequently, throughout a real time strategic change process, there is an intention to work all the salient issues, involve the right people at the right stages, apply the most appropriate methods, and eventually decide upon, define, and implement changes that optimize the impact on the whole system.

The technology you've read about so far in this book needs to be embedded within the larger context of an organization's entire change process in order to ensure maximum positive impact. Change is constantly occurring in organizations (in both planned and unplanned ways) and initiatives like this need to assess and account for this reality. Knowing how to support the overall environment of change, knowing what's involved in each phase of the planned process, and some tips and advice on success-fully navigating your way through them is what this chapter is all about.

Phases of a Real Time Strategic Change Process

Each real time strategic change process undertaken by an organization is unique. The key players, issues, and opportunities determine how the technology can be most effectively deployed in various situations at dif-ferent times. However, a handful of general phases consistent with a sound consultation model help define the scope of work required to ensure success (see Figure 7).

You can reasonably expect to navigate your way through these phases in about two months. More complex change efforts require longer lead times; however, we have been able to move from a "Let's do it!" deci-sion by a leader to implementing follow-up actions in as little as one month. To do so, you will need to free up a lot of resources in a short period of time (e.g., consultants, logistics team members, and locating a facility). Figure 7 shows a rough sequence of phases for a change process, but the phases as described may not fit the realities in your organization. You may find the need to repeat an earlier phase as your organization clar-ifies its position. What is important to note is how the phases work together to bring about real time strategic change.

Clear Contracting

❝ One of the main messages I think you need to get across very early on is that this technology is not a quick fix," emphasizes Ron Frederick, vice president of human resources with Thomson Information and an internal consultant in several real time strategic change efforts. He discusses several key points to address in this ini-tial phase of the work. "It increases an organization's odds a great deal, but alone will never be enough. When you start talking about what else will be required, it strikes people as very time consuming and involved. They say, 'Can't we just take a few people away for a short time instead of a lot of people away for several days?' It all

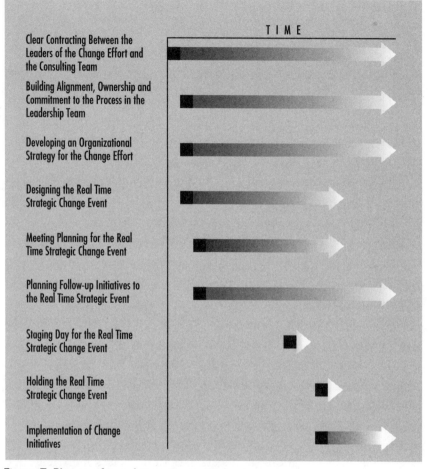

T I M E

Clear Contracting Between the
Leaders of the Change Effort and
the Consulting Team

Building Alignment, Ownership and
Commitment to the Process in the
Leadership Team

Developing an Organizational
Strategy for the Change Effort

Designing the Real Time
Strategic Change Event

Meeting Planning for the Real
Time Strategic Change Event

Planning Follow-up Initiatives to
the Real Time Strategic Event

Staging Day for the Real Time
Strategic Change Event

Holding the Real Time
Strategic Change Event

Implementation of Change
Initiatives

Figure 7. Phases of a real time strategic change process

depends on your purpose. If you want real change in your organization, I'm convinced you have to involve all the people who will be impacted. This process is merely a tool you can use to do real work on critical issues facing your business. It's up to the leader to decide how they want to use this tool, if at all."

The purpose of this phase is to establish a solid relationship between the organization's leader and the consulting team supporting the change effort based on:

1. A fifty-fifty collaborative working agreement of what you each bring to the partnership;

2. Honesty and openness including sharing assumptions you have of each other, your needs, roles you need to play and the work to be done; and

3. Doing work that will make a difference for the organization, its members, customers, and other stakeholders.

The core work this relationship is built on includes defining the scope and boundaries of the process and of the organization affected (i.e., what is addressed and who is involved), the desired results to be achieved from the initiative (e.g., what success would look like), and the particular roles the leader and consultants will need to play throughout the process. Each subsequent phase in the change process may include additional contracting or recontracting regarding issues between the leader and consultants—some expected, others that emerge—with the most common and important of these discussed in the following description of phases.

The clearest measure of success from this phase of work is that the real time strategic change process moves forward with the leader involved, informed, and committed as key issues arise, are decided, and the process unfolds. Because of the accelerated pace of organizational change associated with this methodology—and the far-reaching implications that accompany its application—leaders who opt out, defer, or are left out of key decisions discover their change efforts quickly moving down a path they may not be able to endorse. It is critical that leaders and consulting teams be full and equal partners in this endeavor. A real time strategic change process is not something to be pursued lightly. Profound changes will follow from applying this technology. Make sure they are the changes you want and need to make in your organization. Initial agreements on scope and deliverables may need to be revised and amended as you gather new data and move into new phases of work.

A real time strategic change initiative will lead to uncharted waters for the vast majority of people in organizations and will likely be contrary to their past experiences regarding organizational change. It is important to spend time educating them about the many options and paths available in moving forward. The more fully key players can understand the implications of this technology early on, the better able they are to consider the systemic implications of various choices before acting, and the better spokespeople for the process they can be. As they come to understand the power and possibilities of this approach, they will be able to educate others in their organization as well. People will watch the moves and listen to the words of these key players very carefully to gauge their commitment to and likely success of this change effort. Having a clear contract at all times between the leader of the change effort and the consultants providing support helps ensure that the messages sent around the organization about the initiative are congruent and clear.

Building Alignment, Ownership, and Commitment

❝ When I've talked to some of our management teams and told them they could bring together 350 people from their hotel in one room for an interactive event," describes Asma Ma'ani, the director of human resources and training at the Amman Marriott, "they ask me, 'Are you sure you can handle that many?' A lot of the work with the leadership team involves education. It starts early on in this process and continues throughout it. The more they understand about how this process works the better leadership they can provide for it."

The leader of the change effort must sign up the top leadership team for support. The purpose of this second phase of work is to educate the top leaders in an organization so they can make informed decisions about the real time strategic change process, their respective roles in it, and how they will need to work together in order to ensure its success. The focus of the work for this phase includes identifying and monitoring measures of success throughout the change process (the specific deliverables needed as a result of applying the technology), allocating resources as needed (including money, people, and the organization's time), and making key decisions regarding the positioning of the change process (agreeing on the key internal and external stakeholders who need to be involved and how, as well as clarifying the direction they want to give to the design team).

Success in this phase of a real time strategic change process can be measured in several ways. First, leadership teams will act more as one team and less as a group of department or division heads focused on their own turf (even in teams that seldom exhibit this kind of win-lose behavior). Second, the top group increasingly will be seen as a considered, congruent, strong team by the rest of the organization, modeling the cross-functional collaboration on a small scale that will be borne out of the real time strategic change event on a large scale. Third, over time the organization's leaders will engage in deeper dialogues on strategic system-wide issues and see the real time strategic change technology as a viable and valuable means for addressing these issues. Fourth and finally, these leaders will be prepared to step up to whatever acts of leadership are required throughout the entire change process, within the large group event, outside of it, and beyond it.

No one person, regardless how great a leader, can single-handedly create successful organizational change because it requires the input, ownership, and commitment of others. Especially with the scope, pace, and complexity of the real time strategic change process, there are sheer physical and information factors that preclude sole ownership, apart from the need to secure firm commitment from others through sharing equity in the undertaking. The debates and dialogues leadership teams engage in with each other before making critical decisions are vital in establishing exactly what it is that they agree is worth going after and the results that they desire for their organization. Recall that when a rocket is launched toward the moon, constant monitoring, data gathering and course corrections are required along the way or it misses its mark by a long, long way. Focusing hundreds or even thousands of people to discuss and deliberate on static organizational issues in a fast-changing world yields a similar effect. By listening to see the world through each other's eyes and developing agreements based on an expanded world view, leadership teams develop the alignment, ownership, commitment, and openness to the process needed to make these course corrections in real time. As people in an organization watch and listen to their leaders, they get a continual read on their commitment to the change effort. Further, they positively scrutinize the people they directly report to on the same issues because at this level the potential for impact on their work seems greatest. Real time strategic change in this top group means real business to the rest of the people in their organization.

Developing an Organizational Strategy for the Change Effort

❝ This is really an important step in bringing a top team together," highlights Lynn Brown, director of corporate human resources for Allied–Signal, in discussing the importance of the strategy development phase of the change effort. "A unified leadership group is basically a requirement of this process. The strategy or product from this phase is important, but even more so I think the real value is in the team building opportunity you have. Getting the entire top team involved in setting the strategy for the change effort is a powerful way of developing commitment to the changes you're trying to implement."

The purpose of this phase is to ensure that an appropriate organizational strategy (i.e., the topic and substance of the whole change initiative given current issues and opportunities) is developed and that the leadership team is capable of providing the direction needed to focus the organization's energy on the right things, at the right time in the right ways. Think of this overall change strategy as a big picture plan involving your total organization. In contrast, designing specific real time strategic change events defines subsets of this larger process involving hundreds or thousands of people. The extent to which the strategy developed in this phase is treated as a draft depends on the level of involvement others have in creating it. For example, in certain situations it may make the most sense not to involve other members of the organization, because their most valuable contribution might be made by designing specific events, or in implementing actions agreed to in these events. In other circumstances you may reap great benefits from having others involved in revising or even developing this overall strategy for the change effort. Dialogues between leaders, consultants, and the design team provide insight and guidance into this key choice point in the process.

What is not negotiable is that you have a strategy for the change effort that people can align their actions with. These strategies are developed based on six key steps:

1. Identifying and clarifying the basic, important issues facing the organization as a whole.

2. Agreeing on an overall purpose for the change effort.

3. Deciding which people need to be involved in the change effort and how.

4. Determining how much influence these people need to have over the development of this strategy.

5. Clarifying the information people will need to do quality work and make wise decisions regarding their collective future.

6. Exploring the methods, processes, and approaches that will best support people in making real time strategic changes. (See Chapter 10 for a more detailed discussion of this process.)

Regardless of who develops the strategy in this phase, three key results need to be achieved. First, the strategy needs to effectively respond to the realities of the internal and external environments and the diverse set of needs posed by all key stakeholders. These stakeholders include people inside the organization (from the CEO to the front-line workers), as well as those outside it (customers, suppliers, and communities). Second, the strategy must ultimately position the organization for success in the future. Keep in mind that applying this technology makes the future happen faster. Having people making real time strategic changes in their organization, all aligned with a flawed strategy is a recipe for mediocrity, or even disaster. Third, a stronger team of people to provide leadership for the change effort needs to emerge from the work of this phase. Regardless of organizational titles and grade levels, the strategy for the change effort—and the rationale underlying it—must be clearly presented at the large group event. The creators of the strategy need to be able to articulate it in a simple, straightforward way that breathes life into the words and concepts on paper. Leadership, in this sense, is about drawing circles that include people in the strategy development process. If people cannot easily understand the strategy that has been developed, they are unlikely to discuss it well, revise it wisely, or implement it successfully.

Simply put, by getting the right people together, having them working on the right issues, by providing them with the information they need to make wise choices for their organization, and by creating an open interactive process for them to work within, good decisions will be made in this phase. This formula is the embodiment of a new way of doing business. Making it happen should become a focus for people at all levels in the organization. "The right people" in this case need to be the right people in the organization's eyes. Personally, I represent a strong voice for involving people in decisions that affect their work, and I believe that letting people have a hand in developing their organization's strategy is an exciting and powerful model, a chance to be part of something successful that is bigger than the individual. I also believe this approach—however exciting and powerful—might not be appropriate or effective in all situations. In certain circumstances, people in an organization need and have a right to be able to look to their leadership for direction without detracting from their right to decide how to implement that direction. In other situations, a top group might pull together and develop into the leadership team the organization has been wanting through the work they do in this phase. Involving other people in the process might preclude that from happening. Still other dynamics such as the time required to adequately educate people in the complex web of internal and external challenges and opportunities facing the business might argue against involving a larger group in this phase. In these cases it may make the most sense to carry out certain analyses and draw certain conclusions before opening these deliberations to a critical mass of the organization.

Remember too, that the right issues and the right information are hard and soft in nature. Fact-based planning is a critical component of developing solid organizational strategies, especially when building a common database of strategic information. However, innovative strategies are often borne out of people's intuitions, hunches and unsubstantiated beliefs. Integrating these seeming dichotomies is a key to success in this phase. Finally, the real time strategic change technology can be adapted to support the development and implementation of all manner of organizational strategies representing different schools of thought and different disciplines. We have applied it with equal success to strategies ranging from implementing a new product development process to master-minding solutions to the knotty issues involved in mergers and joint ventures. Other organizations have applied the technology to further training strategies or to develop new information systems requirements. In point of fact, we have yet to discover a change strategy that could not benefit from the commitment, clarity, and collaborative action fostered by the real time strategic change technology.

Designing the Real Time Strategic Change Event

❝ It really is different every time," begins Julie Beedon, an internal consultant in the Employment Service, an arm of the British civil service. She reflects on her own learnings, saying, "Just when you're doing what you needed to for the last group, you realize it doesn't fit for the organization you're now working with. The more times I work with the alignment process, the more I realize how flexible it is. No two events have even been remotely similar, and that's because no two organizations I've worked with have been in remotely the same set of circumstances."

The purpose of this phase is to design an event that is responsive to the issues, challenges and opportunities facing your organization. In short, the challenge is to craft a plan that will get your organization from where it is now to where it needs to be in the future. Two major tasks define the work of this phase:

1. Revisiting and, if needed, refining the overall plan for your organization's change process developed in the previous phase.

2. Designing the cornerstone of that process, the real time strategic change event(s).

The overall intervention strategy helps guide an organization through the maze of key questions and choice points that determine the scope of the change effort. The designs for specific events ensure that you take maximum advantage of the opportunities for synergy and leverage by bringing together a critical mass of your organization at the same place and time. Designs for real time strategic change events are developed through a collaborative process by the organization's leadership team and the event's design team. The work of designing these interactive large group events is described in greater detail in Chapter 11.

The most significant result achieved in this phase of work is a clear plan of action—both at the macro and micro levels—that will serve as your organization's guide for the event and the rest of the process. This guide includes target time frames and the roles key players will have in the event and beyond it, ensuring that each aspect of the overall change effort is set up for success. Another measure of success in this phase is that the people involved—its leaders, the design team, and others—expand their knowledge about, ownership of, and commitment to the change effort. Leaders, consultants, and logistics team members should come to know and understand the event design thoroughly, and while owning it, be prepared to make the inevitable changes needed as the process unfolds.

It is worth remembering that you are engaged in an evolutionary process for the organization that is bigger than the particular change effort, but catalyzed by it. Because organizational changes occur so rapidly through the use of this technology, plans can never be set in concrete. For example, leaders in one organization had decided initially that their overall strategy would involve one system-wide real time strategic change event followed by more specifically targeted events designed for individual facilities. The problem with this plan was that after attending the system-wide event, all of the individual facilities were eager to continue their implementation efforts—and each of them wanted to be the first to have their own events. This created a "high class" problem. People in these organizations wanted to make changes faster than even their leaders had initially envisioned. Our solution was to bring together representatives of the individual facilities at one time, customize certain portions of the event to meet unique facility needs and further reduce the cycle time of implementing system-wide changes.

Stay flexible and see potential issues or problems as opportunities to move further, faster. Don't be constrained by your own past practices, or anybody else's. We have continued to expand the applications of this technology throughout the past decade. The previous story is just one example of a multitude of innovations and improvements we have discovered. I encourage you to be creative with the technology in response to new data and unique circumstances, to push the boundaries and to share your inventions with others. I am confident that at this point, we have merely scratched the surface of possibilities available through this unique and powerful approach to organizational change.

Meeting Planning for the Real Time Strategic Change Event

❝ There are a lot of details that need to be tracked in getting ready for the large group events, and one of the important roles we identified is the interface between the design and logistics teams," explains Gill Thompson, an internal consultant at the Boeing Company. "Logistics can often feel like a second class citizen role if they get conflicting messages. It's one of the consultant's jobs to make sure that doesn't happen. Good teamwork between the consultants, logistics, and design teams is a must. Without it, everybody's job becomes much harder and the more things are sure to slip through the cracks before, during, or after the event."

The purpose of this phase of work is to establish a collaborative relationship to enable the people in charge of managing the event's logistics requirements to successfully plan, stage, and execute them. In so doing, consultants need to form a partnership with the person who heads the logistics team, called the logistics czar. The work in this phase ranges from reserving a facility and copying materials for participants to stage managing and choreographing lights, sound, and the innumerable actions that need to be taken by logistics teams to ensure the smooth and effective delivery of the actual event. Roles and responsibilities for the logistics team and between logistics, design, and consulting teams are agreed upon during this phase. (See the "to do" list for logistics described in Chapter 12.)

A couple of key results can be expected from success in this phase. First, consultants and the logistics czar will, through having developed a good working relationship, give and receive feedback as freely and as often as needed to enhance smooth performance and successful delivery of the event. The need for and direction of mutual feedback leads to more mature, purposeful, and effective dialogues between these key players. Second, the logistics team should be well on its way to becoming a competent, interdependent group capable of executing any and all of the planned (and unplanned) logistics that arise during the event.

Team building is an important aspect of this phase. Clear contracting between consultants and logistics czars about expectations they have of each other, and how they can best support each other, is a good first step. Putting pet peeves on the table soon after you get started can make a world of difference. Although the roles, responsibilities, and focuses of these two players are different by design, they share the common goals of a successful change process and of making the event as user-friendly as possible. One key to any good working relationship is access. Consultants need to make themselves available for updates, questions, and input their logistics czar may have, especially when consultants do not think they need to. Real time strategic change applies as much to the logistics requirements for these events as it does to the decisions and actions taken by participants in them.

Planning Follow-up Initiatives

❝ You really have to plan for the follow-up in this process," says Katherine Funk. Her consulting experience at Corning points out the importance of thinking ahead early on in the process. "The events are only one meeting, and if it doesn't feel like there's going to be any progress after it, you need to wave that flag. Planning and follow-up are both important—without them all you have is one good event."

The purpose of this phase is to lay the groundwork for a series of follow-up initiatives that will support people across an entire organization in building on the momentum generated in the large group event and in continuing to implement real time strategic changes. Because a real time strategic change event is only a point in organizational time, many parallel initiatives to support the changes often add a great deal of value. These parallel initiatives may be thought of as enhancing the organization's capacity to make changes and optimizing the results from them. Pre-planning this support for implementation efforts is usually required when it is unlikely that these plans would be developed during the event, and when these plans need to be in place by the time of the event in order to support implementation plans developed during the event.

If you treat these large group sessions as one-shot meetings and hope for the best, you will be disappointed by the results you achieve. However powerful the technology, and however committed people are, events alone are not enough of a catalyst for change. Follow-up is a must. Because getting hundreds of people pointed in the same direction, committed to implementing changes, and clear about their individual roles in that process makes the future happen faster, follow-up planning is best started as soon as possible after a decision is made to use the technology. Once the scope of the overall initiative is known, there are many areas where follow-up planning can begin at once. Examples of some of these areas are training and development, introduction of new technologies, changes likely to need different systems support from current configurations, workforce planning, involving those affected who were not at the event, and detailed work redesign.

An organization's follow-up initiatives are tailored to its particular needs and situation. However, there are several general options, such as real time strategic change diffusion events, which enable those people who were not able to attend the main event to be informed of and involved in the outcomes and plans made there. Follow-up efforts might also include reunion events three to twelve months in the future; targeted training and development efforts, including well-resourced "action research" initiatives; and various spin-off initiatives and support mechanisms. These follow-up initiatives are described in greater detail in Chapter 13. They often start with ideas generated by the leadership or design teams; however, as more people become involved in the planning and preparations for a real time strategic change event, the number of people participating in these dialogues increases.

Several key results are achieved from this phase of work that support the overall change effort:

- The reality of the organization's present inertia is included in people's thinking throughout the process. The enthusiasm that people enjoy during the large group events needs to be grounded in reality. Thinking about follow-up plans helps make that happen;

- A growing number of people feel and are accountable for making sure the process does not stall at the implementation phase, or lead to a lot of frustration and false starts because support mechanisms for successful implementation are lacking;

- People throughout the organization—even in the early stages of the process—begin thinking future, now.

This skill—and it is a skill—enables managers and front-line workers alike to make real time strategic change a way of life in their organization. Using a common database of strategic information as a touchstone, you ensure that follow-up initiatives support many of the decisions and actions people take on a daily basis to implement planned changes.

In some cases, people fail to see the need to begin planning follow-up initiatives before the event phase of the process. Plans participants make in a real time strategic change event are, to a certain degree, unpredictable; however, thinking through the organization-wide issues from the beginning and developing likely or possible scenarios from which to generate follow-up initiatives has an organization much better prepared for what may be ahead and more ready to support the implementation of change. Follow-up initiatives also need to send messages consistent with those sent during the event. They must inform people's discretion about the organization's strategy and future direction, empower them to make changes in their own spheres of influence, and support them in joining an organization-wide team engaged in creating a future they want to call their own.

Finally it is worth noting that plans for follow-up initiatives made early in the process may need to change to remain relevant later on down the line. Starting these dialogues early is necessary. Continuing them throughout the change process is critical. They make the difference between people enjoying a different kind of meeting and creating an organization in which they are vitally involved, feel valued, and know that the contribution they have made is part of a larger whole.

Staging Day

❝ There's always been a high level of excitement for people who volunteer to be on the logistics team in the agency," explains Anita Dias, project manager for METRO's system-wide cultural change effort. "Even though it's pretty petty tasks, it's a wonderful team experience, and people get a real sense of contributing to what we're creating. They are the heart of this process. If they are not successful, we are not successful. Staging Day (the day before the large group event begins) is time set aside to make sure that people know their roles and that everything is ready to roll for the event."

The purpose in this phase of work is to ensure that the leadership, logistics and consulting teams, and the staff from the facility where your event is being held are prepared to respectively lead, support, and facilitate a successful event. Staging Day is a final checkpoint before hundreds of people begin finding their way to max-mix tables.

Specific staging days vary by organization and event. For example, leaders might want to review the design for the event. In other cases, they may want to get feedback on a presentation they plan to make to the total group. A few leaders even want to make a first-hand check that logistics arrangements are in order. Still others just want to spend some time talking about their leadership team or how other people in their organization are reacting to the real time strategic change process and to the upcoming event.

Throughout staging day, consulting, logistics, and facility teams play planning, preparation, quality control, and coordination roles. A final step-by-step review of the design by consultants and the logistics czar is also done so that every foreseeable loose end can be tied up. (See Chapter 12 for more detail.) Staging Day also provides one last opportunity for the consulting team to prepare before the curtain goes up and their attention must shift focus to all manner of things. During this preparation time, they will need to agree on specific roles for the first day of the event, such as who will facilitate each module. (It is not worthwhile splitting up the entire event's facilitation responsibilities on Staging Day because the agenda often changes during the event.) In addition, consultants need to contract for the type of support they will need from each other during the next few days so that they can focus their collective energy on the tasks at hand.

Staging Day is a major "moment of truth" for the logistics team where, for the first time in the process, they discover exactly how well prepared they are to deliver a first-class experience for participants. It is a day of accelerated growth when roles and responsibilities need clarification, and when a clearer plan of the work required emerges. Attributes of flexibility, responsiveness, creativity, and humor are great advantages both for the logistics czar and the team members in solving existing and potential problems.

The deliverables for Staging Day may seem small to big picture thinkers, but don't be deceived. They are absolutely critical components of a successful real time strategic change event. The facility, its systems (e.g., lights, sound, and catering), and the people involved need to be ready to roll in the morning.

In some ways, Staging Day is similar to a practice session for the next day. The number of stakeholders' needs during Staging Day pale in comparison to the number you will be confronted with during the event, but the practice and experience gained are keys to effectively handling the expanded challenge. The entire organization has a lot riding on what happens during the next few days. Leaders have made a significant investment in this technology, and they are taking a great risk. The logistics team has already devoted long hours to preparing for this event, and their hardest, most intense work still lies ahead. Your consulting team has taken on a complex and demanding task that also requires significant investment and a good deal of risk as well. Tomorrow you take the next step in the process together, so the anxiety and stress levels may be a bit high. A light touch and a little humor can go a long way toward putting people in the right frame of mind to deliver good performance on their part of the process during the next few days.

Holding the Event

66 You have to wear many hats during these events and you're constantly shifting through a wide variety of roles," begins Ian Peters, an internal change agent at Northrop, who has used the real time strategic change technology in a variety of settings ranging from community development initiatives to corporate strategy events. He relates his experiences in facilitating the large group events saying, "Making sure the afternoon assignment will still work given what's happening in the group and coaching leaders at the same time are pretty different tasks. Also, once you move into a new role, you need to be present and accountable immediately. A lot of times the windows of opportunity are small in these events, and you need to be prepared to capitalize on them as soon as they bubble up."

The purpose of this phase of the process is to maximize the positive potential impact of the event. Tremendous opportunities exist in these events for a critical mass of people to agree on and implement system-wide changes. Seeking out and pushing on these inherent leverage points in the process is the basic business of this phase, with the primary work being to balance the diverse, changing, and sometimes competing needs of numerous stakeholders to ensure its success. The trick to competently moving through this phase is to continually gather data from all key stakeholders, then based on that data, know what you most need to do at each moment, as well as who needs to be involved to most effectively move the process forward. Each of the roles that need to be carried out is described in more detail in Chapter 12.

Specific results achieved during a real time strategic change event depend on the particular issues addressed. However, the following list outlines a handful of outcomes you can expect to achieve:

- Increased organization-wide awareness of, commitment to, and even actions taken in support of, a new strategy;

- Expansion of the organization's effective leadership, with more people taking ownership of the organization and feeling accountable for its success;

- Key stakeholders, including customers, experience the strategy as responsive to their particular needs and are excited to see it implemented;

- Individual participants leave the event clear on how they can best contribute to the organization's success, and they are individually and jointly committed to making these contributions.

These large group events can be challenging and exciting. Continually stepping back far enough so you can see the whole process—and all key stakeholders—will help you stay above the fray and keep a balanced perspective. It is important to keep your focus and intent clear and stay well-connected to the dynamics unfolding in the large group. No one leader, consultant, logistics team member, participant, or even an entire team working independently is capable of doing all that needs to be done. As is true in the daily operations of your organization, teamwork and managing well across functions are keys to success, as is following the principle-based processes and practices outlined in this book.

Implementation of Change Initiatives

❝ I'm the kind of person who likes to get things accomplished," comments Fred Mohr, a leader in the development phase of United Airlines' team-based Indianapolis Maintenance Center (IMC). He describes the value added by the technology in designing and developing this entirely new facility. The Center's systems, structures, processes and culture took shape in a series of real time strategic change events attended by the 350 mechanics, engineers and support personnel who comprise the IMC team. "The events we've all been a part of have helped get everybody operating off the same agenda— being a world-class airplane maintenance organization. By focusing people on that higher goal and not exclusively on their individual objectives, we've been able to get a lot more done quicker in terms of designing the organization and how we want to operate it. Now our challenge is to transfer the energy and enthusiasm we've built in designing the organization and culture we want to making it happen in real life. Bottom line, meeting the targets and timelines we've set for ourselves will be our best measure of success."

The purpose of this final phase of work is to ensure that the individual and organizational energy unleashed in the real time strategic change event is supported, expanded, and capitalized on over the longer haul. Change initiatives from real time strategic change events generally take one of two forms. The first of these is akin to the basic fundamentals of organizational life. Individuals, department groups, even entire organizations make commitments in these large group events to do business in new ways in the future. Action plans are developed with associated time frames; responsible and supporting key players are identified. Simply stated, this form of follow-up is doing what you said you would do. Although additional consulting support may add value in this arena, it is likely limited in scope. The day-to-day management and operations of the organization are best left in the hands of managers and operators.

The second type of change initiative stems from the follow-up plans made earlier in the process. These are geared to keeping the fires for change burning throughout an organization. Additional plans for supporting change may be made at the event, and the original ones now may need revision based on data from the event. Supporting initiatives include real time strategic change diffusion and reunion events, targeted training and spin-off efforts of various types. Many types of follow-up initiatives are described in greater detail in Chapter 13.

As you might expect, different organizations seek to achieve different results with their chosen initiatives depending on the purpose and focus of their change effort. However, several common themes have emerged:

- The energy, motivation, and readiness for change built during the event expands throughout the organization;

- The leadership team visibly demonstrates its commitment to the change effort because people see them "walking their talk" back in the workplace;

- Changes are well supported and targets, whatever they may be, are met or exceeded.

You may experience a mental, emotional, and/or physical letdown after the celebrations from the event subside. Others who have helped plan and coordinate the large group event may be feeling the same way. This is a natural response. You have poured a great deal of time and energy into an event that has the potential of changing not only your organization, but people's lives. It is best to capitalize on the energy for change unleashed in the process by having leaders make a few quick and especially meaningful changes immediately after the event. Publicizing these decisions and actions widely reinforces people's beliefs that this time, change is for real.

Because it is important that the people involved in real time strategic change events receive easy, ongoing access to strategic information, follow-up efforts often include the design and implementation of new systems, processes, and structures that facilitate the flow of this information. Also, organizations often see a significant increase in requests for training after these events because participants recognize they need new skills in order to operate more effectively in their changing organization. Finally, continuing to involve large groups of people through various initiatives builds an ever larger community of people committed to the new direction in the organization, further accelerating the implementation of needed changes throughout the system.

❖ A MANUFACTURING PLANT MANAGER'S PERSPECTIVE

Jerry Lewis is the manager of Ford Motor Company's Dearborn, Michigan Glass plant, which has been part of a renewal effort involving the entire division. His work history before coming to Ford was, in his own words, varied and interesting. He served for thirteen years on active duty in both the marines and the army as an officer and enlisted man, earning his college degree at night. He worked his way up through the manufacturing organization at Corning from a shift supervisor to plant manager at Steuben Glass. Jerry also served as the Director of Administration for the Grace Commission under President Reagan in which industry sent business people to Washington to make recommendations on the federal budget. In addition he has also taught courses in management and statistical process control at Florida A & M and Florida State Universities. He came to Ford Motor Company in 1987 and since then has worked his way up to his present position.

"From all my experience, I believe the only challenge within organizations are people. I don't believe the floor sweeper is any less important than I am. Working with these people is how our mission is accomplished, and it's always impressed me how incredibly honest those closest to the production floor are. If people can put aside their differences, the job becomes incredibly easy.

"I found the real time strategic change approach to be a very refreshing communication process. You can see your organization from different people's eyes with the same perspective you get from walking around a circle. I found it to be right on. I can look at a set of issues and you can look at these same issues, and we'll see them differently. But putting everybody's pictures together cuts through an amazing amount of time. If you asked the same questions and worked the same issues you did in these events, but used a hierarchical chain of command, it'd take you one month for something you can accomplish in two days in these large group events. With everybody in the room you get at the real meat— you don't even have to work with the potatoes. You can filter right through to the important elements in everyone's eyes. Here's one example to show you what I mean. If I had asked the chain of command if we had a 'good ol' boy' network in our plant and would it survive this renewal process we're involved in, they'd have told me, 'No, no, no.' But we sat in this large group meeting and sitting and talking about the issues made it clear: it did exist and a lot of people weren't happy about it. The workers surfaced it, we're working it right now, and it's dying.

"I'd say there's really three stages at which I'd recommend using this process. First if I had a new job, I'd push for it immediately. It'll give you a good firm look at the skeleton of your organization—you'll see the bones, but none of the fat. Next if I were told by a customer that things between us were not the way they should be, then I'd use this approach to spread that word and figure out what we were all going to do about it. Finally for strategic reasons, if I had a business that was entrenched and needed to get unshackled, this is the way I'd do it.

"Why bother going this route? To that I'd have to ask you, 'Do you really want change in your organization?' If you do, you have to get all your people involved. If you did it with a memo or order, change doesn't come because you issue it. You need to work the dynamics and people's behavior—you need to involve them. You may be thinking that this costs a lot. In effect we shut down our plant for two days and saw no appreciable cost in our bottom line—and we've got 640 people in this plant.

"We've got a twenty person team that helped design our event and is helping lead our renewal process. They meet weekly shift-to-shift and across different levels and jobs to keep the fire burning, to work through obstacles as they appear. Follow-up is as important, if not more so, than the large group events. There are three follow-up items that I think capture the excitement we've got going in this plant right now:

1. I am absolutely amazed that all of these people turned out to be leaders. There's one accounting analyst who's shown leadership that

I'd have never guessed she had (she never really had a way to exercise it before, either).

2. I am elated about the masses of people in this plant that are craving change, walking around asking, 'How can we fix this problem?'

3. We decided one of the things we were going to go after with this renewal process was quality, and now I've got 640 watchdogs in charge of quality in my plant.

"I can see a need to use this approach in government, starting at the state level and working your way right up to the Congress. A lot of them certainly don't seem to see the world through our eyes. I also see an avid need for this in education at the local and state level. After teaching for four years in two universities, I know from first-hand experience that this process would be valuable for educators. There are a lot of places besides this plant where it could be helpful, but you've got to want change. Everyone wants to say, 'I'm a great leader' but leadership has to be shared. The most dynamic thing about this approach though, was how easy decisions came when we went through the consensus process. You'd think it would take more time to get all these people in agreement, but it was just the opposite. I'm convinced we've gotten a lot more accomplished in a lot less time than if we'd have tried to do this all by the chain of command."

PART THREE

GETTING STARTED IN YOUR OWN ORGANIZATION

CHAPTER 9

UNIQUE PATHS FOR UNIQUE ORGANIZATIONS: FIVE STORIES OF REAL TIME STRATEGIC CHANGE

T he real time strategic change technology is a powerful means for launching all kinds of change efforts in all manner of organizations. In *Part II, Moving Further into the Future, Faster,* I outlined an example three–day strategy development and implementation event. I also explored the working model and presented a roadmap for effectively applying this technology. This chapter describes five specific real time strategic change efforts, each one representing a customized application of the technology. These stories by no means represent the universe of possible applications. Instead, they are intended to stimulate your thinking about the issues and opportunities facing your own organization, and the potential ways in which the real time strategic change technology could support you in moving into your own organization's future, faster.

Ken Freeman, president and CEO of Corning–Asahi Video, the largest U.S. supplier of color television glass, opens the chapter with his story of how the real time strategic change technology enabled 1,200 people to save a business for Corning and jobs for themselves. The second, told by Rick Goldstein, vice president of Marriott's Hotels, Resorts, and Suites division, describes how the technology was used to support a worldwide assault on quality by the company's 100,000 associates. Next Ben Chu, a senior vice president in New York City's Health and Hospitals Corporation, relates how the large group events that form the corner-stone of the real time strategic change technology have accelerated the implementation of a managed care mode of practice throughout his system. This required adopting a patient–centered approach in everything from marketing to appointment scheduling systems. Continuing on this journey we hear from Dick Sandaas, the executive director of METRO, a public agency responsible for water pollution control and transportation in King County, Washington. Dick and 4,000 METRO employees used the real time strategic change technology to directly address some long–standing cultural diversity issues in systemic ways. He believes that using this approach had much more impact than traditional diversity awareness training techniques. The chapter closes with Tom Elliott, deputy superintendent of the St. Lawrence–Lewis Board of Cooperative Educational Services. He recounts how he and others brought together 450 people drawn from across communities in eighteen rural school districts in upstate New York to begin crafting a new role for public educators as partners with businesses, colleges, universities, parents, students, and the communities they serve.

All five organizations targeted an array of changes based on their unique needs. Their stories share three common themes:

1. They needed to bring about significant change in the way they did business.

2. They wished to accelerate the pace at which change was implemented.

3. They believed the best way to make these changes was to involve those people who were interested in or affected by them in a fundamental way.

STORY 1: CORNING–ASAHI VIDEO PRODUCTS COMPANY

"Of all the businesses in Corning, Incorporated," explains Ken Freeman, the president and chief executive officer of Corning–Asahi Video (CAV), "we had the largest improvement in our ROE of anyone in the company last year . . . and we're continuing to make progress." However, good news was not always associated with this Corning operation. Profits had been unacceptably low for many years. "When I came into this business two years ago," continues Freeman, "our customers had quality and responsiveness issues with us, our owners had financial issues with us, and our employees had morale and attitude issues with us. I had a strong sense of urgency and not much time because both owners, Corning Incorporated and Asahi Glass Company of Japan, had told me I had two years to turn the situation around or we'd have to do something different with the business. I was not sure exactly what to change, but I knew I had to get our customers and employees on the team if we ever were going to get our owners happy again. I decided the place to start was with our people.

"I had been exposed to the large group process through a corporate–wide union–management event the previous year and felt its tremendous power. At the beginning of that event, everybody had very different views of what our labor–management partnership agreement was. We had the steering committees from every plant in the company coming together at this event and what we learned was that we all shared some common issues. I saw a transformation before my very eyes in that three–day event as people shifted their attitudes and developed a renewed sense of a willingness to work together. Action came out of the event to support partnership throughout the company and I realized I'd found a valuable tool, which I used the next year at CAV.

"Given the short timeframe we had to work in and my own belief in the power of people, I placed a bet on our people. It really was an easy decision for me to take a $4 million profit and loss hit to have all 1,200 people in our company attend what we called the 'CAV Challenge.' We held three three-day events on consecutive weeks in a high school cafeteria in June and you could multiply by 100 the positive impact I'd seen come out of the previous year's partnership event. I have a fundamental belief that, in the end, valuing the individual will make you or break you. People need to know the goal and feel valued. In our case they needed to feel they were an important part of saving and growing our business. Before we held these events, none of our workforce at any level knew that our customers were very unhappy with our quality. They thought that management was not always straightforward with them and that things were not that bad. Putting the real customer in front of them made a tremendous difference.

"Corning has a great track record in developing and sustaining businesses based on strong technology and revolutionary inventions. For CAV, we took a lot of money that we would normally have put into technology and put it into our people. If there is one single thing that has helped us make the improvements we have so far, I'm convinced it's the 'CAV Challenge.' We've gone from all seven of our large customers hating us to five out of seven loving our quality and two seeing that we've made progress. I like to think that we're still in the romancing stage with the last two.

"I found it very important as the leader to let the design team (the team planning the large group events) provide some leadership in this process, but knew I needed to set out clear expectations of why we were doing this, and what I needed to see accomplished. We worked with 150 people in our business to set the mission, vision and goals to make sure we had the right strategy for saving our business. We have some simple goals to follow to become the best in the world at what we do—making glass panels and funnels for televisions.

"The actual events were very powerful experiences for me and for the hundreds of people who attended them. The first major turning point I remember is when our biggest customer told us 'While CAV is busy trying to get by with poor quality, we're busy trying to get by without CAV!!' People's necks snapped when they heard that—including mine! Being able to ask the customers questions during the open forum burned the message in even further. It was totally different from our traditional way of communicating where the internal leadership tries to convince the rest of the organization the customer is serious this time. We also were very successful in involving the union leadership and its grass roots members in creating our vision. We outlined the vision up front during the event, but we had participation from all levels in deciding on our final strategy. What I remember so vividly is the out–pouring of ideas from people when we were setting up our final strategy. It was the first time in my twenty years with the company that I really felt like we had the power of all our people in action toward a common goal.

"We've done a couple of things to follow up on those events which have helped keep us on course and achieving results. At the leadership level, Steve Groves, our plant manager, and I have done full shift reviews every two to three months. People are seated in table groups of eight and we've used the three open forum questions after our presentations on the current business and plant status. To this day we still use the same format that we learned in the large group events. Other major things we've done have been symbolic like hanging the banners people signed to pledge their support to the mission and vision. We've had action on all of the goals and key result indicators in our plan taken by people at all levels. I can confidently say we're making progress on 90 percent of the action items that came out of those three large group events.

"In terms of what I've learned from this process, I think you've got to take a look at how difficult your situation is. If you don't feel it's a serious issue that you want to accelerate change on, don't spend the money. Be prepared for all of your people to tell you that you have to change, too. You also need to be willing to be flexible enough to incorporate their thinking into yours. At your own core you have to have an openness, a willingness, and the courage to change. The payback from these large scale events is so big, I'd highly recommend this approach. However, the leadership must do more than go through the motions. It must want to lead the change. We took the maximum financial hit that we could, but I didn't view it as an expense. I believe it was a capital investment, not in equipment, but in the people and the business with lasting benefits.

"Finally I have to say that this entire change process has had an impact on me personally. I listen to others more attentively than I used to. The traditional 'top–down' managing doesn't work so well anymore. We must shift from the politics of pleasing the boss to the reason we are in business—pleasing the customer. Seeing so many people in this organization sign up to changing the way we did business forced me to be more introspective. In a way, I've ended up recommitting myself to a more participative and empowering style, one that values the customer, and the individuals who make it happen. I needed to set clear direction and focus for this to work as well as it has. I also needed to let my people run with things once they were ready."

STORY 2:
MARRIOTT HOTELS, RESORTS AND SUITES

"The world was changing for us after many years of success and continually improving performance," begins Rick Goldstein, a key player in Marriott's use of the real time strategic change technology and vice president of organization development for the company. "We had talked for some time about doing more with quality and our performance challenges led to these discussions taking on a new sense of urgency. We were faced with the question of how to get an organization of 100,000 people to think and act differently—and quickly. I felt this process might have the potential to do that so I went and watched how another organization was using it. Then I began looking for opportunities to test it out in Marriott.

"First, I designed and facilitated a 150-person event for our corporate staff and it turned into a very successful event. The real breakthrough in our company came though when for the first time ever, we brought together all 450 senior managers to begin implementing our company game plan. I had been working for some time with the top management group, which wanted the organization to embrace total quality management (TQM). The leadership group agreed to change their own behaviors and practices so that they could lead the way, not be part of the problem. We started with building that team and articulating a new vision for the organization. As a result of this work, they made significant progress and developed real excitement for the vision. They had an urgent desire to communicate the emerging strategic direction to the rest of the organization and to rally people behind them.

"We decided to pull together the entire leadership group in the division—every single general manager at a hotel with a Marriott name, all corporate and regional staff groups, even owners of franchise hotels. It was a chance to get the same message out at the same time and was clearly a turning point for Marriott. We were in the midst of a cash flow crisis because of a downturn in the real estate market, but the event was held anyway. Coming together to plan for the future helped bring us through a significant turnaround. People saw it as a way out of our present problems. This large scale approach enabled us to make a breakthrough.

"Now that we had the senior leadership on board, the next step was to take the message to the individual properties. We had been working for three years or so figuring out how to make TQM work in our business and to train people in 240 hotels in this business approach. We thought it might be possible to use some of these same methods that had worked so well with the senior leaders to deliver the training. It would have taken a long time to get the skills and tools in people's hands in traditional seminars of twenty-five people. After getting the big picture view of why quality mattered, general managers didn't want to wait. We did a test to see what would happen if we included the TQM content on the basic tools in a three-day large scale program. Based on several tests, this approach seemed to make a rapid and powerful impact in getting TQM tools into the hands of many people at one time. The general managers involved in the tests told us they believed it was an effective means to accomplish our goals.

"Now faced with rolling out this message around the world, we trained sixty people from our operations so that we could work our way through all 240 hotels in one year. Because Marriott has very few people in full-time jobs to do training, we used these cadres of trainers to design and facilitate the large group events. Regional vice presidents selected people to work in their hotels and we actually created temporary full–time positions for these sixty people. In this industry that represents an unprecedented commitment to training and organization development. The willingness of the organization to take people out of their regular jobs—that in itself was revolutionary.

"We targeted a minimum of 25 percent of a hotel's staff for any one event and some of the smaller hotels had close to 100 percent of their total employee population involved in these meetings. Training a few people in a hotel was not new. Being able to train hundreds of people at one time was very new. The size of the investment we made is hard to pin down exactly, but the generally accepted figure is $8 million to $10 million worldwide.

"The overall goals of the events were to change the way people thought and saw the world, and as a result, to start changing their business practices. We also wanted to teach the basic tools of TQM such as flow charting and being able to write good problem statements. By taking this process right into each hotel, we wanted our associates to create changes around their own units to improve the quality our guests experienced. We invented some new pieces for these events specifically geared to TQM so that we could teach the quality tools. For part of the agenda, we had a 'home movie' videotape shown that illustrated what our hotels looked like through the eyes of our guests from the moment they walked in to when they left. Different groups then analyzed these "moments of truth" using the basic quality tools as a way to directly apply what they were learning to live customer issues in the hotel.

"As I look back on the massive change effort we're still very much in the midst of, I see one primary issue we never fully solved. It has to do with follow-up and what happens after you unleash the power and excitement in these large group events. You really need a level of organized follow-up and, on their own, many leaders struggle with this task. In hindsight, we needed to focus them on picking three major projects in their hotel and sticking with them to make sure they got done. Some hotels have put together guidance teams made up of cross-sections of different levels and departments to coordinate follow-up efforts.

"There are, however, many examples of success throughout the company. I went to one hotel recently and sat in on a group of lounge employees who were tackling some issues about how to increase their sales and the number of people who came into the lounge. They had tracked when people came in most often and which hours the bar should be open to maximize their sales. The end result of their work is that they are taking responsibility for making their lounge more profitable and giving our guests better customer service. This is one of many examples that show the positive impact of the large scale TQM training program.

"Last January we pulled together a group of eight general managers who were giving this whole effort a serious go to see what we could learn. These were not your one-toe-in-the-water types. Unanimously they agreed that they couldn't go back to their old ways of working. The ones that had followed through the most had the strongest stories to tell about change in their hotels. In each hotel, financial performance and customer service had improved, and they were convinced the TQM effort was a big part of it.

"There is still more fruit to be harvested from the investment we made and we need to keep our follow-up efforts going. However, I am convinced that we have changed the thinking and behavior of a substantial number of people in our organization around the world in a very positive way."

STORY 3: NEW YORK CITY'S HEALTH AND HOSPITALS CORPORATION

"The big issue we were faced with was a new program that was going to make or break us called the New York State Medicaid Managed Care program," explains Ben Chu, New York City's Health and Hospitals Corporation (HHC) senior vice president for medical and professional affairs and a spearhead behind HHC's managed care implementation efforts. "When we looked at our facilities they were woefully unprepared for the challenges lying before us. Morale was low, resources were depleted, and people did not fully understand that a patient-centered approach to health care was the direction we needed to move in order to protect our patient base from eroding to the voluntary hospitals in the city. While many in our system understood that we were in the business of providing quality health care, most did not have the customer focus necessary to survive in the changing healthcare environment. We needed to figure out a way to capitalize on all of the changes throughout the system to redirect and rededicate ourselves to an emphasis on good primary care instead of having people waiting in emergency rooms for basic procedures because they had no regular primary care physician or being able to access our hospitals only when they were in dire need.

"I had a very personal deep, deep sense that there were incredible talents and potential that certain people had in our organization, but that we had to find a way to focus everybody, to tap into the energies of the large pool of workers at HHC in order to make the necessary changes. There are 50,000 employees in this corporation and we needed to get them focused on a patient-focused approach to health care—and quickly. We had just undergone some huge budget cuts and had gotten a slew of bad press. Morale was at an all-time low. We were facing a critical crossroads: how to get people connected to our new mandate as quickly as possible, and how to make sure we got results along the way. Failure meant we would lose our patient base and potentially some of our jobs.

"We needed to make changes on two levels. First and fundamentally we had to get a knowledge base spread across the system of what managed care was going to mean to individual people. Not at a newsletter level though; it had to be visceral for people for this to work. People had to see and understand their own new way of doing business. Second, we had to have people believe in what we were doing, to live these new ways of working in the culture of the institution. It wouldn't be enough to say you were aware of some new way of doing business. We needed to shift people from a punch-clock mentality to customer-oriented practices. It's really a mammoth undertaking when you consider that we needed to re-focus everybody in the corporation on why we're health care providers and where each of us fits into our entire health care delivery system.

"I like to use the medical analogy of an MRI (magnetic resonance imaging) to illustrate what we were trying to do. Most of us learned in basic chemistry about the random nature of particles. We remember the demonstration of Brownian motion. This random, disorganized movement is evidenced in the chaotic motion of particles and shreds of paper in a petri dish. And yet, when you place a person in the intense magnetic field of an MRI, and you align all of their electrical elements in one uniform direction, you can capitalize on the enormous power of molecular energy to create magnificent, detailed images of the human body. To me, the large scale technology served as a powerful magnetic field to help align all the people in our organization with the goal of capturing their energy and applying it to the issues we were facing.

"After forming a leadership team to guide our process and set some direction, we held our first event to introduce the power of the technology into all of the facilities involved in implementing managed care. We captured people's imaginations at this 400-person event, and developed some broad role descriptions for how people would need to do business differently in a managed care environment. We quickly followed this event with a training session for 110 internal facilitators who would be charged with supporting implementation efforts in their individual facilities. In order to make sure the facilities got off to a solid start in their implementation efforts, we held two diffusion events attended by twelve of the seventeen institutions most critical to the success of our implementation plans. In these two day diffusions, individual facilities had fifty to seventy representatives in attendance and were able to lay out their particular facility's plans with a good deal of detail. These max-mix groups from each facility represented the diverse thinking and concerns people had at all levels and from all functions so the plans they put together were realistic and informed.

"After holding only three large scale events, we have a large core of 1,200 people who have experienced this process and who have bought into its power. Our focus has been on helping people understand the underlying principles with which we need to meet the new demands of a patient-centered approach to primary care. If you boil it down to its essence, we're really making sure people know and act on the ultimate purpose of the organization. Everybody needs to change how they work to become more patient-focused.

"I've seen facilities tapping into the creativity you get from bringing together multi-disciplinary groups to discuss where they want to go as a facility in the future. Several of our facilities have already used the technology and held events on their own. We've had other facilities form managed care implementation groups comprised of people who attended one of the system-wide large group events. Historically, most of these kind of major changes have come down from central staff in a fairly top-down style. As part of a new way of doing business, we decided to decentralize the implementation of managed care. People are innovating in the individual facilities, and by bringing together our internal facilitators, we can share these best practices. With 50,000 employees in our system, we needed to seed the individual facilities with this new message and make sure they had capable people who could continue the change process on their own. We've done that, and now it's up to the individual facilities to take it and run with it."

STORY 4:
METRO

"I was in a support department role before I took over as executive director of the entire agency," begins Dick Sandaas, who heads up the 4,000 employees of METRO responsible for water pollution control and public transportation in King County, Washington. "In my department, we hadn't experienced any major discrimination problems. However, I was aware of an issue raised by the agency which later became the Federal Transit Authority that minorities and women were receiving a disproportionately high number of disciplinary actions and terminations in our organization as a whole. At first I figured these problems could be easily managed, but the more I looked into things the clearer it became to me that we were just dealing with the tip of the iceberg. The management style in the operating departments was much different than what I had practiced myself or been used to. It was rigid, harsh, and structured, and that was the basis of some of the problems. Along about the same time, an elected official raised the federal report findings publicly and we had to do something before we were ready. I had been in the job less than a year and looking back on things, I think we started out with totally the wrong approach. We hired some diversity trainers and mandated that all levels of our management staff attend these training courses. As things unfolded, it became clear that this Band-Aid™ approach was not going to do the job. We were trying to put out a forest fire with a garden hose. Fortunately we soon realized we needed to do something far more comprehensive.

"First, we needed to work on issues between our leadership team, the top management group of department directors, and myself. The team I started out with was relatively dysfunctional—we did not work well together, and were not capable at that point of leading any kind of effective change effort. Second, we were involved in divisive labor negotiations with the transit workers, our largest union. Third, we were in the midst of being taken over by the King County government and weren't sure whether we would be a free-standing entity or not. Despite all the uncertainty we were facing, we decided that we needed to at least get started by pulling the top team together. We did want to wait, though, to work through the union negotiations before moving ahead with the large group events because we wanted to make sure that when we began building our new culture, everyone was involved in the process.

"Once we got the leadership team on board, we needed to identify somebody on staff to run this project. Now the old style way to staff that position would have been for me to go into the organization and select the person I thought was most capable. Probably it would have been somebody I'd worked with in the past. However, you have to understand that the hiring and promotion practices were one of the things people were most upset about. In fact, white males who were supposedly getting the best of it were as upset as anybody else with the favoritism in the organization. We started walking our talk about a new culture right away by having an open application and selection process for this project leader. I'm convinced we would have gotten off on the wrong foot with this whole effort and that this person would not have been nearly as effective if I had made a direct appointment in the old way. We also got some strong political support for the change effort and I must admit I still often wonder how. Including staff time, we've spent about $2 million during the past year on this process, but I can rationalize those costs completely. To have 4,000 employees creating a new organization that they're proud to work in, it is not a bad deal. We've been able to absorb the staff time in our budgets—and we've radically changed our organization, instead of sticking to some superficial training courses for managers that weren't making any real difference, other than our being able to say we were doing something about our problems.

"We designed our entire change strategy around using a max-mix model so that all departments and all levels would be represented at each of ten 400 person events. We held one night-shift event and one weekend event for people who couldn't make it to one of the regular daytime sessions. In each of these events people had an opportunity to help design the future culture of the organization, first through developing a strategy and values, and later through explicitly defining behaviors and plans that would support living this new culture. Many good ideas surfaced during these events and we've made a lot of changes in how people are treated in this organization.

"My most powerful memory of this process came when we, as the leaders, revised the mission, goals, and values statement based on feedback we'd gotten from the first large group. Number one, it was a very humbling experience for us directors who had prepared the draft; it wasn't perfect and plenty of people in that group told us so. Number two, after working late into the evening, we finally completed the revised statement, which was then waiting on the tables for people when they walked in the very next morning. I think people were kind of taken aback that we listened and that already there were some signals that the culture was changing. Everybody had an equal say no matter what color their skin was or whether they were male or female. And number three, we got a standing ovation that next morning when we reviewed the revised statement with the total group. At that point we knew we were on to something and that this was going to work.

"We've had plenty of follow-up to do during the past year in addition to all of the large group events. One thing we've done is to make a conscious effort to train our own people to plan and facilitate these large group meetings. We have a core group of internal consultants that have learned the technology and are able to use it competently. Different departments have managed their follow-up efforts in ways that work best for them, but they all can call on these internal consulting resources that are now available. While not everybody in our organization is committed to this cultural change effort, I can tell you one thing: we're outnumbering them, and they are quickly having to decide what they want to do about their old ways. Discrimination is less and less acceptable throughout the agency and it's happening less and less frequently. This change process and the use of these large group events has been one of the most exciting things I've done in my career and I'm very proud of what we've accomplished during the past year."

STORY 5: ST. LAWRENCE–LEWIS BOCES

"In general terms I think you could say we were trying to build community around an expanded idea of what education means and needs to be in the future," explains Tom Elliott, the deputy superintendent for the St. Lawrence–Lewis Board of Cooperative Educational Services (BOCES), which serves eighteen rural school districts in upstate New York. "Traditionally we think of teachers, the board of education and sometimes parents as defining the universe for K-12 education. However, higher education facilities, citizens, employers, and other agencies are key stakeholders and customers of what we do with kids. We brought 450 people together for a two-day conference with the theme of 'Working Together to Build a Brighter Future.' Each of the eighteen component school districts sent a team that was a microcosm of each district, ideally composed of people both from outside the formal school system and those inside it, in an even split. We wanted to create a certain level of dissatisfaction with the status quo, so we had views from various stakeholders as part of our agenda. We also had a very explicit purpose of building partnerships between different groups that hadn't existed before, such as between small business owners and teachers, so that we could be teaching students things that would be useful to them when they went to work for some of these people after graduating from high school.

"Since our BOCES spreads across thousands of square miles and is sparsely populated, we needed to bring in some folks who ran small cottage industries in order to secure enough business people. These people are our stakeholders. We needed their views represented as we looked into the future and made some decisions about the kind of educational system we wanted to create and the purposes it would serve.

"I particularly remember one panel of stakeholders that opened a lot of people's eyes to the extent of changes we needed to make in the future. One of the panelists was a recent college graduate, a product of our school system. She spoke clearly and convincingly about what didn't work for her about her high school educational experience, and this was one of our success stories. She's looking at graduate programs now and she's telling us the school system failed her! If it's not working for our success stories, then you have to sit back and wonder who are we doing a good job for. A small business person on another panel listed what he looks for in hiring somebody to work for him, and none of his items overlapped with the list of basic skills we're now teaching. He told us he looks for honesty, integrity, a day's work for a day's pay, the ability to satisfy the needs of his customers, the ability to communicate effectively with co-workers, and being able to think ahead and problem solve before small problems become big ones. Very little if any of our curriculum addresses these needs. It was quite a wake-up call for people to hear that we're not meeting the needs of a lot of students, or the employers they're going to work for.

"Based on what people learned at our event, each school district team is putting together its own plan of action. As a follow-up to the conference, the North Country Resources for Change Committee has been established to publicize program opportunities designed to help implement change. This committee's efforts are based on supporting pockets of energy in each district. One of these programs is the St. Lawrence Leadership Institute—a leadership training program to prepare community members for leadership roles in St. Lawrence County as library or hospital board members, for example. Using a traditional mindset, that sort of thing is really none of our business. Looking at our role in a broader context though, it's just the sort of thing that's needed and that we can help provide. In addition, we're developing workshops on communication, listening, and consensus building skills so that parents, teachers, and students can work more effectively together on their follow-up plans. We're also offering assistance from our organization for districts to stage local level events modeled after the regional one we did so they can involve more people in the changes they're planning and build further support back home.

"In New York State, the legislature has passed a law that will assure participative decision making in the schools by all of these key stakeholders. We've already met that mandate in a real way with these large group events, and not just superficially. We might have had to resign ourselves to more superficial involvement, even if we wanted to include people in more meaningful ways, if only because we didn't know how to bring them into the process. In terms of building community, the big advantage of this approach is that it enables you to extend a genuine invitation for collaboration to a very wide audience at one time. The regional level of the state department of labor has called us to ask about doing vocational assessments for kids differently because of what they heard during the large group events. They have begun to shift their thinking after hearing the stakeholders' viewpoints.

"After spending only two days together, this diverse group of people found they have a tremendous number of things in common. We've identified a lot of overlaps between social services for students and agencies working with families, and they've started to work together on several projects also. We've seen results like that, which we never expected to come out of just this one event. With our new paradigm about the role education needs to be playing in our communities, it all fits as part of our mission. We have a lot of work left to do, but we've got the ball rolling and a lot of excited people at the local level making things happen."

CHAPTER 10

HOW TO
USE THE
TECHNOLOGY
TO YOUR
ADVANTAGE

"E ven as you get started in the very beginning, I think it's critical that you ask yourself 'What has to be in place in my organization six months from now to really capitalize on the opportunities that will be available from using this approach?' " cautions MaryAnn Holohean, a vice president with the Fund for the City of New York. She offers her advice on getting started with this technology in your organization. "You need to push far into the future in your thinking and identify implications for implementation of choices you're making today. In a lot of ways this kind of thinking cuts to the core of making lasting changes in any organization."

At this point, you may be feeling excited, enthusiastic, and ready to launch a real time strategic change process in your organization. Perhaps you have been intrigued by the concepts and applications you have read about, but feel uncertain about how the real time strategic change technology could apply to your organization's particular mix of challenges and opportunities. Or you may still be feeling skeptical about this approach to supporting change efforts.

The purpose of this chapter is to provide you with some tools with which you can begin exploring how you might apply the real time strategic change technology in your own organization. This chapter discusses a set of key questions to aid your exploration, and a handful of criteria to apply to your thinking. After reading this chapter, identify the key people in your organization who you believe need to be involved in a dialogue regarding the potential for applying this technology. Invite them to join you in thinking through these questions and criteria, adding others as you see fit. Don't forget, though, that each person's truth is their truth, and that others may see the world much differently than you do. So much the better, even if finding the common ground may prove challenging.

The plans you develop may change and evolve over time as you gather new data and people begin to implement changes. Treat this chapter as a starting point for a dialogue in your organization. No definite answers to these questions exist, only hypotheses that must be tested in the real world. A healthy, open dialogue with key players in your organization is the best place to begin.

Key Questions

Figure 8 illustrates key questions you will need to consider in your dialogue with others. It also highlights how the change formula applies to the design of the overall change process, as well as to individual events.

Identifying the Issues

As introduced in Chapter 7, the real time strategic change technology has the capability of addressing an infinite number of issues affecting an organization. Leverage and impact can be maximized in the change process in several ways. A key to success, then, is to clearly define and then address the right issues for your organization. No matter how rapidly people implement changes, if these changes do not respond to the relevant issues—all of them—your efforts will be significantly wasted. Some questions for you and your group of key players to explore are:

- What are the areas of dissatisfaction for people in your organization right now at different levels and in different functions?

- How does your organization stack up competitively in the marketplace and why, including both customer and competitor factors?

- Are you defining the issues to address broadly enough to engage people across the entire organization and clearly enough to be able to act on them?

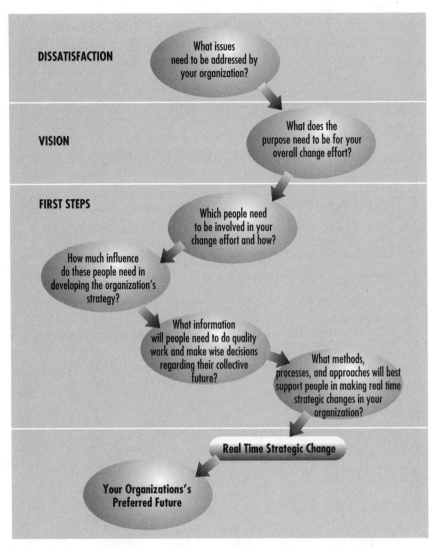

Figure 8. Getting started on your journey into real time strategic change

- Do you have enough different stakeholders' perspectives represented in your dialogue? If not, how can you ensure these other voices are heard?

- Are you defining your organization's issues descriptively and non-judgmentally, or are you assigning blame to one area or function by how you describe them?

- How can you check the accuracy of your perceptions to make sure you have your finger on the pulse of your organization and the issues facing it?

Establishing the Purpose

The overall purpose of your change effort needs to meet the same criteria as a purpose statement for an individual real time strategic change event. That is, it needs to:

1. Account for the varied and complex issues facing your organization, but not be a "reduction of pain" solution tied down by them.

2. Be clear, concise, easily understood and supported by a critical mass of people in your organization.

3. Define what you hope to achieve in your change effort.

Again, the technology is designed to support people in making many different kinds of changes including those related to:

- Attitudes;

- Behaviors;

- Knowledge;

- Skills;

- Structures and Systems;

- Business Processes and Practices;

- Strategy;

- Values and Culture.

First, you need to determine which of these changes are needed in your organization. The next step is to agree on a clear purpose for the real time strategic change process that captures the spirit and intent of these changes.

Also, make sure that your purpose describes the results you will achieve, not the activities people will engage in to achieve these results.

Some questions to consider in shaping the overall purpose for your real time strategic change effort include:

- What needs to change in your organization in order for it to be successful in the future?

- Why do these changes need to be made? What's at stake?

- What is a preferred future for your organization? That is, what does "better" look like?

- What will be different in your organizational world because you have undertaken this change effort?

Who Needs to be Involved?

Answering the question of who needs to be involved in the change effort includes thinking through both internal and external stakeholders. One of the advantages of the real time strategic change technology is the opportunity it affords you to involve many different levels of people from different functions in an organization with customers and suppliers in meaningful ways. A key decision, then, is setting the boundaries of the organization you are working within. For example, we have found that bringing together at least three levels of an organization ensures that we have enough different perspectives in the room to make decisions based on a holistic common database. Another important aspect of this question is deciding which people need to be involved at what points in time. For instance, would some type of functional meeting better prepare people for what they will be experiencing during the organization-wide events? Would the overall change effort benefit from having some groups exposed earlier than others to the real time strategic change technology? What combinations of participants would enable your organization to move further towards its preferred future, faster? Answers to these questions shape the critical components of a real time strategic change effort. The following five types of events may guide your dialogue at this step:

1. *Top of the House Events.* This approach brings together the top levels in an organization at a large group event, which ensures senior man-

agement support for the change effort. Usually top of the house events are followed by some type of diffusion events throughout the rest of the organization.

2. *Total System Events.* In smaller organizations, this approach has proven to be a powerful stimulus for real time strategic change because all members of the organization engage in the process together as one team.

3. *Critical Mass Events.* With this approach, a critical mass of the total organization attends a real time strategic change event to ensure that perspectives from all levels and functions in the organization are represented. This option may meet the needs of either very large organizations or smaller ones that cannot shut down operations while the events are in progress.

4. *Sub-System Events.* When organizations are very big, very diverse, or when the needs and issues are specific and affect a particular unit, they may want to focus their change efforts on a single division, program team, or facility. Within this, there are also other choices, such as the top of the house, or critical mass events described above.

5. *Functional Team Events.* A functional team event usually follows an initial event based on a top of the house or total system approach, and is one form of diffusion strategy. Functional heads provide leadership in these events, and input from other functions can be included through the use of stakeholder panels.

Questions to explore in determining who needs to be involved include:

- Which type of event (or combination of events) seems to best fit your organization's circumstances and purpose?

- Given your initial assessment, who would need to be involved in an initial launch event?

- Who would need to be involved over time in the change effort through diffusion events?

- What specific mix of people would provide the most synergy for making positive changes in the way you currently do business?

- In what other ways could the real time strategic change technology be used to increase the impact of your change effort?

How Much Influence Should People Have?

There are two benefits to creating a change effort that enables people to influence their organization's strategy. First, people develop more ownership of and commitment to strategies they have had a hand in developing. Second, the strategies developed take into account a broader context of reality because they are based on integrated perspectives from many people.

One way to view influence is as a continuum. At the low end of the continuum, leaders present a predetermined strategy to the rest of the organization. Influence is restricted to the action plans people develop to implement the strategy. At the other extreme, leaders develop none of the strategy before the event. Instead the large group creates the strategy and action plans along with the leaders in real time. The most common scenario, in our experience, is for leaders to draft parts of the strategy and receive input from the large group regarding recommended revisions, as in the example described in Chapters 4, 5, and 6.

For instance, the leadership teams in the Marriott and METRO case studies described in Chapter 9 decided to develop draft strategies on their own, yet were open to feedback from the large group. In the Corning–Asahi Video story, the leadership team chose to involve more than 100 people from all levels in the organization in shaping the strategy. This was then added to by participants at the CAV Challenge events. Finally, the New York City Health and Hospitals Corporation and upstate New York educators' cases illustrate how strategies can be developed by participants as part of the real time strategic change events. Depending on your choice and circumstances, you must make different tradeoffs.

Several questions help determine where on the continuum of influence your organization would be best positioned:

- Who has the information and experience bases required to develop a sound strategy for the organization?

- What level of involvement will people want and need for you to gain their support of and commitment to the proposed change effort?

Based on your answers to the above questions:

- How much of the strategy is best developed by the top leadership team or others in the organization before the event and how much should be co-created by everyone at the event?

- How much of the strategy developed beforehand needs to be "locked in" and how much needs to be open for input from participants and potential revision resulting from that input?

What Information Will People Need?

Ensuring that people across an entire organization are operating with informed discretion is a key to making real time strategic change happen. This discretion needs to be based on access to and understanding of a common database of strategic information. Current, accurate, understandable, and relevant information is the life-blood of organizations. With it, people can align the thousands of decisions they make each day with the organization's overall strategy. Without it, people are left to their own devices and limited perspectives.

From the outside looking in, it might seem that people engaged in a real time strategic change effort would suffer from data overload. Integrating so many diverse perspectives goes against our traditional ready-fire-aim approach. However, systems issues require systems responses. To make wise decisions, people need a collective sense of what a preferred future could be and to develop ownership in the strategy.

The information people need may come from outside experts or leaders, analyses of current business practices by people working in the organization, or conversations with customers and suppliers. Identifying the best sources of information shapes the overall process as well as specific event agendas. The kinds of questions to explore at this stage are:

- What do people at different levels and functions in your organization currently know about:

—your position in the marketplace?

—how their work affects the work of others, as well as the services and products your customers receive?

—your organization's overall strategic direction for the future?

- What do people at different levels and functions in your organization need and want to know more about?

- What will people need to know to make informed decisions on a daily basis in the workplace?

How Can You Best Support Real Time Strategic Change in Your Organization?

The following questions will help you determine how to best support people in making real time strategic changes:

- In what ways can you envision using the real time strategic change technology in your organization?

- What affect could this approach have on your people? On your business? On your customers?

- How can you ensure that you are involving the right people at the right times in the right ways?

- Whose support do you need in order to move forward with your plans?

- How well would your plans achieve the purpose you have outlined for your change effort? How well would they respond to the issues now facing your organization and meet people's needs for information and influence over their destiny?

Key Criteria

As you can see from the questions and options outlined, many decisions must be made to customize the technology for your particular organization. This section presents some criteria that may help you weigh and explore the implications of these various options.

Choosing Options That Achieve Your Purpose

The purpose of the change effort serves as your primary reference for all key choice points in planning a real time strategic change process. If you find people disagreeing with each other regarding some of the details, such as who should be involved at different stages of the process, it's possible that there may be conflicting interpretations of the purpose behind your change effort. With a clear, agreed purpose in hand, decisions and their accompanying tradeoffs become clearer.

Walking the Talk

The real time strategic change technology provides an excellent opportunity to start "walking the talk" of the culture in which you want to be living as an organization. Are you making choices about the overall change effort in a manner consistent with the old ways and old culture you are trying to leave behind? Or are you thinking about and aligning with the culture you aspire to create? How clearly do your actions reflect the new culture?

Building Support Capacity

Your overall change effort should support the creation, establishment, or realignment of the structures, systems, and development of the people you need in your organization to best carry out the work that will be done in the future. In essence, you need to be thinking future now. You should also think through your options with an eye toward what will be required to support these efforts over the longer haul. In line with this thinking, it may be helpful to identify potential structures and systems you will need to have in place. How can you design your change effort so that these vital elements develop congruently with the unfolding strategy and plans for action? Who in your organization needs to be involved early on in your change effort? Which groups will be critical in sustaining the momentum for change you gain through using the real time strategic change technology?

What Logistics Constraints Are There?

Your overall change effort must also fit the daily realities of the business you are in. For example, you will need to consider the cost/benefit tradeoffs and practicalities involved in having large numbers of people in your organization attending a real time strategic change event simultaneously. Your shift structure might require some creative changes to achieve organizational unity and alignment with strategy. One of your logistics constraints might be finding an adequate facility. What are your logistics constraints? Which of these are real? Which can be overcome with some creative thinking?

"The Medium is the Message"

People are hypersensitive during times of change and look for underlying meaning in all actions, communications, and decisions. The choices you make in deciding how to use the technology in your organization need to be consistent with the messages you want to send. The change effort begins with the first dialogue you have with others about real time strategic change. Even in these early stages, focus on the impressions you want to make to ensure that they are consistent with the kind of organization you want to create.

The questions and criteria described in this chapter provide a framework for deciding how and if to apply the real time strategic change technology in your organization. You may need to take some risks, as well as educate others. You must also believe that it is possible to make real time strategic change a reality in your organization. Tremendous opportunities exist to move your organization farther into its preferred future, faster. Find the right people in your organization to engage in this dialogue and, if it makes sense, begin mapping out some possible paths. Thoroughness and thoughtfulness at the front end will pay off well down the line.

Sherry McCool has worked in ten different locations over the past twenty-three years with Marriott Corporation. During that time she has been a reservations manager, front office manager, director of services, resident manager, general manager, and regional director of human resources. She is currently once again general manager of a hotel. She says she still remembers that when she joined the company there were fewer than ten Marriott Hotels. There were no such things as vision statements, mission statements, game plans, or strategic redeployment objectives. All decisions were guided by only a few standard operating procedures and one simple concept: If you take care of the employees, they will take care of the customers, and the customers will keep coming back. Sherry believes that concept still guides Marriott's activities. But the company has grown and today's business environment is very different from the one she entered more than twenty years ago. Because of this new competitive environment, changes had to be made in how Marriott did business and 100,000 associates around the world were faced with a personal challenge to change as well. Sherry captured her experience in facing that personal challenge when she said, "There are but a few times in a person's life where there is the opportunity to experience something that alters in a profound way one's personal and professional destiny." What follows is her perspective on the role the real time strategic change technology played for the company, her hotel, and her own personal development.

"In 1990 while I was working on the midwest regional team as regional director of human resources, I was called to Washington, D.C. for a quality review meeting. The format of that meeting was very different from others I had attended because it involved over 150 people representing all levels of the organization. Our corporate training department representatives and an outside consultant guided us through two days of presentations, table group discussions, and large group report outs.

"We had the opportunity to hear from individuals at the highest levels of the hotel division—the people who set our global strategies, who make the policies and create the support systems necessary for our long-term success. Many individuals in the room had never been exposed to regional and staff vice presidents before, much less heard them share their views on the quality process, their roles with the quality process, and how they intended to support the process in the future.

"Before we began our table group discussion, we introduced ourselves to each other because we were seated at tables with people we didn't know. The table seating assignments had been carefully planned so each represented a microcosm of the hotel division with individuals from corporate/regional staff and various levels of the hotels. After our introductions, we talked about what we had heard, how we felt about what we had heard, and raised questions of understanding to ask the regional and staff vice presidents.

"Next the large group was allowed to ask questions. The process was facilitated in an organized manner that avoided debate while allowing clearly understandable responses to the questions.

"Later, working in our table groups we created next step priorities. Each table utilized an organized brainstorming technique. The input of all 150 people was recorded and posted for everyone to consider.

"In a creative and organized manner the total group individually voted on the next steps. The voting process created clearly defined priorities. The regional and staff vice presidents were given the opportunity to report to the large group on the next steps relevant to their specific area of responsibility. One or two of the vice presidents were able to immediately make commitments to the audience. I recall one having to do with the budget process was met with a standing ovation. Others who were not able to make immediate responses committed to report back later.

"Throughout the two days we were taught to listen in order to understand the other person's truth, rather than the more common listening to debate, listening to find fault, listening to convince them I'm right, or not listening at all.

"For me this large scale process was something extraordinary because it allowed everyone the opportunity to be heard and to have a voice in developing the preferred future. I left that event full of hope, energy, and enthusiasm.

"Within a few months, one of the hotels in our region was selected to pilot the large scale roll out of total quality management, and I had the privilege of being on the design and delivery team. The seed that had been planted at the event in Washington, D.C. was about to be nurtured in such a way as to change my personal and professional life.

"As we developed the large scale design for the roll out of total quality management I had the opportunity to work with several very talented people. And in the process, I found a way to do business that was in harmony with my personal beliefs. To have a sense of harmony between what one believes on a personal level and how one goes about accomplishing the necessary duties in a work environment creates great personal synergy. Throughout my career, I had believed that an organization isn't successful because a few people at the top make the right decisions—it's successful because the entire staff is making the right decisions. And a multi-million dollar business isn't successful because one person or a few people have a vision of where they are going. It's successful because the entire staff shares common goals that are meaningful. The difficulty was I had not always been able to live up to making those beliefs a reality for the people I worked with because I didn't have the proper tools.

"My experience with the large scale roll out of total quality management allowed me to learn the techniques and tools necessary to be more in harmony with myself as a person and as a leader. Here are some key points of my experiences with these events:

- It allows the organization to hear from top management their individual and collective goals for the business unit/organization while creating the opportunity for feelings and questions to be shared, setting the stage for better communications;

- It encourages top management to hear the concerns and barriers of the group (whether it's fifty people or 450 people) while creating the opportunity for top management to make change and genuinely respond to their concerns, setting the stage for more trusting and open relationships;

- It is a showcase for external customers to be heard by all levels, creating a wonderful linkage for each individual and each department with how internal processes impact delivery of customer service, setting the stage for continuous improvement;

- It fosters dialogue between departments about what works well and what needs to work better, setting the stage for everyone to serve the customer or someone who does;

- It enables the organization to collectively create a shared vision, setting the stage for everyone to share in the success of the organization.

"The single most important learning for me was that I needed to listen to understand the other person's truth. I must be vigilant in using all my skills to see the world through their eyes, regardless of who they are. When I remember to use this technique, my personal and business relationships prosper. Now, I'll be the first to admit it's hard breaking my old listening habits, but it is worth the effort.

"As a company and an individual hotel we no longer use this technology just for the roll out of major projects—it has become a way we do business. I have personally participated in at least ten of these events, and each has been unique in its purpose and desired results. Yet, each event used a basic format and similar tools.

"I should also share with you that each event has had at least one moment that served as a breakthrough, or caused the group to collectively connect on a physical, mental, and emotional level. I have witnessed and shared tears, standing ovations, the spontaneous response of 170 people clambering to sign a vision statement they created, and the awe of 220 people as a dishwasher eloquently spoke from his heart of the importance of serving each other and the customer. The power of these events is not to be underestimated because they can facilitate people to overcome long-standing barriers, or at least create a bridge for them.

"As you read through these pages I hope you are 'reading to understand' (that's like listening to understand but it's done with the eyes instead of the ears) so that your truth may come to include techniques that allow all levels of the organization to be heard and valued. Best wishes on your journey!"

CHAPTER 11

DESIGNING YOUR REAL TIME STRATEGIC CHANGE EVENT

T his chapter focuses on the process of designing an interactive large group event. Although the prospect of these events captures most people's attention and sometimes awe, it takes good designing, planning, and consulting to ensure their success. This chapter takes a behind the scenes look at who designs these events and why, how decisions are made about which activities occur when, and what happens when you need to deviate from your original plan.

Design Teams

Consistent with the principles underlying the technology, each real time strategic change event is planned by a design team comprised of a microcosm of those people who will actually attend the event and a team of consultants with experience in applying the technology. As consultants, we work collaboratively with this group to determine the purpose and agenda for each event. The design team uses a consensus process to figure out *what* needs to be discussed, *how* it should be discussed, and *when* it should be discussed to achieve the purpose. In short, everyone must agree—a sometimes difficult standard, but one that is essential. In this design phase, consultants provide expertise in the real time strategic change technology, while line managers, front-line workers, and leaders focus on the organization, its issues and their hopes for the future.

A representative team provides a reality check on the design being developed: the design team's reactions help determine what will and will not work in the larger group. We have worked with design teams as large as thirty and as small as ten. Teams at the larger end of this continuum take more time and pose more challenges in the design process, but those at the smaller end may risk not having all the major perspectives represented. Size, however, is not the key factor by which these teams are selected. The most important criteria is that the design team needs to represent an organizational assortment of types, styles, and attitudes, leaving out neither cynics nor optimists. An important distinction to make, though, is that the group should be representative of the entire organization. In this way, design team meetings lasting two to three days mirror the power and possibilities of the large group event. Often during the event itself, people from the design team act as good predictors of the larger group's direction. They tend to be ahead of their colleagues in thinking and action because they have already experienced a paradigm shift through participating in the design process.

Design team members also gather data from their own table groups' experience during the event. These insights, combined with the information gathered through written evaluations, help them make any design adjustments that may be needed for the next day. Healthy team dynamics developed during design meetings before a real time strategic change event enable these people with widely varying perspectives to achieve agreement on changes that need to be made in real time during the event.

Finally in some organizations, design teams assume additional responsibilities as leaders of change in the organization. For example, the knowledge, skills, and commitment fostered through the design process enabled one team to assume the role of an implementation team after their real time strategic change event. In this role, they took charge of coordinating the many and varied initiatives created to support the changes and actions that evolved out of the event.

An Overall Framework for the Design Process

This section outlines the models, concepts, and flow of activities that shape the design process for a real time strategic change event. As a broad conceptual base, design teams follow an overall planning process model—data, purpose, plan and evaluate (DPPE).

Data

Data gathering ensures that the design team gains a broad understanding of the real time strategic change technology and each other's perspectives of the total organization. By sharing, comparing, and integrating their perspectives, the design team acquires a collective picture of the successes and frustrations, realities and rumors, worries and threats, and opportunities and desires currently alive throughout the organization. One person's success, however, can be another person's frustration. It is therefore important and a challenge for design team members to be cognizant that their own judgments, prejudices, and interpretations are only part of the picture. A key to being an effective design team is the ability to listen to, understand, and accept each other's perspectives, even when they seem to be in conflict. Because the design team represents a microcosm of the larger organization, these diverse views reflect similar distinctions in the total organization—important information to have when deciding on the event's purpose and design.

Purpose

Once the design team has developed a representative picture of the organization, it must define the purpose of the event. To do so, the design team relies on its own data and the needs that organizational leaders have. The purpose serves as a guiding light for the design team to follow, and helps event participants to better understand the rationale behind the flow of activities they experience. If the purpose is on target, the participants will read it and say, "Yes, that's a good reason to pull all of us together!" They will usually be excited by the prospect, even if they find it hard to believe it is possible to achieve.

Plan

The next step is to design and plan the event. As the design unfolds, it is regularly checked against the purpose to ensure that the plan will deliver on the purpose. The design team must often ask questions such as, "Is this what I would want to be doing right now? Am I interested in what's happening? What do I want to know from this speaker? Do I need a break?" The Change Formula described in Chapter 7 becomes a touchstone for the design group to ensure that missing ingredients in the formula are addressed and that the large group achieves the paradigm shifts necessary for the required changes to occur. The design team determines the content, processes and agenda that serve as the roadmap for participants.

Evaluate

Evaluation occurs throughout the design process. For example, the purpose and agenda are evaluated by allowing outsiders, especially the leadership group, to road test them. Individual module options are measured against the purpose and outcomes to assess the value they would add for participants. Design team members also evaluate how effectively they themselves are working as a team as a basis for continuous improvement. Written comments gathered from participants after each day of an event are used to redesign the agenda as needed.

An Example Design Team Meeting

Figure 9 illustrates the purpose and agenda flow for an example design team meeting. This figure also highlights which elements of data, purpose, plan and evaluate (DPPE) apply to each item on the agenda.

Generally one to two days of actual design time is required as a minimum to plan each day of a real time strategic change event. More time may be needed, depending on the complexity of either the organization's environment, the event itself, and the design team dynamics. In fact, it is not unusual to finish the first day of a design team meeting without agreeing on a purpose for the large group event. Additional time may be needed for scheduling, preparing, and coaching outside speakers, for "marketing" the event, and for tying up loose ends.

The following sections provide a closer look at the purpose underlying each agenda item, the processes used to determine these purposes, and some tips and advice that should make it easier for you to work your way through a design team meeting.

PURPOSE: To ensure we take best advantage of the time, energy and resources we'll have available to us during the real time strategic change event so that we can move further, faster into the future we prefer for ourselves, our organization and our stakeholders.

AGENDA FLOW

DATA	Welcome/Purpose Agenda/Logistics Personal Introductions Background and History of the Technology View from Design Team Members
PURPOSE	Identifying Desired Outcomes from the Event Agreeing on the Purpose Statement
PLAN	Brainstorming Elements for the Agenda Laying Out the "Chunked" Agenda Designing the Detailed Agenda Next Steps/Loose Ends
EVALUATE	Reviewing the Design Evaluation/Close/Debrief

Figure 9. An example design team meeting agenda

Welcome and Purpose

The purpose of this module is to provide a broader context for the role of design teams in the process of planning large group events, and how these events enable people at all levels in the organization to contribute to creating their preferred future. Usually the leaders of the change effort make some opening remarks at the design team meeting. Deciding who makes these remarks depends on who the group needs to hear from in order to legitimize and sponsor the change effort. These comments send a clear message about the initiative and demonstrate the support key players in the organization have for the process. By encouraging design team members to probe for further understanding at this early stage, leaders set the norm for deeper dialogue throughout the rest of the meeting. At the same time, they clarify their needs and perspectives for the design team.

Because the real time strategic change technology represents such a radical departure from business as usual for many organizations, whoever opens the design team meeting needs to make a clear case for why this new approach is being used. That person must link the organization's current issues and challenges, such as cross-functional relationships, customer satisfaction, or the flow of information through the organization to the technology's strengths. This helps to achieve two objectives:

1. Design team members begin to experience a new way of doing business by having direct contact with their leaders, and by hearing the strategic dialogue they engaged in when deciding to invest in applying the technology.

2. It is clear that the leaders have done their homework and are committed to seeing the process work.

Agenda and Logistics

This module, like the Welcome and Purpose, parallels the large group events. It reduces the mystery of the design team planning process by examining what will happen, why, and how it will happen. One of the consultants reviews the agenda, which is usually recorded on flip chart paper. The consultant describes the process in terms of a journey that starts with a collection of people, many of whom do not even know each other and results in an effective design team that has created an engaging, productive agenda for the upcoming real time strategic change event.

This early in the process people are still pretty skeptical and reserved. The flip charts send the message that this is a working meeting. It is also important to let people know that this meeting is not to rubber stamp a purpose and agenda handed down from above. During the next couple of days, the design team creates the agenda. Anything the consulting team can do to signal that this meeting is not business as usual will enable people to get on the playing field and out of the spectators' stands sooner. From a logistics perspective, look for a well-lit room, preferably one with windows. A little sunshine and fresh air can go a long way toward getting people's creative juices flowing—and every little bit helps. Generally people sit around a board table in horseshoe or square configuration. Small breakout areas in the same room can be a helpful addition. Light lunches and snacks delivered to the meeting or a nearby room for a change of scenery allow the design team to better focus on the task at hand. Plan on taking breaks when people need them—at least once in the morning and once in the afternoon. They can help a group break through on tough deliberations, especially when the group is larger, or in organizations where open debates are uncommon.

Personal Introductions

Brief personal introductions serve two basic purposes:

1. They increase people's conscious awareness of the whole organization by calling attention to the various levels, functions, and roles represented in the room.

2. They begin laying the foundation for the kind of teamwork required to succeed in designing a process so critical to future organizational success.

A small set of easy-to-answer, relevant questions set the stage for engaging team members in the design process. It helps everyone know who is on the team, where they work, what they do, and something about their organizational and career backgrounds. It also helps to know what, if anything, each person knows about the need for change, how they came to be in this group, and what is expected of them. We often suggest using a "Quaker Meeting" style ("When the spirit moves you, speak up").

These introductions generally take one to two minutes each so you need to be conscious of time and interest levels with a large group; asking a few follow-up questions breaks the string of brief presentations and signals that seeking data from others is encouraged in this meeting. People may have known very little about the need for change prior to the Welcome and Purpose. Discussing what people know helps shape the next item on the agenda, the Background and History of the Technology.

Finally, observers often attend design team meetings for a variety of reasons. They need to introduce themselves to the design team and explain why they are there. In this context, observer is code for "one who does not talk." In some situations, observers may be learning how to facilitate design team meetings. In other cases, they may be representing other divisions or parts of the organization that are exploring applications of the real time strategic change technology. If seated away from the design team's table, they quickly blend into the background, but are able to gain valuable knowledge for themselves and their organization.

❝ When I looked around the room in that first design team meeting, we were a pretty diverse group of people," described Leonard Carone, a first-line supervisor in Ford Motor's Dearborn, Michigan glass plant. "I wondered how some of the others could help since they didn't work on the floor. All of us were uneasy. As time wore on, hourly and salary employees came together—we all agreed there had to be changes made on both sides. We battled a bit over the agenda, and were concerned that we'd be seen as a special group. We were concerned that we would be part of a scam—that management wasn't really serious about change. But there was an energy I sort of loved in those meetings. Everybody was telling the truth, and I took that as a good sign for the future."

Background and History of the Technology

The primary purpose of this module is to educate design team members about the real time strategic change technology so that they can make informed decisions about the purpose and agenda for the event. A brief presentation from one of the consultants provides an "easy to digest" helping for design team members. The presentation should describe the technology, how it has been used in different ways in various organizations, and what makes it work. It sometimes makes sense during this session to introduce the "Arthritic Theory" and Change Formula, but be careful. Too much theory too early in the day is just that. One of the great strengths of this technology is that it is based on principles, the most fundamental of which is common sense. A slick presentation is likely to detract from the basic message: get the right people together, enable them to address the right issues, provide them with the right information and opportunities, and they will do good work.

Even if people are familiar with the technology, nothing substitutes for breathing life into these concepts by engaging people in discussion. The more real-life examples and connections made between the technology and design team members' experiences in their organization on a daily basis, the better. Sometimes we show a brief video of an actual real time strategic change event so the team can see what the large group meeting looks like with people working at max-mix tables or circulating around flip charts. In this way, they get some vicarious experience of what it will feel like at their event. Because it is hard to describe in words, pictures often help. Although the design team is more passive than active at this stage, the next module, a View From Design Team Members, shifts the air time from the consultants back to the other team members.

View From Design Team Members

The purpose of this module is to build a composite picture of the current state of the organization from the various perspectives represented. When armed with this holistic perspective, individuals are able to exercise their newly informed discretion as a team and make decisions based on the collective intelligence in the room, not just on the more limited, biased view they had when the meeting began.

Several options are available for how to share this information within the design team. In a smaller group (of 15 or so), a free flowing group dialogue usually works well. All it takes to get things started is to ask people to take a few minutes to think about what's working and what's not in the organization. As people contribute their views, it is helpful to highlight themes and differences as a way to distinguish key issues, opportunities and interdependencies or conflicts between sub-groups. Another option is to use the ingredients from the Change Formula (dissatisfaction, vision, and first steps) as the framework for questions. Larger design teams can be broken down into smaller max-mix groups, each of which answers the same questions, and then reports their findings to each other.

It is also helpful to summarize these dialogues on flip chart paper at the front of the room. Summarizing brings a sense of closure to this portion of the meeting. Recording it on flip chart paper ensures that you have an accurate record to refer back to during the rest of the design team meeting. This entire part of the agenda routinely takes several hours.

It is critical during the data gathering process for the team to understand that there are no right or wrong answers to the question, "What's happening in the organization?" It is often helpful if the group adopts the notion that they are solving an organizational jigsaw puzzle in which each perspective represents another piece. The more pieces they identify, learn about, and fit, the clearer the picture becomes. Imagine yourself as Sherlock Holmes. Look for clues, ask naive questions, read between the lines. Often, metaphors are a helpful way to share insights in the design team. For example, the program manager in one organization suited up for his visits with project teams in much the same manner that a medieval king toured his land holdings—with much advance warning, pomp and splendor, and plenty of preparation by the people. In this way, he was never disappointed, and his employees never surprised because he never saw or heard anything wrong as he visited his cross-functional teams. The metaphor made it easy to identify what the program manager and his people needed to do differently. Of course, not all of these ideas easily translated to their organization, but several did and the design team had discovered a useful way to describe what had long been considered an "undiscussable" in their organization.

During this phase of the meeting, expect plenty of venting and frustration to surface. For many, this dialogue represents the first time in a long time (if ever) that they have really felt listened to. In some instances, the design team may be too overwhelmed by their own negativity and feeling of powerlessness to make any significant dent in their organization's old ways of doing business. These reactions are natural. Through this dialogue, we are making the dissatisfaction (from the change formula) explicit and conscious in the total team. The next module, Identifying Desired Outcomes from the Event, starts the design team on a course for developing its own vision. The team begins to see the possibilities for the organization in terms of outcomes from the whole change effort, and specifically, those outcomes they want to see result from the real time strategic change event.

❝ When I first walked in that room, my motivation was to let folks know what I thought needed to be changed about the county," admits Kevin Bomhoff, a program manager at the mental health department in Sedgwick County, Kansas. In talking about his experience in being on a design team he explains further: "But something happened pretty early on that really shifted my thinking. There were some guys from the roads crew on the design team, and we were told to stop talking and to listen to these people. They hadn't said anything until then, but basically everybody with a college degree shut up and listened. At that point, I knew this was going to be different. Those guys from the roads crew actually had a big impact on the purpose statement for our first large group event for 350 people. It had a big impact on me personally as well. I think I listen a lot better than I used to, to a lot more people."

Identifying Desired Outcomes from the Event

The purpose of this module is to clearly define what success will look like from each design team member's perspective at the end of an organization's real time strategic change event. These desired outcomes become the design team's stepping stone between the current reality (the data they generated in the View From Design Team Members) and the path into the preferred future (the purpose and agenda for the real time strategic change event). Generally we use an open-ended question to solicit outcomes from the design team. One example of this type of question would be, "Given what we now know about our organization from each of our perspectives, what needs to be different, and what must we have achieved during the event that would tell us we have been successful?" For larger design teams, it may be helpful to have them explore possible outcomes in smaller groups before reporting to the entire design team. These outcomes are then discussed, clarified, and recorded on flip charts.

Desired outcomes identified by the design team must be realistic and achievable, but should also represent a "stretch" for people in the large group event. Listing additional funding and staffing levels as the results from a three day interactive session attended by several hundred people is proof that the design team is still operating out of an old paradigm: money is the only answer, or at least the best one to solve our problems. Some realistic desired outcomes might be to identify and commit to new business practices, understand and own the organization's strategy, and have each individual leave the event with a clear understanding of what they can do differently right away for the total organization to succeed. These types of outcomes also pack a lot more punch in the long run. The desired outcomes need to be stated in results-oriented language, not as activities. For example, "to discuss" anything begs the question of "to what end?" In this way, evaluation becomes much more meaningful because you can measure the difference you will have made against the benchmark for success established here.

Finally it is important to note that an individual event may not provide all outcomes targeted by the total change effort. Multiple initiatives, including those developed during large group events, are often required to support organizations in shifting from business as usual to real time strategic change. Chapter 13 describes examples of these other initiatives in greater detail.

Agreeing on the Purpose Statement

❝ When you start out with a design team and walk through DPPE, they'll nod their heads, but don't realize the significance the purpose statement has," explains Gill Thompson, manager of organization development for Boeing's Large Airplane Development group. "People really tend to appreciate the purpose after the process much more. What most people tend to want to do is talk about the agenda and order of things. And they spend a lot of time arguing about what we each want. With the right purpose statement, the agenda falls right out. One of the values of a purpose statement is that it serves as a reality test of the leaders' desires, given where the organization is. It doesn't always end up being what a vice president wants either. Otherwise, it just becomes another 'Go do' command, which is counter to the organization we're trying to create."

The purpose of this step in the design team process is to distill the numerous desired outcomes generated by the total group into a single, simple, easy to understand statement of purpose for the real time strategic change event. This statement should:

1. Be integrally linked to and reflective of the data generated by the design team.

2. Be motivating and ennobling to all participants in the large group event.

3. Provide clear direction to the design team in developing the agenda for the event.

One way to get started might be to have people call out words or phrases to be included in the final statement and record them on flip charts so that sub-groups can later draft purpose statements. With smaller design teams, it is often possible for each person to have a crack at drafting a separate purpose statement. Another option is to have design team members work with each other in pairs to describe how they would tell an outsider why they are having the large group event. The only limitations on this step stem from our level of creativity, knowledge of process, and quality of response to the group's dynamics.

After you have a few draft statements to work from, roll up your sleeves and settle in for a true consensus-building dialogue. Some purpose statements take days to arrive at, although that certainly is not the norm. It is essential to "nail the purpose" in everyone's eyes because it directly informs the agenda for the event, and even determines who will attend the event. Although the invitation lists for these large group sessions are often predetermined, the participant list should be checked against the purpose statement to ensure that the right people will be in the room. On occasion, the participant list needs to be revised as a result. You know you are ready to move on to the plan step of DPPE when you have consensus on the purpose and you have a clear sense of the difference the event will make for the organization and for the people who attend it.

Whatever you do, don't hurry through developing a purpose statement. The time will be well spent. The design team will emerge stronger, clearer, and more effective. Choice points in the agenda of the event become easier to make when weighed against a clear purpose. Participants in the large group immediately understand the event and its purpose as soon as they hear it because it makes good sense and would be worthwhile to achieve. Good purpose statements are clear, capture people's imaginations, are responsive to the organization's current challenges and opportunities, and call forth people's best selves to the process. Poor purpose statements are boring, vague, or signal a business as usual mentality.

In the case of purpose statements, "we are just wordsmithing" or "it is just semantics" often signal differences in real meaning or ambiguity that warrant pursuing a deeper level of dialogue. If the purpose does not speak to all members of the design team, other people will feel confused or disillusioned by it in the real time strategic change event, as well. Distilling a simple statement from the complex array of data on the walls, and from the list of outcomes, is a challenging task. However, you can pay now, or pay later.

Brainstorming Elements of the Agenda

The purpose of this session is to identify all of the possible activities the large group could engage in or experience that would support the purpose of the event. The free and open exchange of ideas that characterizes this step is welcomed by design team members; the hardest work is now behind them. Although most design team members are not familiar with the modules that would work in real time strategic change events, they know the organization and their own needs for information and engaging activities. In some situations, it is best for consultants to actively offer ideas, possible elements, or activities in the brainstorm. In other situations, it works equally well to have the design team write down all the things they want and need to hear, see, or do during the event to achieve the purpose and outcomes. Using this brainstorming session as a starting point, they can then sort the output into themes or topic categories, and begin designing actual activities for the event. For example, "get different functions working together" eventually could evolve into a Valentines module customized for the particular event. "Making commitments to carry out agreed-upon changes" might translate into a Back Home Planning module.

Different data and purposes for events suggest the need for unique elements. The more ideas generated in these brainstorming sessions the better because a crazy idea could be just the one to fulfill a unique or complex need. One of these large group events actually opened with music from West Side Story. The leaders of two long at-odds parts of the organization entered menacingly from opposite sides of the ballroom, only to meet in the middle, put down their knives, and shake hands. In one design group, the brainstorm lasted more than one hour, and generated plenty of good ideas that were included in their real time strategic change event. Because organizations have unique needs, we regularly invent new elements, which continually expands the technology's power and breadth of application.

To tap into the full creativity and wisdom of the design team, you have to give them a lot of room to roam in this part of the meeting. Some people will still be all too willing to have a consultant or organizational leader who happens to be on the design team run the show. But as process experts, consultants make their most valuable contribution by advising design teams on how to best address specific content issues, such as hearing customer feedback and analyzing current work practices, in the large group setting. Sometimes team members get caught up in design details, such as the wording for assignments, and end up saying, "This will never work!" because they lose sight of how it can be done in such a large group. Once the team has completed this brainstorm, you are ready for the next module, Laying Out the "Chunked" Agenda. Remember that new ideas can always be added as you move through the rest of the design process.

Laying Out the "Chunked" Agenda

❝ I love it when they say, 'That flow will never work,' " begins Julie Beedon, an internal quality support consultant with the United Kingdom Employment Service. She continues describing the give and take that characterizes a good design team meeting. "I believe it's marvelous to know it now in the design team meeting rather than finding it out before 600 people in the middle of the event! I regard the cynicism you sometimes hear during the design team meetings as healthy, and if you use it wisely, you can save yourself a lot of headaches down the road."

The purpose of "chunking" the agenda is to develop a rough outline for the event. It is the agenda, minus the fine detail. This rough outline organizes individual, selected elements into the journey that will take participants in the event from where they are now to where they need to be, based on the purpose and outcomes.

Four lenses, or filters, help the team design and determine the appropriate elements and sequence for the agenda:

1. The conceptual filter.

2. The visceral filter.

3. The linkage filter.

4. The purpose and outcomes filter.

The conceptual filter guides the design team's sequencing and selection of elements through the application of different models and concepts. For example, the Change Formula served this purpose in the example agenda in Chapters 4, 5, and 6, as did the Strategic Planning Model. Different types of real time strategic change processes call for the application of different concepts and models. For example, Deming's "Plan-Do-Check-Act" mantra was embedded in the design for the TQM implementation effort at Marriott described in Chapter 9.

However, do not blindly apply any of these concepts or models. The conceptual filter is counter-balanced by the visceral filter. This is usually the easiest to apply, and the most accessible to the design team, because it is based on the team's own sense of what will feel and be right for them as participants in the event. Because design teams are a microcosm of the total large group, what feels right to the design team is likely to feel right to the hundreds of people in the event itself.

The linkage filter ensures that the risk levels of different elements, and the skills and knowledge required to do the work within them, are sequenced, staged, and graduated appropriately. In this way people in the large group event feel wise, empowered, and capable of doing their best work. For example, in the sample agenda described in Chapters 4, 5, and 6, the Valentines module is positioned prior to lunch on the second day. Participants heard from their customers the previous afternoon about how they needed to do business in new ways in the future to meet these key stakeholders' needs. The Change Possibilities Panel on the second morning provided proof that change of significant magnitude is possible, even in similarly large and complex organizations. Knowing what they need to do differently, and armed with new listening skills, as well as the awareness that each person's truth is truth, participants are ready, willing, and able to assume the additional risk associated with giving and receiving open, honest feedback in a highly focused and productive way.

The purpose and outcomes filter provides an overarching perspective to the other filters, as well as to the whole design and event process. This filter demands that the design team estimate how much value any particular element or sequence of elements in the design add to achieving the outcomes and stated purpose. Inevitably, this leads to some additions and changes.

One of the most fool-proof tests of whether a design team is on the right track with a chunked agenda is whether they would be eager to be participants in the event they are planning. If the event feels boring, disempowering, or like a jumbled mess of activities, it probably is. At this point, the best move is to go back to the purpose and start over with a clean sheet of paper. The design process is much more art than science. It is a balance of designing both from your gut and from your head. The chunked agenda may well change as the team gets further into designing the detail of each element and how the elements fit together; however, this rough cut just created is their ticket to move on to the next step in the design process, Designing the Detailed Agenda.

Designing the Detailed Agenda

The purpose of this module is to put flesh on the bones of the chunked agenda. It should detail the form and flow of each element, and should answer who, what, how, and when in addition to estimating the timing and logistics of each element. The highly structured product of this step is in many ways an illusion (see the Appendix for a sample detailed design). No event ever has gone exactly according to plan, but the structure, discipline, and clarity derived from the detailed agenda is absolutely critical. As the saying goes, "A plan is very helpful; it gives you something to deviate from, and you know why you are choosing to do that." Each element in a detailed agenda is the result of a handful of choices made by the design team. The section below is a guide to each of these choices, linking them back to the example strategy development and implementation event described in Chapters 4, 5, and 6. While this section provides a menu of options, observation, specific training, and working with skilled practitioners are the best ways to develop those skills.

What or Who are the Best Sources for the Required Information? For some modules, like Organization Diagnosis, the whole large group is the best source of information. In modules that use outside presenters, many choices need to be made based on what the group needs to hear, from whom, and from how many people. In still other modules, like the View From the Leadership Perspective, one individual or a whole executive team may have the information that the group needs to hear. In some situations, the required information should come from sub-sets of the large group, such as cross-functional quality task forces, a department, or a section team.

What is the Nature of the Work to be Done? The nature of the work to be done in each module varies from understanding (as in the leaders' and customers' presentations) to analyzing (as in the Organization Diagnosis), to creating (as in Preferred Futuring), to recommending (as in Participant Feedback on the Draft Strategy and System-Wide Action Planning), to deciding (as in Leadership Turnaround and voting on System-Wide Action Planning). These various types of work influence everything from how modules are introduced to the form, flow, and detail of wording for assignments that the group works on.

What is the Most Appropriate Work Group Composition For Each Task? The configuration of working groups changes throughout a real time strategic change event depending on the task at hand. In the example agenda described in Chapters 4, 5, and 6, and detailed in the appendix, participants stayed in max-mix groups throughout the entire first day of the event. They shifted to department groups for the Valentines, worked as individuals in writing Post-it notes about their preferred futures, collaborated as self-select groups for the System-Wide Action Planning, and met in natural work groups for their Back Home Planning module. There are endless options within each module. These include presentations, question and answer sessions, and in-depth discussions. The choices you make should evolve out of your unique needs and available opportunities.

What Level of Influence Do Participants Need Over the Output of the Module? The level of influence participants have over particular modules is determined by a combination of their desires and the needs of their leaders. In some organizations, certain parts of the strategy are not open for input from participants. In the example agenda, participants had the opportunity to suggest changes to the strategy. In some organizations, participants have been involved in both developing and revising the strategy. Finally, the majority of the modules are designed to encourage co-creation. The Organization Diagnosis, Valentines, and Back Home Planning modules are all examples of this sharing of responsibility and accountability.

What Is the Dimension of Time Addressed in Each Module? Different modules focus on different dimensions of time, and therefore, serve different purposes. The Telling Our Stories assignment, for example, provides participants with an opportunity to look at the past years' experiences, the evaluations at the end of each day of the event represent a current snapshot, and the Preferred Futuring and System-Wide Action Planning modules enable participants to venture into their future.

How Are Different Styles Accounted for By the Process? The vast majority of traditional large group meetings require participants to spend a majority of their time sitting passively theater-style and listening to lengthy speeches, looking at slide or overhead presentations, and waiting for brief opportunities to have their voices heard. In contrast, real time strategic change events make use of a wide variety of techniques and processes. Models and concepts such as the Change Formula appeal to people at an intellectual level. Preferred futuring taps into their visceral hopes and desires. Presentations are almost always followed by table discussions, and are balanced by "post and read" and "post and vote" sessions. While some portions of these events are devoted to talking with others, opportunities are also available for individual assimilation of new data and personal reflection. Shifting these methods and processes throughout a several day event keeps participants interested so that they are encouraged to make their best contributions—regardless of their personal styles and preferences.

In What Ways Are Participants Able to Share Information? We employ a number of methods to ensure that each person's voice is heard in the small group settings. These include individual presentations, brainstorming, and discussions. In large groups, other useful techniques to use are the presentation/open forum process, report outs, call outs, post and read sessions, and post and vote sessions. These categoris provide design teams wih a range of options from which to draw either individually or in combination as they develp a particular module.

Here are some tips and advice for this phase of the process. The design team must keep the participants' needs in mind while working through the detailed design by asking themselves, "Could we answer the questions in this assignment in this order? Would we want to? What would this get us? What would we then want to do next?" The team also needs to consider how many different groups people will need to work in, how often each person will have to move, and how long they will work in these new groups. Will people feel herded like cattle? Will they be able to function at the level required in the new group given the task at hand? The design team needs to answer these sorts of questions before making a final decision.

Small things like scheduling "post and votes" and "post and reads" are best done in conjunction with an extended break to save time. The design team also should look for different ways to accomplish similar tasks so that participants never feel bored. For example, you may decide to use two "post and votes" in the same event. In one, you may have participants put check marks by the items they agreed with the most, while in the other they might use stars and dots. Even minor variations such as these ensure that participants do not experience similar tasks as repetitive.

The design team must also be patient. Designing a two or three day event is arduous. Given time constraints, you may want to focus on issues only the organization's members can answer, such as how to word specific assignments or selecting topics for speakers to address. Consultants can then fill in things like logistics details between design team meetings.

Another way to put time to the best use is to keep an eye on the energy levels of design team members. If people feel disempowered and that there is little hope for real change, it is often helpful to hold a "God, ain't it awful" brainstorm to get all the negativity out, and then return to the task at hand. Also, look for learnings in the group dynamics of the design team. As a microcosm of the entire organization, they may get design insights by reflecting on their own process.

One last note: the best design team meetings are also fun. Deciding how to make the wisest use of hundreds of people's time is a huge task. A little bit of humor goes a long way toward making the work enjoyable, productive, and effective.

Reviewing the Design

❝ The design needs to respect the design team's thinking," explains Rob de Wilde, an external consultant in Amsterdam, who has used the real time strategic change technology with his clients. "But it also has to be something the organization's leaders can support and believe in. Although these large group event designs might be seen as a 'black box' with certain aspects such as max-mix seating and open forums in common, each design is different and needs to fit the needs of a particular organization and what it's trying to accomplish. Reviewing the design in the design team meeting is the first step of quality control. Continuing to review it during the actual event is also required to succeed."

The purpose of this module is to carry out a focused evaluation of the design. Although some leaders choose to be members of their organization's design team, the need for balance precludes whole leadership teams from participating. This module provides an opportunity for all key players, including consultants, to review the purpose and detailed agenda for their real time strategic change event.

The evaluation process educates those joining the meeting-in-progress and places the purpose and agenda in the larger context of the issues and challenges people are now experiencing in the organization. Having one of the design team members read the purpose out loud and explain the meaning behind it to their leaders is powerful proof of the clarity achieved by the design team.

We have found it most effective to go through the agenda module by module, highlighting the leaders' particular roles, the purpose of each module, how each fits with the ones preceding and following it, and how it might feel for participants to engage in this process. If leaders have significant "hiccups" with the design as they listen, this is the time to iron them out.

It is critical that the design team listens to what these "outsiders" have to say. The group can always benefit from a fresh perspective, especially from other key stakeholders. Even after several days in a room together so close to the issues, deliberations, and plans there can still be a few holes or loose ends. Leaders have a great deal invested in this process. Design teams need to listen to their reactions, make sure they understand them, and then work together to improve the design. This review also enables design team members to listen for gaps, inconsistencies, and other problem areas in the design. It is probably the first time anyone has sat back and gone through the entire agenda from start to finish. The overall impression gained can prompt leaders or the design team to come up with points of view and ideas that are very different from those raised earlier. It is much better to catch a flaw in thinking or identify a potentially sensitive issue at this stage than to discover it with several hundred people in the room.

Remember too, that leaders who cannot make the design review should feel free to drop in on the meeting at any time to observe and answer questions or offer suggestions. However, they should guard against taking over the meeting every time they appear. Further, if the design team has not finished when the leaders arrive use the design review process as a "stop-action" to check on your progress and make any necessary course corrections. You will be pleased with the results when you take the time to ensure the quality of the event. Too much is riding on it to do a rush job.

Next Steps/Loose Ends

The purpose of this part of the design team meeting is to ensure that the leadership team, design team members, logistics team, and consulting team members all know the game plan between now and the event. It is always a good idea to review the agenda one last time to make sure people leave the design team meeting clear about their particular roles, responsibilities, and tasks.

The saying, "The devil is in the details" certainly applies to the real time strategic change technology. Minor slip-ups when under the magnifying glass of several hundred people's eyes, become a big deal. A typical loose end at this stage is finding the best speakers to make presentations at the event. Some next steps include assigning logistics tasks, such as creating the max-mix table groupings, planning catering, making travel and accommodation reservations and setting other design team meeting dates. The design team needs to discuss how and when participants will be invited to the event, and what preliminary information, if any, they will find useful and empowering. Design team members need to be informed about staying to read the evaluations after each day of the event. They also need to arrange their transportation and home lives. As a final evaluation, it is a good idea to have each person say a word or two about how they are feeling as they leave the design team meeting.

Redesign in Real Time

❝ This is a living process—you're likely going to have to redesign parts of these events on the spot with hundreds of people in the room," warns Anita Dias, who heads up the internal consulting team working on culture change at METRO in Seattle, Washington. "This method is a pretty powerful tool, and part of its power comes from its flexibility. You've got to know your stuff in terms of what to change when, but being able to make last-minute changes helps make sure you've got 400 people working on the right things, instead of blindly following an agenda that was developed weeks before—even if it was done by a representative cross-section of the people in the room."

With the satisfaction of a good design team meeting under your belt, let me not mislead you: the design process has just begun. The need to redesign the agenda in real time during the event could be caused by one of two sets of circumstances. The first situation, which occurs most often, arises when the actions, decisions, or behavior of the large group are different from that predicted by the design team. The second is when the design team, for one reason or another, missed the mark and planned an event that does not deliver anything really worthwhile. This happens if the design team does not even closely represent a microcosm of the actual participants in the event, if the team's dynamics are extremely poor, or if parochialism and hidden agendas exist and are not worked through during the design team meeting. This can happen when there is a failure in leadership, or when the team itself does not experience a paradigm shift during the design of the real time strategic change event.

"Live" redesigns can be exhilarating or excruciating for consultants and design teams. They necessitate a short turnaround time so that several hundred people are not kept waiting for the next activity. In one situation, we had asked participants to add their thinking to the work being done by groups on other organization issues. We tied the post-read-give feedback assignment to a coffee break. Participants chose to take their breaks, and for the most part, skipped giving feedback to the other groups entirely. Faced with rather sparse groupings of comments on the walls, it would have been a waste of time to have groups read through the input they received, sort it and integrate it into their final recommended changes in business practices. Some quick thinking and good teamwork enabled us to redesign that assignment while the large group was still on break. They were none the wiser for the change, and we created a new module we could use or adapt when faced with a similar situation in the future.

Redesign work can also occur at a relatively more relaxed pace. For example, this sometimes occurs after evaluations are reviewed at the end of each day. After reading several hundred evaluations and exploring the numerous options that emerge, design teams often decide to "stay the course." In other situations, minor to radical redesigns are completed. Participant evaluations, combined with design team members' actual experiences, provide another round of data for the DPPE design process. The same principles and models used in the design team meeting apply to redesigning. The only major difference is that when redesigning, you are working within a condensed period of time. The data you have gathered and the structure created in the design team meeting give you something to deviate from, when needed. In terms of designing real time strategic change events, though, I believe baseball great Yogi Berra said it best: "It ain't over til it's over."

❖   AN INTERNAL CONSULTANT'S PERSPECTIVE

Gary Jusela, director of continuous quality improvement for the Boeing Company, has worked with the real time strategic change technology in various settings since the early 1980s. Always having been fascinated by group process, theory, and how organizational systems work, his career really started through a large scale change effort at Ford. It was there that he came across this large scale methodology.

"When I first saw it, I was awed by the way it integrated what I had known from several different sources," he begins. "These events provided tremendous learning settings, much larger than I had ever imagined possible. It took the most competent models I knew about group process and expanded them so many more people could be involved in a meaningful way in these events. Ford was going through a massive adaptation at the time—so much had to change, and we had so little time. We had to impact vast numbers of people and how they behaved. This large scale process served as a tremendous vehicle for including people in shaping the future destiny of the company.

"For the last four years, I have been supporting a major cultural and strategic change effort at Boeing. I brought the large scale model with me, but in this situation we have a different challenge than Ford faced. Whereas Ford was in a crisis, Boeing wants to avoid one by anticipating change. We haven't been on the same firm ground here in Boeing in terms of having a clear policy direction to support our efforts and that's made it a lot tougher than it was at Ford where everybody knew "Quality is Job 1," and employee involvement was a part of the UAW contract.

"Ultimately any change you want to bring about happens through people and how they understand the context of their business and current situation. If you really want to bring about change in your organization, this is the most efficient and effective way to do it. You can spend a lot more money and time trying to change large organizations with small scale approaches than you will by using these large group events. If you're just bumping along and not really interested in any significant changes, or you're in the midst of ambivalence and mush, though, it probably won't work. You've got to be up to something big to justify its use.

"All organizations are being pressed more and more to respond faster and faster to what's going on in the world around them, or they'll ultimately get left behind. I ask myself, what is the magic of this approach? And there is some magic in it, because I don't know how else to say it. There is a positive energy alive in the room when you get hundreds of people pointed in the same direction. I've had three people come up to me in the last six calendar days saying, 'I was with you in Wichita in February of 1988. Remember that event?' I was supposed to be talking in that meeting for five hours with people seated in rows of chairs. Well, we did that event differently than anybody would have imagined with everybody seated in round circles talking to each other much more than I talked to them. More than five years later the magic of that event is still alive in their souls. Part of the magic of this approach is that they give people some control over their own destiny. People feel they can and do shape their future. Combined with rigorous planning and follow through, you can move a system in ways that seem incredible.

"However, I also know that this methodology is not a complete panacea. It doesn't—and can't—take the place of consistent and committed leadership, careful planning and course corrections, and making sure you have quality disciplines in place throughout your organization. This technology's only one tool in an entire arsenal you'll need to build a world class organization. But it's an important piece for bringing the whole system together, and I have yet to find a more powerful and embracing way to do that."

CHAPTER 12

WHO DOES WHAT TO SUPPORT SUCCESSFUL REAL TIME STRATEGIC CHANGE

P articipants, leaders, design teams, consultants, logistics team members, and outside presenters each have specific roles in creating a successful real time strategic change process. The purpose of this chapter is to clearly define these roles so that you:

1. Understand their context within the events and in the whole change process.

2. Are able to more concretely think through the implications of a real time strategic change approach for you and your organization.

3. Can begin preparing yourself and others in your organization to engage in this process.

The Role of Participants

❝ I've found it exciting as hell to be able to say exactly what I think in these meetings, even if it goes against what used to be the corporate grain," says Jim Barker, a lead mechanic in 767 plane overhaul for United Airlines, who has been involved in several real time strategic change events aimed at designing a brand new maintenance facility and accompanying work processes. He shares his views on being a participant in these large group meetings. "I've had my share of frustrations with the old ways and see these get-togethers as a quantum leap forward. The way I think about it, we've been able to start holding hands instead of holding weapons. The more people see and understand the big picture of where we're headed, the more inroads I've seen being made. People start thinking, 'Maybe it doesn't have to be status quo forever.' I've gotten some new ideas in these meetings and even seen the light go on in some people who used to just be head-bobbers—the people who talked a good game but never played one. We've got a completely 180-degree different approach to this new facility and how we'll work in it because of these meetings and what we've learned in them."

No matter how many people attend a real time strategic change event, certain basic roles exist for all participants. Although there are always a handful of optimistic souls in any organization, most people are initially doubtful about the chances of anything productive or successful emerging from a large group meeting. However, the meeting process itself needs to encourage people to move beyond their initial skepticism and get down to work. As they shift between max-mix, functional, self-select and back home teams, participants are supported in making three critical contributions:

1. Listening for and integrating different perspectives into their thinking and actions.

2. Jointly exploring ways to develop and implement new business methods.

3. Engaging in the messy and sometimes frustrating business of change.

Each of these contributions challenges people's long-held assumptions about how the world works. The next few pages will explore each of these contributions in greater detail.

Integrating Different Perspectives

A core principle of the real time strategic change technology is the creation of a common database of strategic information. In line with this, participants need to learn to listen for and integrate different perspectives. As people listen, the mood, energy, and dynamics of the meeting process shift accordingly. The most obvious of these shifts is in the views participants have of the challenges and opportunities they and their organization are facing. The question of why change is needed is answered by various stakeholders, each of whom adds his or her own reasons to the common database. In addition, listening for and integrating different perspectives leads to a collective awareness and insight that is broader and deeper than any one individual could realize on their own. Therefore, subsequent decisions, whether individual or collective, are wiser and more informed.

It also sends a clear message that each person in the organization matters, that everyone's knowledge, skills, and experience are valued. A good example of the value this adds to the process can be seen in the experience of Kevin Bomhoff during his first design team meeting, as related in Chapter 11. His organization's roads repair crews had an important influence on the purpose statement the design team created. The process used to shape that statement was as important to the roads crew as the content of the final document. As a result, the design team decided to include the phrase "having our voices heard" at the beginning of the purpose statement. To have your voice heard requires that someone else be listening. The value added by having people in an organization listen to each other leads to more informed, effective decisions.

Listening for and integrating different perspectives are key skills required to bring about real time strategic change. We design large group event processes to make the acquisition of these skills easier for participants. We do this by carefully increasing the challenge over the course of an event, by discussing how to listen without being defensive, and by providing a whole host of other tips, advice, and frequent reminders. When people return to their day-to-day work in an organization there is no consultant to introduce and frame specific assignments. They are left to their own devices. However, the methods available to people who have participated in real time strategic change events are many and varied. I have heard countless stories from clients of how people have adapted and integrated information learned at an event on the job. These people have planned and implemented changes, worked through conflicts, improved cross-functional collaboration, and developed many other useful applications. One of the best insurance policies any organization can have for staying in front of the power curve of change is to have members who listen for and integrate different perspectives as a way of doing business.

Exploring Opportunities

The bottom line deliverable of any real time strategic change effort is a new way of doing business that leads to new and more desirable results for the organization and the people who work there. Exploring these new ways of doing business is another role participants play in the change process.

I characterize the nature of people's experiences in a real time strategic change event as a joint exploration because individual actions are guided by the total group. Participants also begin to see change as an opportunity, instead of a problem. With this paradigm shift in thinking, participants are more motivated to seek out and make needed changes, rather than sweep issues under the carpet.

A joint exploration of opportunities by people from all parts of an organization also leads to synergistic plans and actions that are unlikely to be conceived by small groups of people working in isolation. The free and open exchange of ideas between participants in a large group event paves the way for entirely new ways of doing business across an entire organization. Old ways that have long outlived their usefulness are discarded by consensus, thereby making room for the future.

Changing Yourself and Your Organization

For most people and all organizations it seems, change is disruptive, painful and difficult. As individuals and organizations, we exhibit great focus, energy and ingenuity in the process of rationalizing and procrastinating our way around making fundamental changes. This reality leads us to the third contribution participants make to a successful change effort: engaging in the messy and sometimes frustrating work of changing themselves and their organization.

One vital aspect of this issue relates to the ownership people assume for creating their existing situation, and how potent they feel about influencing their future one. It is easier and more convenient to blame someone or something else for our problems, but this form of abdication does nothing to move an organization toward its preferred future. The large group events are designed to support people in taking charge of their own destinies. Through the event, people are encouraged to take charge by running their own small group meetings. They also carry out their own organizational diagnosis and ensure their own understandings through question and answer sessions with speakers. They learn that their leaders don't pretend to have all the answers, and are openly invited to influence the proceedings and their organization's strategic direction. Later, they hear about possible initiatives, and give and receive feedback on how they and others need to change to ensure future success. As the event progresses, individual participants come to realize the scale of the collective impact they can have. Years of powerlessness and helplessness evaporate as people gain a sense of their own worth and contributions.

Participants also gain a greater sense of clarity at these events. Although awash in a sea of complex and sometimes conflicting data, by working together participants are able to discern which changes really need to be made for the entire organization to succeed. Understanding the interconnections in the common database of strategic information enables them to weigh tradeoffs and consider the probable implications of choosing different paths, which ensures that informed decisions are made and that ultimately, the desired results are achieved.

The crux of the issue is whether people are committed to being different tomorrow than they are today. Although very few, if any, participants arrive at an event ready, willing, and able to change, the number grows as the event progresses. In the final analysis, however, the success or failure of a change effort is not based on the commitments made during an event. Instead it is based on whether the commitments made to both internal and external stakeholders are carried out over time. After a decade of seeing people in a wide variety of organizations engage in this process, it is clear to me that the vast majority are successful. What leads people to change their behavior and, as a result, the organizations in which they work? The answer is enlightened self interest. If the commitment required from people to make change happen relied on altruism solely, this commitment would soon disappear. But where personal and organizational payoffs are aligned through strategies and plans that are responsive to reality, it endures.

The Role of Leaders

❝ We had an extremely diverse participant base in our meeting. Our goal was to derive a vision for the game and business of golf in the United States—a pretty tall order," begins Joe Beditz, president and chief executive officer of The National Golf Foundation. The Foundation had used a traditional conference format for many years in sponsoring its biennial industry leadership conferences, called the Golf Summit. Joe continues in this quote to describe the key distinctions in his own role, and the results achieved by the total group as they shifted to a real time strategic change approach for their most recent meeting. "First of all, we had representatives ranging from CEOs of all the major golf equipment companies to leading journalists from national and regional publications, representatives from the PGA, LPGA, and the major golf associations, owners and operators of golf facilities, golf course designers, architects and builders, and resort owners and operators. In terms of my role in this event, a major challenge for me was to ensure that something different happened this time around. We needed something tangible, some key areas we could all work on together. As I look back on it, one of my main jobs throughout the event was making sure that my own contributions and the presentations made by others were all focused on delivering that tangible result—that we got out of the meeting what we needed to."

The greatest challenge for leaders in a real time strategic change process is to strike the appropriate balance between sharing their perspectives with others and having others share their perspectives with them. Who gets defined as a leader depends on the culture of the organization. In some situations, the leader would be the individual at the top of the organization's hierarchy. Other organizations might include this person's direct reports, such as an executive board, while in some cases, they may include middle managers and others with ideas and vision. In any of the above scenarios, leaders support the success of a real time strategic change process in seven key ways:

1. By making the initial commitment to the process required for the change effort to succeed.

2. By clearly articulating their rationale, needs, ideas, and desires for the initiative.

3. By modeling behaviors consistent with the culture they aspire to create.

4. By engaging in events as fully contributing participants.

5. By clearly conveying their thoughts, beliefs, and values in the presentations they make to the total group.

6. By thinking through and deciding on design revisions in collaboration with the design team.

7. By reinforcing new ways of doing business over the longer haul.

The Initial Commitment

Certain commitments must be made by leaders early on in a real time strategic change process in order for their organizations to succeed down the road. Much in the same way that an ante allows one to play in a card game, leaders must first clarify the results they wish to achieve. They then must gain buy-in from other members of their team and allocate the necessary resources to enable their organization to engage in a real time strategic change effort. Although making these initial commitments does not guarantee success, not doing so can ensure failure. From both symbolic and practical perspectives, these contributions—even so early in the process—lay the groundwork for an effective, considered, system-wide approach to the challenges and opportunities they and their organization are facing.

Clearly Articulating Their Case for Change

Another contribution leaders need to make early on is to clearly articulate the rationale, needs, ideas, and desires for the initiative. Explicit reasons make it evident to others in the organization why change is needed. Cogent explanations of a leader's own needs shape the purpose of the overall process and sometimes influence certain aspects of individual events. Because of the collaborative nature of this approach, leaders are also encouraged to freely share their ideas about promising paths to pursue. This might be with their consulting team during initial contracting dialogues, or in setting a context for the design team. It may also be with themselves in honestly assessing the current state of the organization. This articulation of the leader's rationale, needs, ideas, and desires becomes a mirror for the rest of the organization. The clearer the presentation, the easier it becomes for others to visualize their preferred future.

Modeling New Behaviors

Every interaction between leaders and others that occurs during a change effort serves as an opportunity for leaders to model behaviors consistent with the culture they aspire to create. What these specific behaviors are depends both on the current culture and on the definition of the desired culture. The important point is that everything leaders do and say during a real time strategic change process is duly noted by those present and quickly disseminated through the grapevine. This dynamic is magnified during an event, thereby creating a great opportunity to set a positive example, or to reinforce damaging old ones.

As an example, one leader had a habit of "thinking out loud." Although this behavior never left anyone in his organization wondering where he stood on an issue, it didn't leave much room for others to share ideas. During one of his organization's real time strategic change events, I learned that his max-mix table was in the midst of a silent revolt. His tablemates were convinced that he had already mapped out the organization's entire strategy and that he was merely waiting for the right time to announce it. I knew these assumptions were flawed, so I told him what I had heard, adding, "You know, some of the people in your max-mix group might have some pretty good ideas you'll never hear if you're the only one talking." A big grin creased his face, showing the message hit home. The rest of the event was a radically different and more positive experience for the leader and all the groups he worked in.

A final word on how leaders' behaviors can contribute to establishing desired culture comes from a concept developed by Stan Davis (1987). Davis argues that organizational leaders need to act in the future perfect tense in order to most effectively support change. That is, in Davis' words, ". . . to lead from a place in time that assumes you're already there, and that is determined even though it hasn't happened yet." I believe the mindset Davis describes is an appropriate and useful framing for leaders to use as they think through the messages they want to communicate to the organization during a real time strategic change process. They need to think and act as if the future were already here, and to modify their behavior accordingly to maximize the positive impact they have on others.

Being a Fully Contributing Participant

This contribution from leaders is based on the principle that leaders are both different from and the same as everybody else in the organization. Each of the aspects of a fully contributing participant (described in the preceding section) are equally relevant for leaders. People often listen differently to their leaders than they do to front line workers—even if the front line workers happen to have a much clearer understanding of the issue at hand. Nevertheless, leaders must act as fully contributing participants. There is another side to the coin though. Most leaders find it refreshing and informative to see the world through the eyes of others in the organization. However, it also can prove frustrating when they realize the gulf of understanding that exists between them and the rest of the organization. Engaging as a fully contributing participant in the large group events serves as a first step in bridging that gulf.

Conveying Thoughts, Beliefs, and Values

Presentations are opportunities for leaders to clearly convey their thoughts, beliefs, and values to the rest of the organization. Open forums can transform traditional speeches into genuine two way dialogues. Much deeper levels of meaning can be found by connecting organizational strategies with personal beliefs and values. A certain vulnerability is called for in order for leaders to be able to make this contribution. However, the payoff can be huge. By sharing their thinking, beliefs, and values, they become real to the rest of the group. My colleagues and I share a belief that honesty is the true charisma. People want to follow leaders they can believe in, and a powerful means for capturing their support is for leaders to clearly convey their thoughts, beliefs, and values to the large group.

Collaborating with the Design Team

Because the success of a real time strategic change event is highly dependent on its responsiveness to the needs of the large group, a sixth contribution leaders can make to the process is to think through and decide on design revisions in collaboration with the design team. As described in Chapter 11, these design revisions could occur at the end of each day or while the event is actually in progress. In either case, leaders have a significant stake in the outcome of any design revision, and a unique and valuable perspective to add to the design team's thinking. Leaders monitor the meeting agenda to ensure that the event time is used most effectively and that the large group continues on a productive path to achieving desired outcomes.

One organization could not agree on whether the design team or the leadership team should decide on design revisions. The design team didn't want to review the event agenda with its leaders because members saw their new role as an opportunity to call the shots. But the leaders were not willing to let go of the meeting process entirely. Ultimately, a third option based on a collaborative approach was created in which these two teams listened to each other's perspectives, and in so doing, discovered shared common ground.

The result of this collaborative approach is more informed and higher quality decisions with a broader consensus. Although there is usually at least one leader on the design team, it is also common to solicit comments from an entire leadership team on the initial design, and in actively working on revisions. This ensures that the top team's desired outcomes are reflected in the agenda, that they solidly support the event design and overall change effort, and that they are providing role models for collaborative decision-making.

Reinforcing the Change Effort

Numerous opportunities are available for leaders to reinforce new ways of doing business in their organizations over the long haul. Behavior reflects a person's true objectives, and leaders are no exception to this. In personal interactions and broad-based policy decisions, choices leaders make can either strengthen or undermine these new ways of doing business. For example, leaders can ensure that new information, reward, and performance appraisal systems receive adequate resources of time, money, and dedicated people. On the other hand, people in organizations attach great meaning to the conversations they have with their leaders, transforming even casual discourse into a strategic choice point. From start to finish, leaders play significant roles throughout a real time strategic change process in supporting its eventual success.

The Role of Design Teams

❝ We've had a lot of stress in our organization the last couple of years and have needed to change the way we do things on a day-to-day basis," explains Stacey Nakamura, a middle manager in the quality organization at NASA's Lyndon B. Johnson Space Center in Houston, Texas. In the following passage he reflects on his experiences as a member of two different design teams who were working in support of a change process at the Center. "In the planning for our events, people on the design teams—including me—have experienced great synergy and optimism. The key to success then is to transfer that same synergy and optimism to the larger group.

"As a design team member in the event, you have to sit back and soak up what's happening around you. If you keep your ears and eyes open, you can pick up on people's energy and interest levels. Because of the real-time flow of these events, you can't stick to a set agenda at all costs. In fact, if the purpose or agenda we develop as a design team is not on the money, it's our job to make sure we make the changes needed during the event to get the maximum payoff possible from bringing all these people together."

The roles design team members play during an event alternate between thinking and acting as participants and thinking and acting as a design team. At times this dual experience can prove challenging because design teams are typically at least one step ahead of the total group based on the paradigm shift they experienced in planning the event. Although leaders, and even consultants who are part of the design team, can hypothesize about how the event is going for the rest of the group, design team members have reliable access through their friends and co-workers to a broader, less biased, more realistic assessment of the total group's experience. Design teams play two primary supporting roles: they keep their fingers on the pulse of the total group's experience in the event, and they redesign the agenda to meet emerging needs of the total group.

Keeping Their Fingers on the Pulse

Design team members, consultants, and leaders rely on several sources of data to make decisions regarding redesign options. The first is the design team members' own reactions and feelings. Although design team members are not "average" participants, their personal experiences in the event provide valid and valuable insight into the larger group's mood and dynamics. Listening to other participants as they work through assignments in max-mix, self-select, functional, and back-home teams is another information pipeline for design team members. Once design team members begin consciously observing other people's experiences, it becomes clear to them to what extent the design is effectively engaging people in the work that needs to be done. A third source is to actively seek out and collect data regarding people's experiences. Simply asking, "How's it going?" often prompts many participants to respond thoughtfully and honestly. A fourth data source is the written evaluations participants complete each day. Even after a full and fast-paced eight hours of work, we regularly receive a seventy-five percent response rate on evaluations. This creates a clear, composite picture which enables us to accurately track the large group's progress, needs, misgivings, and desires.

Redesigning the Agenda

The agenda is analyzed and integrated by the design, leadership, and consulting teams in real time during large group events, which enables them to make considered and informed decisions regarding redesign options. A fuller discussion of design revisions appears in Chapter 11. The needs of design team members and individual participants are balanced against needs of the total group, based on the principle that nothing is done in the event for an individual at the expense of the total group and nothing is done for the total group at the expense of an individual. In addition, these ongoing course corrections go a long way toward ensuring that the ultimate purpose of the event is achieved.

The Role of Consultants

❝ You start out with several balls in the air at the beginning of the first day and keep adding more as the event progresses," begins Zoe Wilcox, Consumers Power Company's director of business operations analysis and head of its re-engineering consulting practice. Zoe has had experience applying the real time strategic change approach in both corporate and community settings. She describes her perspective this way. "From the minute you walk in the room you're constantly checking and monitoring what's happening and making course corrections. I like to include a lot of different vantage points in this assessment so that I can sort and sift through the significant data from the leaders, participants, logistics team, and other consultants. In that way you can validate your observations with others' before deciding what actions to take. The real trick in these meetings in the consulting role is to be focused on the right stuff at the right time to keep things on track, given the particular purpose you're trying to achieve."

The ultimate challenge for consultants in supporting real time strategic change is in balancing the diverse roles they are called on to play. The scope of work involved, complexity of the simultaneous dynamics set loose by the technology, and the ripple effects that small changes have on the overall event process make working in a team a basic requirement for consultants. A team of two works if both consultants are well-versed in the principles and practice of real time strategic change. Teams of three, and even four or five, are also common. In fact, we organized thirteen consultants to support the 2,200-person event held at Ford's Dearborn, Michigan assembly plant.

Each role a consultant plays is part of a larger whole. Working together, a team of consultants needs to continually monitor, balance, share, and rotate all the required roles so that all the bases are covered. Ignoring any one of them can be cause for trouble. In many ways, the consulting team operates as the hub of a wheel with other support teams linked to this center. Unique consulting demands are posed by each of the phases outlined in Chapter 8. However, this section focuses only on the consultant's main roles in the event. Although by no means exhaustive, this section highlights those areas that make particular demands on this key support team.

Teaming with Other Consultants

The ability to work as part of a team is critical for consultants in a real time strategic change process because teamwork is the glue that holds everything else together. Throughout the process, and especially during an event, consultants are continually comparing their data with each other and with the design, logistics, and leadership teams. They must continually analyze it, explore options and implications, and decide on a plan of action. Consulting teammates might support each other by collaborating to develop clear, relevant, and timely instructions for educating participants on what to do in particular modules. They might also jointly solve a logistics weakness in a design or offer constructive feedback during an event. Finally, because it is easy and even seductive to get lost in the details, good consulting teams keep each other grounded and focused on the major issues.

Coordinating with the Logistics Czar

The consulting team is involved with logistics throughout the process. This includes communication, planning, preparation, and scheduling aimed at making the event feel seamless for participants. It also includes re-planning, re-preparing and re-scheduling. Because of the dynamic nature of these events, consultants must develop a solid partnership with the logistics czar in order to handle the demands for openness, trust, honesty, vulnerability, and mutual support.

Relationship Building

Throughout the process, consultants need to continue building ever stronger relationships with the leader and the top team as well as with participants, speakers, and observers. All of these people are sources of data about what is happening. Having access to more data means consultants can make more informed and better decisions. When these relationships are built on mutual trust, honesty, and a commitment to success, the consultant's job becomes easier to manage. In essence, this network enables key players to exercise greater influence over the organization's real time strategic change effort.

Designing Ahead

Events rarely follow the exact detailed agendas that have been carefully crafted by design teams. The dynamics of the large group require consultants to regularly assess progress toward achieving the stated purpose, and against emerging data. This data can include subjective and qualitative opinions about the large group's mood and state of readiness for whatever is scheduled next. Sometimes, designing ahead pertains to the wording of particular assignments. It may also involve re-planning or re-scheduling. Being at least two steps ahead of the hundreds of other people in the room is an absolute must for any real time strategic change consulting team.

Data Gathering and Interpretation

Just as people within the organization need to build a common database of strategic information, so do consultants. During an event, everybody in the room is a potential source of data that can be used to guide and inform design decisions, just as it does during design team meetings. Gathering this data and interpreting it appropriately ensures that the consulting team takes advantage of opportunities to move further faster as the event unfolds.

Leading "Up Front"

This role involves introducing assignments, giving instructions, telling background stories, explaining underlying concepts, sharing illustrative examples, and facilitating group activities such as question and answer sessions. This adds up to a complex and demanding task for consultants—one that must be delivered simply and clearly, so that hundreds of people can understand and act immediately on what they hear.

There are no second chances to remove ambiguity or reverse confusion when working with large groups. It is often quite a challenge to keep the process moving along its prescribed path from up front. If consultants are too direct, participants may feel punished. Worse yet, they may complete assignments without understanding why they are doing what they are doing, merely jumping through hoops for the leader's or consultants' benefit. Consultants can also be too passive. When that happens, they may find themselves in the middle of an event that is out of control. Striking the right balance between these two extremes is one of the challenges of facilitating an event from up front.

Coaching Leaders and Presenters

What is said and how it is said in a real time strategic change event carries a lot of weight. Therefore, another requisite role for consultants is to coach anyone who is speaking to the total group. If honesty is the true charisma, a little coaching can make sure presenters are prepared and focused before they begin. Coaching also includes value-added support, such as helping nervous presenters relax, advice on where the group's energy and interest lies, or getting an early read on tough questions panelists may face during a question and answer session. For example, briefing panelists on what to expect gives them time to think about questions. Participants, in turn, benefit from the more considered responses they receive.

Facilitating Small Groups

Consultants occasionally need to facilitate small groups within large group events. Individual group facilitation is needed occasionally: larger breakout groups (more than twenty people working together) may benefit from having a professional facilitator; small table groups could also benefit, especially those who are having trouble on particular assignments. In the first case, active facilitation is usually most helpful because keeping a sizable group focused on the task can be challenging enough without their also worrying about how to run a breakout meeting. Small group facilitation, on the other hand, calls for an "intervene and move" strategy. With as many as one hundred tables to potentially check in on, it would be impossible to actively facilitate all of them. Consultants must also be careful not to take over a small group's meeting. This would send a mixed message about the principle of empowerment. Most groups learn to facilitate themselves quite well in these events. The ones that do encounter problems often only need a light touch to get them working effectively once again.

The Role of the Logistics Team

❝ I find you go through many different emotions being in charge of logistics for this process," says Lisa Feist, who has played the role of logistics czar at Corning for the past several years. "It starts with excitement because you've been asked to play an important part. Then soon after, it shifts to your feeling overwhelmed with all of the things you know you'll need to do. Deep down I know it will all work, but when you prioritize what needs to happen, it's a pretty impressive list. Then it's fun when you know what needs to get done and you can start making some lists and crossing things off. There's a certain anxiousness and nervousness that comes with the approaching event as you wonder whether your team will work well together and how things will fit together. At the event, you have a combined feeling of pride and stress. Pride in all that you and your team have accomplished and stress that something—anything—may slip through the cracks. After the event, everything's worked out, or at least been invisible to the participants if it hasn't worked perfectly. You look around at the empty room and sigh to yourself saying 'Wow, it's over! Great!' "

Logistics for a successful real time strategic change process is a lot like stage management for a Broadway play. You don't notice when it is done well, but without it, the show would not go on. Participants in large group events tend to be unforgiving regarding logistics errors. One minor slip up is okay. Two or more misses and people start complaining, "There are too many people at this event," or "Who's in charge here? Doesn't anybody know what's going on?!" Confusion is quick to multiply when hundreds of people feel lost or confused by a logistics mistake.

The logistics team, headed by the logistics czar, is a group of people charged with carrying out all of the behind-the-scenes activities that ensure the event runs smoothly from start to finish. One major role of the logistics czar is to coordinate all communication, work, and assignments between the consulting and logistics teams. Having one point of contact streamlines communication and minimizes conflicting messages between the two groups. Some organizations assign co-czars to help balance the workload before, during, and after the event. Another advantage of this dual leadership approach to the logistics team is that two heads are better than one: more creative ideas are available to solve the numerous logistics issues that crop up in any large group process.

The number of people needed on a logistics team depends upon the size of the event and the complexity of the design. However, a general rule of thumb to use would be a logistics team member for every twenty to forty participants. Although anything but glamorous, the work of moving easels; collating, counting, and distributing paperwork to participants; and carrying microphones affords people an opportunity to experience a real time strategic change event in their organization that they might otherwise not have. For example, when the size of the organization makes it impractical for everybody to attend, working on the logistics team is a good way for some people to be involved. Although logistics team members are not full-time participants, they do have the opportunity to feel included. Anyone can serve on a logistics team, including internal consultants, trainers, administrative staff, technical and production people. In one case even a line manager who was next-in-line for a large group event served on a logistics team. A different problem exists when it is decided that everybody from an organization will attend as participants. Apart from finding people to mind the shop, whole logistics teams, often including a czar, need to be recruited from temporary agencies.

The work of the logistics team often begins with finding an adequate facility. Long after the last participant leaves the event, the logistics team continues working on typing action plans and paying bills. The following sections lay out the team's major areas of responsibility before, during, and after an event.

Securing a Meeting Facility

Given the size of most events, they must be held in special off-site facilities, such as hotels, sports arenas, or convention centers. If the facility does not measure up to standards, even the most motivated group working on the best design will face an uphill struggle. One of the primary responsibilities of the logistics team is to ensure that these problems are headed off from the outset. Lower order needs for adequate space, ventilation, light, and bathroom facilities cannot be left until an event is underway. Certain minimal specifications must be met—and the list is long. These include location, transportation, and accommodations. The main room, breakout areas, and meal arrangements must satisfy the requirements dictated by the group size and design. For example, large group meetings call for a superior sound system. A real time strategic change event is probably different from any other function held at these sorts of facilities. The interactive nature of the event process, combined with shifting for break times and many other factors, demands extremely high standards of customer service and flexibility on the part of the facility's management and staff. Try getting 400 people through a lunch line in three and a half minutes. (The secret is in having a dozen separate, well-spaced stations well-laid out for self-service. Each must be double-sided, and there must be a plan for who goes where.) In addition participants, leaders, and consultants count on the logistics czar and team to work with the facility's representatives to continually anticipate and have plans for potential logistics issues that might materialize regarding the meeting facility. A final thought: the reaction of facility representatives to your clearly articulated expectations at the start of negotiations is likely to parallel their performance during an event.

Meeting Materials

Ordering and storing materials is another pre-event task of the logistics team. Easels, flip chart pads, markers, and tape comprise the basic meeting materials, with stars and dots for voting. You will also need pens, note pads, and individual assignment handouts. All handouts need to be copied, collated, counted into sets, and ready to go by the day and time they will be distributed. Also, having extra copies of the detailed design helps observers, presenters, and design team members follow the behind-the-scenes event process.

The team should distribute materials based not on efficiency, but rather on user-friendliness for participants. For example, if participants could be confused by a handout not yet called for, it should be handed out "on cue." On cue simply means that the facilitator would announce, "The logistics team is now distributing . . ." cueing the logistics team to immediately distribute handouts to the table groups.

I would be remiss in describing how materials are used without mentioning a strong aversion we have developed to the use of overheads and slides in large group events. These tools have never worked well. Turning the lights down signals to people that interaction time is over. Handouts have proven to be a much more empowering way to share information with large groups. People can take notes directly on the material, rather than having to copy what is on a screen they might not be able to read. Handouts received after presentations have been completed do not encourage participants to engage and learn. Speakers also tend to connect more to the people in the room when they use handouts. Finally, no slides or overheads for presentations in most organizations is also a sure sign that new ways of doing business are already being practiced.

A massive amount of information is produced at an event, the vast majority of it on flip chart paper. By checking with the design team and/or leadership team, the logistics crew can identify what materials need to be typed, in what time frames, and what needs to be saved for other uses. Those things to be saved need to be accurately labeled, including the activity, page number, and group, if applicable. The faster material gets distributed to participants the better. In our work with Marriott, for example, they often began turning around all the necessary documentation in real time during the event itself. Output from morning sessions was typed, copied, collated, and ready for distribution in the afternoon. Although this approach costs more because of the need to provide additional computers, copiers, typists, and space, the payoff can be worthwhile. This is particularly true where the demands of building the common database, sharing learning, and discussing implementation of initiatives requires quick consolidation and turnaround of data in a highly usable form. This output can also be used by participants to explain what happened during the event to people not in attendance.

The logistics team's responsibilities regarding materials concludes whenever documentation is completed at the close of the event. This needs to be typed, edited, copied, and quickly sent out to participants, along with a summary of the final day's evaluation supplied to the logistics team by one of the consultants. Time is of the essence, whether the documentation is used to inform non-attendees of the deliberations and outcomes of the event, whether it forms the basis of further, detailed planning in a work group or whether its purpose is to refresh memories about the initiatives being undertaken.

Organizing Support Systems

It is critical that the logistics team is always clear that the ultimate customers are the participants. Working on a logistics team throughout one of these large group events provides an object lesson in the fine art of service. Design and logistics decisions are always made in the best interest and support of participants. Whatever enables them to do the best work they are capable of is always the right answer. Look at the role of logistics in these events as an opportunity to make life easier for participants, even if doing so puts undue strain on the logistics team.

Several support systems are put in place when participants are identified and invitations to the event are sent. Different seating configurations need to be created from the database compiled by the logistics team. Whoever creates the max-mix seating list should know the organization well, have access to the most recent organization chart, and use established criteria to assign seating. Support systems can vary enormously by group, characteristics, event location and facilities, duration, season and weather. Logistics people find themselves arranging parking spaces, passes, transportation, and child care; providing emergency bases; making signs; ordering special meals; and considering the needs of the physically challenged.

The logistics team is also responsible for guiding participants to and from breakout rooms, and warning them of time limits during lengthy assignments. Logistics roles run from the mundane (e.g., replacing worn out markers and flip chart pads) to the complex (e.g., configuring breakout room allocations that maximize the available space), and from the mechanical (typing a revised strategy document) to meeting the special needs of individual participants. A good support system can be the difference between, "Nice try. You worked really hard," and "Every base was covered; everything went superbly and people felt well looked after."

The Role of Outside Presenters

❝ I think one of the contributions I was able to make was to help people anticipate some of the issues they would be facing in moving toward a modern operating agreement," begins Steve Babson, a labor program specialist at Wayne State University's Labor Studies

Center. Steve made a presentation to the total group on modern operating concepts in manufacturing facilities during the 2,200-person event at Ford's Dearborn, Michigan assembly plant. He speaks to the value outside presenters add to the process. "These kinds of changes in work practices have happened other places and, because of my outside perspective, I could link what these people know with what's happened elsewhere. In that sense, I guess you could say I was also able to bring some more reality into the room. Change is not easy, and it's been my experience that the best path is not to oversell the change process. In this situation, that strategy took the shape of opening people's eyes to the issues and continuing conflicts they'd be facing *before* they had to deal with them."

Industry experts, customers, suppliers, representatives from outside organizations, change possibilities panels, and experts on leading-edge thinking relevant to the organization all fall under the general heading of outside presenters. None of these people should be introduced as having the answers. Instead, they play valuable roles in stimulating participants' thinking and in enriching the common database. What they say needs to be held up against the unique set of challenges and opportunities facing the organization. Presenters add value to the process in two ways:

1. By challenging participants' thinking and current paradigms.

2. By creating a larger context for the organization's change effort.

Challenging Participants' Thinking

Outside presenters can challenge people's thinking and current paradigms in a variety of ways. For example, change possibilities panels can help participants understand that what they may have considered impossible to achieve actually already exists in other organizations. Current assumptions are called into question by industry experts using hard data. Other leading-edge organizational thinkers can provide new perspectives and insight into long-standing problems. Simply put, opening people's thinking opens more possible paths into the future. Even when an organization's own leaders could tell the same story, hearing it from an independent, non-vested voice can prove quite powerful.

Creating a Larger Context

Because outside presenters live and work outside the organization, their perspectives provide a broader slant on the issues driving the need for change in the first place, and on what possible organizational responses might be. Participants sometimes need to recognize that they are not alone in their need to develop and implement new ways of doing business in order to reject the status quo and engage in a quest for real time strategic change. By expanding the context within which participants see themselves and their organization, outside presenters help create spaces for people to explore new ways of doing business.

Everyone Is a Key Player

Participants, leaders, design teams, consultants, logistics teams, and outside presenters all play critical roles in delivering on the promise the real time strategic change process holds. It is also important to highlight the interdependence of these relationships because a dropped ball can be picked up by other groups. Just as people begin to feel responsible for the success of their entire organization's change effort, at some level each of these key players feels responsible for the success of a large group event. Rather than creating artificial boundaries between these roles we encourage people to take a big picture perspective of the contributions they are making. In this way, fewer balls are dropped and more effective changes get made.

❖ A SENIOR EXECUTIVE'S PERSPECTIVE

Mary McCormick is the president of the Fund for the City of New York, an operating foundation mandated to respond to the problems facing government and non-profit organizations in New York City. The Fund was created by the Ford Foundation in 1968 and now concentrates its efforts in five main program areas: children and youth, housing, the urban environment, AIDS, and government and technology. It operates a broad array of programs and acts as management and computer consultant, banker, grant maker, neutral convener, broker, and incubator of new programs. In these roles, the Fund's overriding purpose is to introduce innovative technologies into government and non-profit organizations that support implementation of needed changes. Throughout her career, Mary has focused on how to improve management practices in government agencies and non-profit organizations to address implementation issues, as opposed to policy development issues.

"What concerns me most personally has to do with a general failure to implement agreed upon policies and procedures at a sufficient level of quality," she begins. "Because we don't implement well, people are led to believe that the problems we're facing are more intractable than they really are. In many ways, I think we've lost confidence in our ability to get things done. At the Fund, we work to ensure that when initiatives are adopted, they respond to the impetus behind the policy. As a country and as a city, we stop too often at policy making and devote scant resources and attention to implementation. If a person were a casual observer of government, and received information mostly from the newspaper, he or she would probably conclude that there are lots of plans and proposals but few that yield the results promised.

"One of the issues the Fund has been working on for the last decade is making it more possible for government officials to engage in setting strategies, allocating resources, coordinating services, and implementing action plans. We have worked successfully with methodologies that are effective in doing this with small groups. But most problems do not confine themselves to one agency or institution. In the past two years we have actively sought out innovative planning techniques from around the country and around the world that will allow us to bring together people from across divisions, agencies, government levels, and sectors to address the multi-faceted dimensions of complex problems.

"A striking example that involves several city agencies was the newly emerging problem of controlling tuberculosis in New York City. Potentially a major epidemic, an approach was needed to enable many city agencies to do real planning simultaneously on this issue while there was still time. Controlling TB required that we find a way to shorten the time between planning and implementation—and that we do so quickly.

"Tuberculosis is a disease of poverty and the vast majority of people who contract it regularly move among temporary shelters, health clinics, hospitals, and prison. Making sure that people do not slip through the cracks between agencies, get the care they need, and religiously take their medicine is the key to controlling TB. The Department of Health has ultimate responsibility for a public health issue like TB, but it could never control this epidemic without several other very large government agencies—the Health and Hospitals Corporation, the Department of Correction, and the Human Resources Administration—acting along with it to develop and implement its blueprint for TB control. The public hospital system in New York City has approximately 50,000 employees. The Department of Correction is responsible for 20,000 inmates at any given time. The Human Resources Administration, responsible for administering the shelter system, provides food and living accommodations for around 11,000 people daily.

"We used this approach because there was no other way to do it. We had an urgent need to deal with the issue and successful implementation depended on the coordinated response of hundreds of people. When people understand the overall goals of an initiative and the particular role they need to play, change happens. We had to find a way to get information communicated comprehensively and quickly to a wide audience. Through the large scale process, public servants better understood how their roles needed to change and felt responsible for controlling TB. In some ways, you could say this process broke down traditional hierarchies and constructively put them back together again.

"The leadership team invited approximately 100 people ranging from the commissioner to front-line workers from each of the four key agencies responsible for the control of TB. Corrections officers, nurses, shelter directors, epidemiologists, primary care physicians, admissions clerks, budget analysts, building engineers, union officers, and lawyers worked together for three days—all the individuals who make decisions on a daily basis that affect the success of TB control.

"We achieved several key outcomes on what I hope and believe is the path to beating tuberculosis. First, there are now 400 people in a very complex system made up of several city agencies who have a clear understanding of the threat posed by this epidemic and the major steps the city and its individual agencies are taking and need to take to respond to it. Second, new networks and working relationships were created, some formal and some informal, between and among individual agencies, so that people are now able to work in a much more fluid way. For example, a number of inter-agency working groups were established at the large group event, and are now focused on important issues, such as the design and implementation of a technology and information system, which will be used to track TB patients throughout the city. Another committee is working on employee health and safety matters to ensure that employees do not contract TB. Also, instead of sending in individual budget requests to the Office of Management and Budget for TB funding, which was the traditional way of working (and pretty much guaranteed little coordination down the line), all four agencies came together and pooled their collective needs. People balanced and weighed a lot of tradeoffs in these dialogues, and I'm confident we ended up with a better plan out of the process. A third key outcome, and an unanticipated consequence, was that individuals within agencies also created new working relationships, and felt empowered to take more responsibility for TB control. Finally, a powerful by-product of this process is the respect it engenders for the kind of knowledge that is required to implement public policy. In one planning meeting for a large group event, a doctor was uncomfortable because he acted as if he were the only one in the room concerned about primary care. However, after being surrounded by housekeepers, custodians, MIS directors, nurse practitioners, and laboratory technicians for several hours, he realized that he had only one part of the picture, and that his success was totally dependent on the actions of the other people in the room.

"From my experience, the aspect that is hardest to communicate about this process is that participants are doing real work on real issues while they are in these large group events. They are fully engaged with the essence of the issues, and there is nothing passive about it. The result of these events is not just planning to meet again and talk about what to do, it is actually getting things done. In my estimation, too many meetings never get anything accomplished. With this technology, large numbers of people integrate a vast amount of information, develop a shared vision of what the goals are and what constitutes success, and then apply this information to their own jobs. They are then able to begin to act as soon as they walk out the door."

CHAPTER 13

KEEPING THE FIRES BURNING, ONCE YOU HAVE THEM LIT

T he real time strategic change process unleashes extraordinary energy and optimism, with significant dividends realized as a result. People see a future they prefer and they claim it for themselves and for their organization. A critical mass of people within the organization develops a new paradigm. They believe that they can bring about fundamental, system-wide changes in a shorter period of time than they previously thought possible. With the dissatisfaction discussed, vision created, and first steps in place changes begin to take hold across the organization. Back in the workplace, people are not alone in making these changes, but are surrounded and supported by hundreds of like-minded and like-motivated partners collaborating to create their collective future.

However, whatever magic occurs during a real time strategic change event is not enough to sustain a system-wide change effort. This technology is not a magic elixir about which you can say, "My organization has had its two real time strategic change events. Let's check in and see how successful things are in six months' time." Although it may seem preposterous to adopt such an attitude, it is not outlandish when you stop to think of how many other change efforts have followed a similar story line. Unfortunately, too many organizations expect people to keep the fires of change burning by giving them a small supply of flint, some twigs, a few dry logs, a rough indication of where the forest is and sending them off to make change happen with an inspiring, "Good luck, we're counting on you!"

In a real time strategic change effort, for the first time in what for many is a very long time, people believe in and are committed to creating a future that is better than their past. However, navigating your way through this process without adequate follow-up greatly diminishes the potential for progress to be made. At worst, it does more harm than good. Through this approach, people substantially raise the expectations they have of themselves, their colleagues, and what the total organization can accomplish by doing business in new ways. These expectations will eventually fall as the time, energy, and money invested in the process yields poor returns, unless it is backed by an adequate follow-up effort. If the people in your organization were resistant to change before a real time strategic change process was launched, wait till you see them after they have finally given up waiting for promised follow-up initiatives to materialize. Applying the power of this approach carries with it the responsibility for using it wisely and the payoff for using it well. Following up is not something to be done as an afterthought. It needs to be a conscious and considered part of an overall strategy for making effective, powerful, permanent, and positive change in an organization.

As more new ways of doing business become institutionalized, an organization makes further progress toward achieving its preferred future. These positive results provide even more impetus and momentum for people to continue making changes over the long haul. Purposeful, positive, ongoing change efforts also exert powerful influence on the culture of an organization and on how people in it operate on a daily basis as continuous improvement becomes a way of life and change itself becomes a regular part of people's real work.

There are two ways to keep the fires burning. The first way is aimed directly at institutionalizing these new ways of doing business. The second is designed to support the institutionalization of those new ways of doing business. In practice, the distinction between new ways of doing business and the effective support required to implement these new ways of doing business can become blurred over time.

The remainder of this chapter describes new ways of doing business that various organizations have institutionalized. It also includes some examples of follow-up initiatives. You may find some of these options more appropriate for your organization than others. Their purpose here is to stimulate your imagination so that you can keep your organization's fires for change burning.

Successfully Institutionalizing New Ways of Doing Business

This section outlines four examples of new ways of doing business that various organizations have institutionalized as part of their real time strategic change processes. Although not an exhaustive list of the possibilities, their variety demonstrates the breadth of issues organizations have addressed and reinforces the universal application of this approach. The examples cover how to:

1. Focus people's time and attention on achieving key business results.

2. Ensure that a common database of strategic information is sustained throughout the organization over the long haul.

3. Draw circles that include rather than exclude people in the process of change.

4. Realign an organization's strategy, culture, systems, structures, work practices, and processes.

Focusing People on Achieving Key Business Results

❝ Right up front I stated that I didn't want to get involved in any of this if people were not totally committed," explains Leonard Carone, a laboratory supervisor in Ford's Dearborn, Michigan Glass plant. "People in this plant are like family to me and what we committed to in that large group event was for real. We've continued to meet once a week as the design team for this renewal process because you don't finish the work at the end of the big events. That's just the start. We're real careful not to turn these weekly meetings into bitch sessions either—we need to talk about glass and windshields, our customers, and quality numbers. That's the only way things will change around here."

In a real time strategic change approach, focusing people's time and attention on achieving key business results expands their thinking and actions to answering the question, "What's best for the entire organization?" In this way, participants in a real time strategic change process begin to explore the systemic implications of the myriad choices available to them, and subsequently, how to make considered, congruent plans and act on them. Also important is the emphasis on results. These results can include cost, quality, cycle time, and customer or employee satisfaction levels.

Difficulty in institutionalizing this focus on organization-wide results is related to four factors:

1. How isolated is each work group, both in terms of other work groups (especially those closely related in the "value chain") and in terms of the organization as a whole?

2. How entrenched is the current basis for setting priorities, measuring and communicating results, and getting rewarded?

3. How clearly and successfully can organization-wide results be interpreted into back-home priorities and local measures that can really let people know how much and how well they are contributing to overall organizational performance?

4. How much capacity, support, and encouragement is there for a work unit to reconfigure criteria and systems for the measuring, reporting on, and rewarding performance?

Depending on the particular case, work units make different degrees of progress on these factors during real time strategic change events. In the above example, Ford's Dearborn, Michigan glass plant decided to use a temporary structure—the design team—as a task force to continue defining results and developing measures for resetting priorities and institutionalizing this new way of doing business across the entire plant.

The variety inherent in each of these four factors can lead to a wide range of devices and strategies to help institutionalize an organization-wide results focus, such as:

- Establishing groups responsible for cross-functional work practices and processes, each with representatives from many work units. Their purpose could include developing a thorough understanding and insight into the interrelationships of various work units and the potential value added by each. Such a group would likely be assigned to redesigning work processes or developing a continuous improvement initiative in line with the values and philosophy of total quality;

- Forming a single work unit task force charged with dismantling obsolete systems based on inappropriate measures for assessing and rewarding performance. For example, this type of group could choose several parts of the real time strategic change technology to carry out their studies and implement new systems;

- Forming a work unit to advise on and support the establishment of systems to assess and be recognized for contributions to overall organizational performance.

Sustaining a Common Database of Strategic Information

❝ We've found the technology to be a tremendous vehicle for keeping people informed on large and complex development tasks, like our new 777 airplane program," explains Gary Jusela, director of continuous quality improvement at Boeing. "Every six to eight weeks the whole program team comes together for a two hour meeting to make sure no one falls back into their own little boxes, and that everyone stays connected to the big picture of where the program's headed. Bringing everybody together like that allows for co-creation because people are able to network with each other all at the same time. What excites me the most is that these meetings aren't even a direct follow-up to any specific large group event—they're just the way this program is being managed."

The development of a high quality common database of strategic information is a critical component of any successful real time strategic change process. Sustaining this flow of valuable information over the long haul is equally fundamental. People usually recognize and appreciate the relevance and value of current information to a much greater degree after they have been engaged in a real time strategic change effort. This is because they feel more freedom to exercise their own discretion regarding a multitude of key business decisions.

The methods used to maintain a current, complete database of strategic information accessible to all members depend on three factors:

1. The nature of the strategic information itself. That is, how qualitative or quantitative is it? How objective or subjective? How stable or variable is the information over time? Although the specific information needed by a particular group may change over time, the nature of these characteristics usually remains consistent. For example, the kind of information required by a research and development group in the aerospace industry would differ significantly from that needed by the accounting department of a large bank.

2. How systemic or idiosyncratic are the implications that arise over time from changes to the common database? For example, changes may amount to an individual work unit noting and monitoring a particular situation that has little relevance for other units. On the other hand, changes may warrant across-the-board deliberations and a new consensus at the organizational level.

3. How systemic or idiosyncratic are the decisions made based on changes that evolve in the pool of strategic information? Any number of responses may be appropriate depending on the situation because of the complexity added by different parts of an organization making decisions based on their own interpretations of this new information. For this reason, considered study should be given to which decisions should be systemic and which idiosyncratic.

The methods used in different organizations to most effectively institutionalize real time strategic change can vary from a monthly organizational newsletter with quarterly meetings of key stakeholders to a sophisticated combination of enhanced management information systems and regular large group meetings. Computer-based communication methods, such as groupware, can also help sustain a common database. Adaptations of real time strategic change events like that mentioned by Gary Jusela not only help to sustain the database, but also ensure that the information base continues to reflect many different perspectives. Within short meetings, people can assess new data in real time and make the decisions required to set new plans and actions in motion.

Drawing Circles that Include, Rather than Exclude

❝ One of the things that has changed dramatically in our organization," relates Bill Buchanan, county manager of Sedgwick County, Kansas, "is that people are thinking differently on a daily basis because they've been involved in our real time strategic change process. A perfect example of this has to do with how we've transported people from the county up to the state psychiatric hospital for the past twenty-five years. You see, we used to wait one to two weeks before transporting people (so that the sheriff would not end up running a continuous transportation service), and because there were so many people who had to go by that time, they had to be shackled when the sheriff took them up. It was a stupid system that didn't work for anybody—it was demeaning to the patients, inconvenient for the sheriff and costly to the taxpayers. For too long, all we heard from the sheriff was that they couldn't do much, the judge couldn't provide any help, and the people at the state welfare department said it wasn't their responsibility either. One of the main messages out of our whole change effort was to include key stakeholders in decisions, so that's what we did in this situation. We got everybody together in the same room and figured out a way to end a quarter century of people having to be shackled for these trips so that we could transport them with a sense of personal dignity and have as many trips as we wanted in a week. The local hospitals these people are now staying in will gladly pay for a private provider to transport them to the state hospital as soon as they are ready, rather than having to wait for the sheriff, and the courts signed off on the whole plan. We're saving taxpayers' money to boot. We're giving people in our organization the opportunity to succeed in this change effort, and this is just one of many examples of the new ways we're doing business on a daily basis in the county."

As outlined in the beginning of this book, most common approaches to organizational change "draw circles" that exclude significant numbers of people from an organization's change effort, if only because effective ways to include them are not known by those charged with leading these ventures. Therefore, one of the new ways of doing business experienced in a real time strategic change process is the concept and practice of "expanded boundaries of participation" through inviting all the key players at any point to join in the process of making changes.

The more people who have a stake in the outcomes of a change effort, the more people there will be committed to making it succeed. However, as evidenced in the story related by Bill Buchanan, the number of players is not always the limiting constraint. In some cases, people's mindsets are the culprits. Although the notion is simple, establishing a mindset that looks at expanding organizational boundaries and including stakeholders as an opportunity to form entirely new collaborative relationships is a major breakthrough for most organizations. Although pockets of people in organizations often think "outside the box" like this, this approach to organizational change expands those pockets to include at least a critical mass of others in the organization.

Sometimes the organization's existing culture prevents these new ways of doing business from becoming institutionalized. Whatever leads to people saying:

- "It's not my job, it's outside my area/control";
- "I don't have the authority to make that decision, talk to them, act on that request, etc.";
- "It doesn't pay to question the system around here";
- "We're always being told that we have to do the best we can with things as they are, and not to expect miracles to happen";

is what needs to change for this new mindset to firmly take root.

Some predictable factors underlying such responses are autocratic management styles, narrowly defined performance appraisal systems, limitations on regular access to strategic information, task-oriented reward and recognition systems, and people having little involvement in the decisions that affect their work and how they do it.

It is difficult for an organization to adopt a real time strategic change approach without dealing with many of these issues. Their negative impact goes way beyond a myopic mindset concerning stakeholder inclusion. Specific strategies can be employed to address these factors. These strategies could range from training and development initiatives to self-managed work teams to reconfiguring performance measurement and reward systems. Establishing a process for effectively involving key stakeholders and ensuring broad exposure of everyone to overall organizational issues becomes a basic rule of thumb that supports this new mindset.

Total Realignment

❝ I've used the cultural change process in our organization as a stepping stone for all of the new strategy work we've been doing in our HR (human resources) group," explains Suzanne Elshult, director of HR for METRO of Seattle, Washington, describes her experience with one total realignment initiative. "What we heard in these large group events was that we were seen by the rest of the organization as reactive, activity oriented, compliance based, and internally focused. The organization wanted a results driven, customer oriented, externally focused HR group. Ultimately what they wanted is part of our vision: to be their strategic business partners. We actually started our cultural change process in HR talking about our own role and what we wanted it to be in the future. We went out and conducted 150 face-to-face interviews with all of our different customer groups, from transit operators to senior executives. I think it's been really valuable for people to see how the cultural change process plays out in real programs in HR. This work may have happened without the cultural change process because I was a new leader and wanted to make changes anyway, but I had a concept, framework, and buy-in handed to me on a silver platter because of the earlier work done agency wide. There are two clear results I can point to as success markers:

1. The spirit in our department is incredible. We're functioning as a team and communicating across sections. Teams come into play and dissolve when the work is done. We have fewer boundaries and are more focused on our customers.

2. The whole HR department is engaged in a continuous improvement process, actively redesigning all of our HR systems and processes with input from our customers. We've changed our hiring and promotion policies—two hot issues that came out of the large group events—using an agency-wide task force. I think what we've done is given people the okay to go ahead with all this stuff, and other people are making things happen all over the agency, like we are here in HR."

Because a real time strategic change approach is systemic by definition, it is especially well-suited for totally realigning an organization's overall strategy as well as the culture, systems, structures, work practices, and processes that support that strategy. From conceptual, technological, and practical application perspectives, this approach has the power to bring about radical change.

However, the need for radical change must be established as a considered response to a compelling gap between an organization's current strategy and its vision of the future. When the new strategy is vastly different from the old one, many new ways of doing business need to be established. At the same time, people need to let go of their old ways of working. Significant transformations call for the development of new structures, systems, practices, skills, and processes to support the successful institutionalization of these new ways of doing business.

To attempt to bring about significant change without also changing all the trappings and support for old ways of doing business leads to confusion and organizational schizophrenia because people receive contradictory messages. For example, a new strategy may lead to the call for cross-functional collaboration. Unless the individuals involved renegotiate their current roles or have their performance appraisal criteria changed, the old incentive systems can encourage people to maintain the status quo rather than engage in these new business practices.

How radical or broad changes need to be depends on an organization's particular situation and the urgency with which it must respond. The usual approach favors incremental change, ostensibly to bring about controlled, predictable results and maintain organizational stability. A major problem with this approach is that the notions of control and stability are illusions. The school of thought to which I subscribe says that organizational change is a natural and constant phenomenon. It follows then that if you support a change effort, you need to ensure that you are creating a good match between the changes you want or need to create and those that occur naturally. When a lot of changes are being made through a real time strategic change process, organizational life can be unsettled. However, when the right people are working all at once on the right things and are given adequate resources, encouragement, and the freedom to act, new ways of doing business emerge logically and naturally.

In the case of METRO, the HR group was responding to a loud call for a new culture. In addition, their internal customers wanted them to do things differently in line with this new culture. Whenever an organization's new strategy calls for a radical change, its HR group must also change radically. This is because they exert a major influence over an organization's culture through policies, procedures and practices related to hiring and firing, training and development, competency profiling and skill building, workforce succession and career pathing, pay and promotion as well as benefits, rewards and recognition.

What other issues face organizations when they try to change radically and to institutionalize those changes? Even where the initiatives are real time and systemic, versus incremental, paced, and affecting only part of an organization, there are still several potential traps, most of which relate to leadership attitudes and perspectives. The following sections discuss these considerations.

Getting Enough Perspective on the Organization   It is important to be able to stand back far enough to see where the organization needs to go. The most likely repercussions from not getting enough distance on the organizational scene are that progress will take the organization only part of the way required and that it will not achieve sufficient results. Worse, the organization may actually embark on the wrong journey.

The following safeguards should prevent leaders and others from developing this skewed perspective. When deciding in the design phase on the nature, scope, and elements of the common database of strategic information, leaders, and their design teams, need to be thorough and creative to ensure that they have a comprehensive and multi-faceted view of the organization's current reality. Too little diversity in perspectives discussed in the larger group can lead to organizational myopia, which inhibits the development of a responsive strategy.

Secondly, during real time strategic change events, leaders must use discretion in determining how much interpretation of the common database should be carried out by the large group. In the case of radical change and total realignment, it pays to develop various scenarios of the realistic and probable outcomes for the organization. It is in this phase that people need to make sense of data from the turbulent and probably ambiguous environment that triggered the need for total realignment in the first place.

The third safeguard then is to not let current realities impair your vision of where the organization might go in the near future. At some level, organizational leadership must envision a preferred future to define a new draft strategy (one of the many right answers to the puzzle of getting from the current reality to a desired destination). To help ensure success of the realignment process, you should be careful to keep these phases separate, and to create a preferred future based on, but not limited to, the common database of strategic information.

Developing an Implementation Plan   A substantial amount of planning needs to happen after a real time strategic change event. The challenge for leadership in this case is to significantly support, promote, and guide the development of plans and their implementation so that all key stakeholders are making decisions from the highest vantage point. Focusing on and understanding the systemic implications of alternative decisions and plans can make the difference between synergy and fragmentation—the difference between multiple positive effects and conflicts, resulting from people working at cross-purposes.

Another downside potential is that if this systemic audit is not done, the old ways of doing business will interfere with the new ways. Leaders need to be champions, collaborators, and scene setters during this phase. Plans will be developed within and across work units. All the key stakeholders will participate. Leaders need to help make the systemic connections obvious. They must also truly be managers of strategy development, not managers of tasks or the people who do them.

Deciding On the Magnitude of the Organization's Change Effort
Leadership sets the tone for the pace, level, and style of response to new strategies and plans. Even though the real time strategic change methodology demands action on a wide front, discretion is still needed regarding how changes are made, and how fast they are implemented. Imbalance, whether a phase is too slow and passive or too aggressive and unduly disruptive, is best avoided. Ideally, people should be enthusiastic about progress without being anxious about the toll that the total realignment effort may extract from them or from the organization's potential for success. Because of this, leaders need to pay attention to the throttle of organizational change; keep closer than ever to stakeholders, especially internal ones; stay flexible; and continually review plans and progress. By modeling new attitudes and values, leaders support new ways of doing business for the total organization. This has a powerful, positive impact on any change effort. This does not mean that leaders can control the realignment. But they can show others how to stay on course during the journey.

Forging Courage and Commitment   It is easy to be committed and courageous, even tolerant and empowering when outcomes don't really count, or the cards are highly likely to fall in your favor. It is a totally different matter when the stakes are high, when things are not going smoothly, or when people's frustrations are growing. However, these are things you would expect to face as part of a total realignment effort. It is at these times that leaders are most likely to grab for control, or the illusion of it. And it is at these times that such behavior will be most damaging. Potentially leaders can irreversibly sabotage the total realignment process and the organization's future success. Leaders send strong messages about trust, faith, and values; the nature of the leader-follower relationship; and the hope for things ever really being any different. Leaders must pay particularly close attention to their thoughts and feelings and act only after thorough consideration. They must be open and honest with affected stakeholders and risk being vulnerable. And they must involve these key stakeholders in any decisions. Especially during a total realignment process, leaders should seek tangible support to be and act their best. One final word: the secret of good leadership is "ask questions." Focusing on this will serve you well in overcoming the control trap.

Marshalling and Dedicating Necessary Resources   The challenge of using the real time strategic change approach is that total realignment and radical change must happen in real time. This depends heavily on adequate resources being available so that "transition time" does not translate into "down time." The type of resources needed in a manufacturing operation will be different from those required in a hospital, a software company, a county road commission, a hotel, a pharmaceutical research and development division, or a social advocacy agency. One consistent thread is that substantial resources will be required. Some of these requirements will include logistics and a commitment to the process on the part of leadership. Another resource will be creativity and broad-based thinking. For example, expertise of all sorts both from within and without an organization can add enormous value. This expertise may be industry specific, or it may be business, financial, or human resource-related. It may also involve information technology and systems, or work process and systems redesign. Partnering with people who have this expertise can provide solid support for a realignment effort.

In sponsoring the effort to adequately resource the overall change process, leadership exerts a positive influence on the rest of the organization. In some cases, this even creates a self-fulfilling prophecy. Because of this, you can finish up not knowing whether your success was due to having the right resources, or whether it was because the organization's leaders engendered enough collective commitment, energy, and action to pull off the necessary changes. Of course, the answer is merely academic.

Providing Effective Support

This section describes three types of support initiatives for new ways of doing business that have proven to be effective. These three examples are all extended applications of the real time strategic change technology. They could be built into a change effort from the start or added over time after the initial phases of the process. Also, there are an infinite number of smaller scale initiatives that could be applied to leverage the institutionalization of new ways of doing business. Most of these are themselves new ways of doing business. They are also covered in the previous section of this chapter as additional considerations organizations need to keep in mind when adapting and assimilating new ways of doing business. The three examples discussed here are:

1. Real time strategic change diffusion processes.

2. Real time strategic change reunion events.

3. Targeted training efforts.

Real Time Strategic Change Diffusion Processes

In many organizations, even bringing together hundreds of people in a large group meeting means leaving the vast majority of members uninvolved. The process of diffusing the change effort throughout an organization involves more and more people in a process similar to the initial event. Experience, supported by vast amounts of literature on adoption theory, natural diffusion, and cascade effects, shows that effective diffusion does not happen by itself. It requires one or more diffusion events modeled after the initial event. These should be broadly consistent in purpose and design, and they often share several similar modules. However, different people are involved. Also, because changes made as a result of the launch event have already altered some realities in the organization, each diffusion event requires its own design process. The generic purpose of these events is to further accelerate implementation of an organization's new ways of doing business by:

1. Involving more people in the change process in significant and substantial ways.

2. Building a common database of strategic information so that these people can make informed choices about their collective future.

3. Empowering these people to make needed changes throughout the organization in real time.

Numerous options are available to organizations in designing their diffusion strategies. These include those described in Chapter 10, such as "whole-system, microcosm" designs, and "functional," or "project or process," team approaches. Where organizations choose to have the "top of their house" as the target population for their launch event, we recommend a strategy whereby some participants who were "followers" in the launch event become "leaders" in diffusion events. This role transition pays dividends in two ways. First, people playing these dual roles gain a better understanding of their organization's strategy and a deeper insight into what they and others at different levels of the organization need to do to support it. An example of this is preparing for, presenting, and answering participants' questions during a View from the Leadership Perspective. Second, participants attending diffusion events see and hear that the people they report to are committed to doing business in new ways. These ways are directly applicable to them and they can immediately relate to these new ways because the strategy is presented at a level relevant to the work that they do. This sends an unmistakable message— changes are going to be supported at every level in the organization.

66 In my area I have 1,200 staff working at twenty-one different locations," explains Janice Saunders, an area manager with the Employment Service in the United Kingdom. "We had only 400 people at our large group event, so the first task all office groups committed to was holding mini whole day events for people who couldn't attend the first event. The focus of these events was on looking at what their actual office could do in line with the area strategy, and the local office managers have really taken hold of this process. Lots of work is being done in the offices, and that led us to do some focus groups to find out how things were going. One of the questions raised by these focus groups was what value we added as a senior management team in the area. We set aside some time to better understand that question and got clearer on our own purpose. After sharing it with others, we've been able to measure our own activities against it, and it's helped us sort through what we should be doing together and what we are better off doing separately. Our initial purpose of the follow-up work was to involve more people in the organization in our alignment process. What we've found out is that we as leaders need to be more involved, too."

In larger organizations, several levels of diffusion events might be required to ensure that each member of the organization can be involved. The further you go toward the front line, the more people there are to involve. Therefore, for practical purposes, many organizations opt for two-day diffusion events following a three-day launch event. Not as much can be accomplished with the reduced time frame; however, people attending diffusions benefit from the momentum created by the launch event. We have designed and facilitated one-day diffusions, but there are clear tradeoffs in going this route. One-day diffusions in a large organization significantly reduce the overall cost and ease the logistical issues associated with the change effort (less downtime and lower facility fees, for example). However, participants sometimes complain that they have only one day to learn what took top managers in the company three days to get a handle on—a reasonable protest considering that changing traditional business practices which this three day-one day difference exemplifies is one of the stated goals of the effort. These choices send important messages to people in your organization and need to be decided on a case by case basis.

Real Time Strategic Change Reunion Events

Kurt Lewin's theory of action research forms a conceptual basis for real time strategic change reunion events, as well as for the initial process. Lewin, the ingenious social scientist whose work laid the foundation for much of what we now know about the field of planned change, invented action research in the 1940s. It has not only stood the test of time, it has rightly experienced a resurgence. Its focused, practical, reality-based, real-time approach to learning and change is equally applicable to individuals, small teams, or large organizations. Lewin's approach to change advocates a continuous cycle of process improvement in which actions are taken, their impact analyzed, learnings gathered, and future actions planned based on these learnings. Deming's Plan-Do-Check-Act quality process shares the same core principle.

Consistent with these concepts, the purpose of reunion events is to integrate new learnings gained from the changes decided upon in the launch event into the future plans of the organization. In doing so, you increase the efficiency and effectiveness of the organization in general, and of the specific change effort in particular. The reunion event embodies a continuous learning and feedback loop process. This process functions at the individual level, as well as at the work unit or team level. This is not to say that reunion events are the only opportunity for the organization as whole to take stock of progress made. Organizations commonly reconfigure communications channels and systems so that the common database can be updated and accessed by people in all parts of the organization. In this way, whole organization, big picture strategic thinking established at the initial event is supported and encouraged. However, there are three main advantages to the reunion that you cannot get from a totally new effort.

Reunion events generally occur between six weeks and one year after an initial event. The wide variance in interim periods is explained by differences in the magnitude and nature of the changes required, and the rate of change in an organization's environment. Our experience suggests that an organization-wide common database has a life of between three months and one year.

These "stop action" events usually begin with participants rejoining their back-home groups and revisiting the commitments they made there. These free and open dialogues achieve three outcomes:

1. The dialogues create opportunities to celebrate successes publicly—often a counter-cultural event in most organizations.

2. Participants learn about plans that did not work or were not lived up to. They are also able to identify system-wide issues that need to be resolved in order to further support their change efforts.

3. The entire process models a new culture that promotes learning from mistakes, rather than being punished for them.

Reunion events focus on addressing system-wide issues that stand between the organization and its vision for the future. These events should be based on an up-to-the-minute, common database of strategic information. Finally, reunion events provide an opportunity for participants to get a "double loop" of learning (Argyris, 1977). That is, they are able to learn *how* they learned to make change happen. This double loop of learning leads to course corrections in behavior and action plans that ultimately result in more successful change processes for the organization.

❝ Originally, we started out this process with a two-day, off-site event a couple years ago," says Allen Gates, the leader from Kaiser Electronics, who has used a reunion strategy in his company to sustain the momentum gained from earlier real time strategic change events. "We followed that up with two-hour events every six weeks, and another off-site event six months later. The process will not work unless leadership at the top is unwaveringly committed and clear about what needs to be achieved. Last year we had another two-day, off-site event, and we have another scheduled for this September so that we can continue to gather people, and build commitment and motivation to the vision we've created as part of this process."

Targeted Training Efforts

❝ We went through a county-wide process of offering empowerment to employees, but managers were left in a bit of a quandary, asking,

'What's my role now?' " explains Jerry Harrison, assistant county manager for Sedgwick County, Kansas. "We felt it was necessary to train our managers in how they could add value in the new organization. For us that answer came in the form of them learning how to manage strategically. We probably waited too long to get started with this training, because there was a great period of confusion between the large group events and the training. We heard some feedback saying, 'Why didn't we do the training before the strategic planning events?' but I don't think it would've worked that way. Until people saw outside the county organization—and the impact they had on other people and the citizens—the awareness was just not there. We now have people thinking about who else needs to be involved in decisions and what's the value we're getting from certain programs for what we're investing in terms of money and time. These are really different questions people are asking and I've seen our managers evolving very rapidly. We've got a new 'County Way' of operating based on our mission, goals, and values, and our managers are using it more and more."

Real time strategic change events often trigger a deluge of additional training requests from people who attend. Although participants develop skills in holding dialogues and reaching consensus, conflict management, listening, teamwork, and system-wide action planning, they recognize that they will need to do business in new ways in the future for their change efforts to be successful. This represents a high class problem for the organization, and this time it ends up in the training department's lap. Rather than publishing corporate directives and mandates of minimum training and competency requirements to ensure that people develop the skills they need, trainers have to prepare themselves for a mass of eager learners. The type of training requested depends on the issues addressed by the organization's change effort and how different the culture being sought is from that which currently exists. In some organizations, a call for technical training closely follows real time strategic change events. However, participants often identify "soft skills" or non-technical development needs as well.

Given that traditional training approaches are usually limited to under fifty people, trainers can quickly find themselves buried under a pile of requests they cannot hope to meet for months (and sometimes even years). That means people are sometimes prevented from expanding their skill base. Without them, motivation and momentum is slowed. Sometimes entire change efforts can be held up as a result. One method of addressing this potential bottleneck is to apply the real time strategic change technology to an organization's training needs. Bringing together hundreds of people at the same time for skill building workshops ensures that more people get up-to-speed on the new ways of doing business faster. It also provides the added benefit of having the common database of strategic information available in such a large group. Marriott's total quality management case study described in Chapter 9 illustrates how groups of up to 500 people—many of them having had no previous training in quality tools or techniques—learned and competently applied Deming's seven basic quality tools, all in a three-day real time strategic change event. Not all training done in organizations needs to use the large group format. However, when you need to expose many people to new concepts, tools, and techniques in a small window of time, the real time strategic change technology provides an excellent option.

❝ We realized a consultancy approach was actually a very effective tool for managers to have," says Martin Raff, a regional director in the United Kingdom's Employment Service. He explains, "We had been grappling with empowerment for some time, but really didn't have the skills we needed to make that shift. Some of the consulting concepts, such as developing a fifty-fifty relationship based on inter-dependence, actually replaced empowerment as our goal. We opened up the internal training sessions so that we could create a group of consultants capable of supporting our work in the region, while also developing key senior managers' consulting skills that they're now using in their day-to-day work."

A Closing Comment on Follow-Up Efforts

In terms of follow-up efforts, focused, comprehensive support for implementing change is not an option if you hope to be successful with a real time strategic change effort. These examples were intended to trigger your thinking about what changes and follow-up support might make sense in your organization. Some follow-up initiatives are best planned and coordinated centrally. Others are most effective when they bubble up from various pockets in the organization. By involving key stakeholders in thinking through the design and delivery of centralized efforts you ensure that all key needs are being met. By finding ways to support and publicize initiatives taking root out in the field you ensure that momentum for change is spread throughout the organization and that other groups can "steal" these good ideas. Whatever you target and however you approach this work in your organization, remember one thing about follow-up above all else: it definitely needs doing!

PART FOUR

PUSHING THE BOUNDARIES OF REAL TIME STRATEGIC CHANGE

CHAPTER 14

THREE PATHS TO REALIZING THE FULL POTENTIAL OF THIS NEW PARADIGM

T he real time strategic change approach described in this book has proven to be effective in addressing a wide range of issues for organizations around the world. However, even given this substantial impact, I am convinced that we have only begun to scratch the surface of its ultimate potential. Three separate paths need to be pursued simultaneously to realize the full potential of this new paradigm: application, innovation, and collaboration. Each path is different, yet essential in continuing this pursuit. Fundamental, far-reaching, and fast-paced change is a realistic, achievable result for organizations committed to a real time strategic effort. This new world view breaks through existing barriers, thereby enabling organizations to change as whole systems.

The three paths of application, innovation, and collaboration have always been inextricably linked to how the real time strategic change approach was invented and how it has evolved over time. Each serves as a catalyst for the others. The application of team-based action research, or learning-by-doing, has led to innovations in the technology. Innovations in the technology have, in turn, paved the way for new applications.

The path of application focuses on the potential this approach holds for you and your particular organization right now. In short, the more organizations that engage in real time strategic change efforts, the closer we come to realizing its full potential. Innovation refers to the potential of real time strategic change to continue to add value for all organizations in the future. Continued innovation ensures that this approach will remain responsive to the emerging trends in organizations and in their efforts to change. Finally, the path of collaboration leads us toward the next generation of concepts, tools, and technologies that will most effectively support organizations and the people in them in realizing their preferred futures. This open system approach can, when combined with other innovative methods, provide raw materials from which to create a blueprint for the future of the field of change and its application in organizations.

Before exploring these paths in greater detail, I want to briefly reflect on some past "new frontiers," which have since become fundamental aspects of the real time strategic change approach. I offer these images as a backdrop to the remainder of this chapter, to point out that what once seemed impossible, or at least improbable, is now commonplace.

We began ten years ago working with groups of sixty participants. At the time, we believed that this was the upper size limit for the technology. Through our work at Ford's Dearborn, Michigan assembly plant we learned that we could confidently engage 2,200 people, achieving remarkably similar results to those of a decade ago. In fact, 500-person events are now commonplace. Language barriers between participants in multilingual organizations initially seemed to demand more than the technology could deliver, but our experiences with simultaneous translation proved that assumption to be flawed. We questioned the validity of our North American model in supporting change efforts in other cultures, and have found the core constructs equally applicable in such diverse locales as Eastern Europe and Asia.

Over time, we have also continued to invent new design modules, logistics systems, and planning processes. For example, the concept of change possibilities panels emerged out of the needs of certain organizations to quickly and clearly have their insights about other organizations shared with a broad audience. Although we were originally trapped by our own paradigm that an event must take place in one main meeting room, we pushed this boundary through the use of closed circuit television, which enabled us to significantly expand the number of people who could participate in one event. Ten years ago, we planned these large group gatherings by interviewing a representative cross section of participants, then used consultant-only groups to design the actual event processes. Today, the use of participant-based design teams enables us to develop higher quality, more responsive agendas in less time than we could ever craft on our own. Initial beliefs about the real time strategic change approach have given way to new ways of doing business within the overall process. The remainder of this chapter explores possible paths of application, innovation, and collaboration that provide an action agenda and promise to continue to break new ground in the future.

The Path of Application

There are three critical success factors along the path of application that are required for an organization to effectively apply this approach and realize its full potential. These three critical success factors are courage, clarity, and commitment.

The Need for Courage

First, courage is needed to let go of outdated, less productive ways of doing business. As an advocate for real time strategic change, you make a strong statement in support of discovering and institutionalizing new ways of doing business. Since an entire organization becomes involved in a real time strategic change effort, sacred cows are regularly called into question, pet projects put on alert.

Courage is called for in order to shift investments of time, money and energy needed to adequately support a real time strategic change effort. The approach I have outlined marks a radical departure point for how organizations can and must change, and in doing so, represents uncharted territory for those in charge of allocating organizational resources. The results described by the many people in the organizations represented in this book highlight the potential benefits afforded and risks associated by this process. Although tested in a wide variety of organizations, there are no guarantees of success with this approach. Therefore, courage is required to act in the face of this risk and uncertainty.

Third and finally, courage is needed in order for an organization to move into an uncertain and unpredictable future at an accelerated pace. Creating an environment in which all members plan and implement changes in real time shatters any remnants of the illusion that an individual or small group of people can control an entire organization. Establishing a common database of strategic information throughout an entire organization makes it easier to "trust the process." In fact, ensuring this common database is current, accurate and readily accessible is probably the single most important organizational resource people have in preparing themselves and their organization for an uncertain tomorrow.

The Need for Clarity

Clarity of purpose is needed because the real time strategic change technology is only a tool. When it is applied with a lack of focus, its value is largely lost. Your organization's leaders, their words and actions, as well as the designs for the large group events and all follow-up initiatives, must be aligned with the overall purpose of your change effort. Without this alignment, potential synergies disappear. Even more costly though are the inconsistent messages that will be sent throughout the organization. These mixed messages undermine any progress already achieved. The result is that the real time strategic change technology will be no more effective than any of the common approaches discussed in Chapter 1.

A thorough understanding of the process of real time strategic change is another key component for success. Great flexibility is possible in applying this approach; however, violating one or more of the principles underlying the technology is to invite failure. You need to develop a deep understanding of the approach and the process behind it to ensure that all key players understand their roles.

The Need for Commitment

One appeal of this approach is in the speed at which an organization can move further into its preferred future by applying it. Nevertheless, change efforts succeed or fail based on what happens over the long haul. Various people have pointed out through these pages that the large group events that form the foundation of this approach are merely starting points. Real time strategic change efforts cannot work as test cases or small pilot programs. They must be high-profile initiatives that require a significant commitment of resources and personal conviction on the part of organization leaders.

Real time strategic change efforts also require that people throughout the organization assume personal responsibility for changing themselves. In essence, they must assume an attitude of "change begins with me." Organizations comprised of hundreds of thousands of people can be transformed through the individual commitments people make to think, act, and be different on a daily basis.

The Path of Innovation

The path of innovation is another avenue from which we can realize the full potential of real time strategic change. In this section, I outline several scenarios involving potential innovations. Some of these images are close to current reality, while others represent more remote possibilities. Read through these scenarios with an eye towards the future, for if we can continue to stretch the boundaries of what might be possible in our minds, we can then begin to transform these same possibilities into reality in our lives.

Remote Location Events

One of the most difficult logistical issues associated with a real time strategic change event is how to bring all participants to the same location. This first scenario introduces the possibility of remote location events as a solution. We had good success in adopting closed circuit television technology for Ford's 2,200-person Dearborn, Michigan assembly plant event. New methods, combined with video conferencing technology, could also support the staging of successful remote location events. Remote location events could even be held on different continents and in different languages. One benefit is the potential for significantly expanding the number of participants. With 2,200 people working together at the Ford event, can 4,400 or 6,600 be far in the future?

Although a number of compromises would likely have to be made in this scenario, including less diverse max-mix table groups and no visceral interactions with participants at other locations, new communications technologies could minimize the impact of these. In other cases, simply being able to include groups from different locations in the same real time strategic change event could far outweigh any trade offs.

"Virtual" Events

The concept of virtual reality technology and the increasing interest in and experimentation with virtual organizations and virtually co-located teams are challenging commonly accepted practices of how work should be organized. What might a virtual real time strategic change event entail? Based on the principles described in Chapters 4, 5, and 6, virtual real time strategic change events would always be in progress as people continually added to their organization's common database of strategic information. Once again, current technology constraints make this scenario appear unlikely. However, a thirty-five–fold increase in the number of participants would have sounded equally unrealistic ten years ago. The continued emergence of new ways for people to organize themselves to work will greatly increase the pressures and opportunities for this approach and its accompanying technology. So even though I can only offer a cursory description of virtual real time strategic change events at this time, as the need increases, I suspect so will the innovations.

Applying the Technology to More Complex Change Efforts

We have enjoyed consistent success in applying the real time strategic change technology within single organizations. We have also worked with multiple organizations for specific purposes, and with community-based groups. The technology may also pay great dividends as a method for organizing and managing large one-time group events, such as the Olympics. These one-time initiatives, characterized by years of planning followed by rapid implementation, face huge obstacles in creating and sustaining a common database of strategic information. Applying the real time strategic change approach as part of the preparation process in such settings would almost certainly speed up the whole process.

Town meetings have become a common forum used by political leaders and others in the United States as a means for limited two-way communications with constituents. Town meetings have created opportunities for people to be involved in the political process as never before. But they result in only a fraction of the value people realize by participating in a real time strategic change process. The results could be similar to those achieved at the community or individual organization level: faster paced, higher quality changes made by more informed people committed to creating their collective future. Political dynamics add another level of complexity to a change effort of this magnitude. However, that is not reason enough to preclude exploring these options more fully. Perhaps the real time strategic change technology would have to be adapted in some way to account for this additional complexity, or perhaps the capability for this work exists in its present form.

The Path of Collaboration

Collaboration holds great promise as the third path for realizing the ultimate potential of this new paradigm. Seeking out, understanding and combining what is now known about real time strategic change with other innovative approaches to organization change can yield potent practices for the future. In some ways, the commitment required to invest in this type of exploration is akin to that which is needed for basic scientific research. Immediate applications of knowledge gained may not be clear at the outset; however, significant advances in practice become possible through collaborative efforts as representatives from different schools of thought push each others' boundaries of current beliefs and assumptions. By transferring, integrating, and testing knowledge and practices, this approach holds the potential for uncovering powerful new insights into the fundamental nature of organizations, and how and why they do and need to change. I believe these open-ended quests for knowledge provide a path toward the next generation of concepts, tools, and technologies that can best support organizations and their people in making changes and crafting their collective futures.

Where to From Here?

The question, "Where to from here?" is both yours and mine to answer. Organizations around the world need to learn how to change faster and more effectively than ever before. The real time strategic change approach is a powerful means to that end. For some organizations, it can mean the difference between mere survival and continued viability. For others it may mean extending past successes into the future.

With this approach, you have the opportunity to transform your organization through the practice of democratic ideals. Thomas Jefferson believed the only safe repository of power resided in the people themselves. That concept holds equally true for organizations. When using the real time strategic change approach, participation becomes more than just a buzz word. Involvement becomes more than another passing fad. People have a hand in shaping their organization's future, as well as their own. Each person's voice is heard in creating a tomorrow that is better than today.

People's hearts, minds, and imaginations are set free, thereby enabling them to create organizations they want to call their own. After ten years of doing this work I still find magic and wonder in the impact it has on people's lives and on the organizations in which they work. I am amazed at the wide-ranging possibilities generated during the large group gatherings, and I am humbled by the influence an entire organization of people can have over their collective destiny. Each of us is called on to carry out deeds of greatness during our lives. However, it seems that we are seldom afforded the opportunity to do this work together. This approach makes that partnership in greatness possible. At its essence, I believe the real time strategic change approach is about rekindling the human spirit. And in the end, that is the most important work we can do. The time to begin is now. The place to start is in your own organization.

APPENDIX

In the three-day, detailed design that follows, the "Time" column contains the start time for each day of the event with the design team's best guess at how long (in minutes) each part of a module will take to complete. The "Content" column explains what is to be done during that module. The "Process" column contains specific logistics instructions ranging from when handouts need to be distributed to breakout room assignments.

Real Time Strategic Change Event

PURPOSE: To work together as leaders of this organization to:
- Build a common picture of where we are right now,
- Explore and agree on where we must be in the future if we are to be successful, and
- Make commitments to each other on what we need to do differently, individually and collectively, to get there.

AGENDA
Day 1
8:00 AM	Coffee, etc.
8:30	Welcome and Purpose
	Agenda and Logistics
	Telling Our Stories
	View from the Leadership Perspective
	Organization Diagnosis
	Lunch
	Content Expert Input
	View from the Customer's Perspective
5:00 PM	Evaluation/Close/Debrief

Day 2
8:00 AM	Coffee, etc.
8:30	Feedback on Evaluations/Agenda for the Day
	Change Possibilities Panel
	Valentines
	Organizational Norms
	Organization Strategy: Revisit
	Feedback on Strategy by Participants
5:00 PM	Evaluation/Close/Debrief
	Leadership Turnaround on Strategy

Day 3
8:00 AM	Coffee, etc.
8:30	Feedback on Evaluations/Agenda for the Day
	Response from the Leadership Group: Finalized Strategy
	Preferred Futuring
	System-Wide Action Planning
	Back Home Teamwork
	Back Home Planning
5:00 PM	Wrap-Up/Evaluation/Close

Real Time Strategic Change Event

Purpose: To work together as leaders of this organization to:
- Build a common picture of where we are right now;
- Explore and agree on where we must be in the future to be successful;
- Make commitments to each other on what we need to do differently, individually and collectively, to get there.

TIME	CONTENT	PROCESS
Day 1 8:00 am (30)	**Coffee, etc.**	Registration table set up. Participant packets on tables, including: • One-page purpose and agenda; • "Telling Our Stories" assignment; • Rules of brainstorming, roles of facilitator, recorder, and spokesperson handout; • List of design team and leadership team members; • Map of facility; • Strategic Planning Model handout; • Change Formula handout; • Organization strategy document; • Name tags with table numbers on them. Open Forum questions on table tents.

TIME	CONTENT	PROCESS
		Alphabetized max-mix seating list on the door. Open forum table grid taped to podium. Podium up front on side of risers. In boxes on tables, pencils and pads of paper at each place. Easels, markers (dark colors only), and masking tape for each table.
8:30 am (10)	**Welcome and Purpose** • Why we're having this event; • Why everyone needs to be a leader if we are to be successful; • What I hope we will accomplish during the next three days.	Leader up front. Participants seated at max-mix tables.

TIME	CONTENT	PROCESS
8:40 (15)	**Agenda and Logistics** • Briefly review history of real time strategic change technology; • Describe three-day agenda, linking it back to the purpose; • Introduce the design team; • Cover norms: -Where phones and bathrooms are; -Breaks in the morning and afternoon; -Smoking areas; -"It's your event."	Consultant up front. Refer to purpose and agenda in participant packets.

TIME	CONTENT	PROCESS
8:55 (30)	**Telling Our Stories**	Reference assignment in packets.
	(03) Introduction	
	Assignment:	
	Take two minutes to prepare to introduce yourself to the rest of your table group by answering the following questions:	
	• Who you are, your job right now, how long you have worked in the organization, and other jobs you've had in the past;	
	• What contributions you are most proud of making during the past year;	
	• What has frustrated you;	
	• What do you see as the most significant challenges and opportunities facing this organization in the coming year;	
	• Given all that, what do you need to see accomplished in the next three days to make this event worthwhile?	
	(Each person take three minutes maximum to introduce themselves.)	
	(02) Individual time to think about answers	
	(25) Group Work (8 people x 3 min./person)	Choose a facilitator to keep time.
		"Listen to see the world through each other's eyes."

TIME	CONTENT	PROCESS
9:25 (10)	*Assignment:* Take ten minutes to identify common themes and significant differences in your stories, as well as key outcomes your table group needs to achieve from the three days.	Verbal instructions; demonstrate recording format up front and reference examples hanging around the room. Choose a recorder and get an easel. Recording format:

Themes	Differences
Outcomes	

TIME	CONTENT	PROCESS
9:35 (20)	Post, Read, and Break	Name signs for leaders up front on panel table. Leaders up front to focus and prepare for the view from their perspective. Hang topic headers for Organization Diagnosis around the room.

TIME	CONTENT	PROCESS
9:55 (25)	**View from the Leadership Perspective** (05) Facilitator briefly summarizes for the total group the themes, differences, and outcomes posted during the break. Also introduces purpose of this module and the open forum process to be used Suggested Tick Points for Leaders: • The challenges and opportunities we see for the organization from our perspective; • Strengths and weaknesses we believe we have in this organization in meeting those challenges and opportunities; • Our vision for the organization's future; • Key thrusts we believe we all need to focus on to be successful. (20) Presentations	Leadership team up front. Facilitator makes arrangements to time them and contracts with them on ending times. Refer to strategy handout in packet.

TIME	CONTENT	PROCESS
10:20 (60)	Open Forum (15) Table Discussion: • What did we hear; • What were our reactions; • What questions of understanding do we have? (45) Questions and Answers	Choose a new facilitator, recorder, and question asker. Remind participants: questions of understanding only—no speeches! Logistics to help with flip charts and work the crowd with the microphones. Remember to save the last ten minutes for burning questions.
11:20 (35)	**Organization Diagnosis** (5) Introduce assignment *Assignment:* • Choose a facilitator, recorder, and reporter; • Agree on a common definition of your topic; • As you look back over the past year, brainstorm all the things you are glad, sad, and mad about in your topic area; • Record your brainstormed lists on flipchart paper as shown below, leaving three inches blank under each item for voting.	List of glad/sad/mad topics for each person, with one topic highlighted handed out on cue, along with assignment for each person. Review rules of brainstorming. One table per topic identified to report out on the voting. Voting "implements" in in-boxes.

TIME	CONTENT	PROCESS

PROCESS

Topics:
- Decision making
- Communication
- Team work
- Promotion/Hiring/Career Development
- Conflict Management
- Events
- Policies/Procedures/Implementation
- Customer Relations
- Planning
- Rewards and Recognition
- Discipline
- Training
- Employee Participation
- Affirmative Action
- Budgeting
- Safety and Security
- Grievances

Logistics: Hang sheets from tables as they finish them.

CONTENT

Topic: _____
Definition: _____

Glad	Sad	Mad

3"

3"

3"

(30) Group Work

TIME	CONTENT	PROCESS
11:55 (60)	**Lunch** Circulate, read, & vote over lunch: two gladdest glads —>two checks per topic two saddest sads —>two checks per topic two maddest mads —>two checks per topic Reporters tabulate votes on their topics and prepare report outs. (one minute reports) (Make sure you have at least one table's reporter for each topic).	Call reporters up front to give them instructions before they go to lunch. Give lunch and voting instructions to total group.
12:55 (20)	Report Outs	Logistics needs to be ready with mikes. Reports given from around the room under each header.

TIME	CONTENT	PROCESS
1:15 (25)	**Content Expert Input** (05) Introduce expert (20) Presentation: These are the key trends that I see impacting your industry over the next five to ten years: • Marketplace; • Competition; • Government/regulatory; • Labor; • Any other meaningful areas. Characteristics of the kinds of organizations that will succeed in that environment.	Design team member up front, along with expert. Remind participants that we will be using the same open forum process as we did before lunch with the leadership panel.
1:40 (55)	Open Forum (15) Table Discussion: • What did we hear; • What were our reactions; • What questions of understanding do we have?	Choose a new facilitator, recorder, and question asker. Logistics be ready to help with flip charts, if needed. Logistics be ready with mikes to work the crowd.
	(40) Questions and Answers	Save last ten minutes of Q and A for burning questions.

TIME	CONTENT	PROCESS
2:35 (15)	Break	Change name signs on podium and bring customers up front. Customers seated at panel table.
2:50 (35)	**View from the Customer's Perspective** (05) Introduce customers (30) Suggested Tick Points for Presentations: • What are the challenges and opportunities your organization is facing in the next few years; • What will you need to do differently as a result of these challenges and opportunities; • What will we, as suppliers, need to do differently to be more helpful to you? Three presentations (ten minutes each)	Leader up front.

TIME	CONTENT	PROCESS
3:25 (75)	Open Forum (15) Table Discussion: • What did you hear; • What are your reactions; • What questions for understanding do you have; • Of whom?	Choose a facilitator, recorder, and question asker.
	(60) Questions from tables	Save last ten minutes for burning questions.
4:50 (10)	**Evaluation** • How did today go for you: - Highs; - Lows; • What advice do you have for us for tomorrow?	Handed out by logistics on cue. Invite leadership and design teams to stay and read evaluations.
5:00 pm	**Close**	Logistics team stay by the exits and collect evaluations from participants as they leave.

TIME	CONTENT	PROCESS
Day 2		
7:30 am (30)	**Coffee, etc.**	Participants seated in max-mix tables. Names of Change Possibilities Panel up front on podium
8:00 am (15)	**Feedback on Evaluations/Agenda for the Day**	Consultant upfront
8:15 (45)	**Change Possibilities Panel** Presentations: • Who we are/what we do (size, products, etc.); • Why we needed to change; • What worked, what didn't; • How change impacted people in our organization; • How we are doing now and what our future looks like; • What we learned.	Need to identify who will introduce panel.

TIME	CONTENT	PROCESS
9:00 (65)	Open Forum (15) Table Discussion: • What did you hear; • What are your reactions; • What questions for understanding do you have; Of whom?	Choose a facilitator, recorder, and question asker.
	(50) Questions from tables	Save last ten minutes for burning questions.
10:05 (15)	Break	
10:20 (75)	**Valentines** (05) *Assignment:* • Describe the Valentine process and specific assignment verbally; • Choose facilitator and a recorder (to write on valentine sheets); • Remind participants to brainstorm every thing they can think of to write to each department.	List of functions and packets of Valentines delivered to in-boxes.
	(10) Functional Groups move to breakout areas.	

TIME	CONTENT	PROCESS
	(60) Groups write valentines: To: _____ *(Specific Group Name)* These are the things we need you to do differently in the future so we can better meet our customers' needs: From: _____ *(Department Group)*	Headers and blank flipchart sheets for each functional group posted around the room. Provide pieces of tape for posting Valentines.
11:35 (45)	Deliver Valentines, Circulate, Read, and Eat **Lunch**	Return to max-mix tables at 12:20 to get instructions for responding. Distribute four-step response assignment to in-boxes. Post four steps up front and in any breakout rooms on flipcharts.

TIME	CONTENT	PROCESS
12:20 (100)	**Valentines** (*continued*) (15) *Assignment:* • Read and vent; • Read again and listen; • Summarize your feedback into major themes; • Prepare a non-defensive response to these major themes. Describe "hissing" process and practice in large group.	
	(10) Each department take your Valentines to your table or breakout area and begin by choosing a facilitator, recorder, and spokesperson. Be prepared to give a one minute report to the total group on key themes you hear and your non-defensive commitments to change.	Have easels and markers in breakout rooms. Send facilitators to check on and work with large groups, as needed.
	(45) Group work	Tell participants to return from group work (or shift after group work) into max-mix tables again.
	(30) Reports from department groups (one minute each, plus some slack time)	Have mikes ready at each group's header.

TIME	CONTENT	PROCESS
2:00 (65)	**Organizational Norms** (05) • Give definition of a norm, examples. Ask table group to brainstorm norms in this organization; (15) • Tables brainstorm norms: How we have always done things around here; (10) • Put a +,-, or 0 in front of each norm to indicate whether it will help us achieve our goal, make it harder, or have no impact; (05) • Circulate among the tables and read other groups' lists of norms; (15) • Return to your table, then as a group, choose one negative norm that you feel *must* change if we are to live up to our Valentine commitments and meet our customers needs; • Identify the new (positive) norm that needs to take the place of the negative norm; • Be prepared to convince others to join you in the change you are proposing; (15) • Roomwide callout of proposed changes.	All verbal instructions. Participants get easels.

TIME	CONTENT	PROCESS
3:05 (15)	Break	Handout Feedback on Strategy assignment to in-boxes. Make sure leaders' name signs are up at panel table.
3:20 (20)	**Organization Strategy: Revisit** (05) Facilitator explains process for rest of afternoon and the work the top leadership team will be doing during the evening. (15) Leaders briefly review strategy again • Make sure you ask for feedback and say why you want it; • Make the strategy come to life. (In your own words, what will it mean for how we do business in the future?)	Leaders up front to present strategy.
3:40 (75)	**Feedback on Strategy by Participants** (45) *Assignment:* Read and discuss the draft strategy, then identify: • What are the things we agree with; • What are the things we disagree with; why; • What changes do we recommend, and what is our rationale for those changes? Record your recommended changes on a self-explanatory flip chart sheet, leaving a six-inch margin on the left side for voting.	Choose a new facilitator and recorder.

TIME	CONTENT	PROCESS
	(45) Group Work	
	(30) Post, Read and Vote	Logistics team passes out evaluations to in-boxes as participants are voting.
	Check as many recommendations as you agree with. (Only one check per recommendation.)	
4:55 (05)	**Evaluation**	Leaders and design team stay and read evaluations.
	• What were the most important things you learned today;	Logistics people at the doors to collect evaluations.
	• What still feels unfinished for you;	
	• Do you have any tips and advice for tomorrow.	
5:00 pm	Close	
5:30 (?)	**Leadership Turnaround on Strategy**	Logistics organize voting sheets for leaders while leaders, design team, and consultants read evaluations.
	Leaders decide how they want to organize themselves, given the task before them. Consultants observe, and are available if needed.	Logistics needs to be prepared for overnight typing of revised version of strategy.
		Dinner delivered to leaders and facilitators.

TIME	CONTENT	PROCESS
Day 3		
7:30 am (30)	**Coffee, etc.**	Revised strategy distributed to participants' places. Voting sheets hung behind leaders on stage. Post-its and felt-tip pens in in-boxes for preferred futuring. Headers for each part of the strategy posted around room. Sign-up sheets with assigned table numbers posted.
8:00 am (15)	**Feedback on Evaluations/Agenda for the Day**	Consultant up front.
8:15 (30)	**Response from the Leadership Group: Finalized Strategy** Leaders describe: • How we worked together to integrate your feedback with our thinking; • What we heard you say in your voting; • What we changed in the strategy; • What we didn't change and why.	Leadership team up front.
	Check with group to see if the leaders are on target. If not, move to emergent design.	Consultant or leader?

TIME	CONTENT	PROCESS
8:45 (35)	**Preferred Futuring**	
	(05) Introduce what preferred futuring is and where it came from	
	Assignment: It is two years from today.	Verbal assignment.
	• We are pleased and proud of how effectively we have achieved each part of our strategy;	
	• What do we see, feel, and hear that tells us this is true?	
	(30) Individuals or pairs write one note for each idea.	Logistics and consultants circulate, pick-up Post-its, sort them and post them under appropriate headers.
9:20 (25)	(05) Give instructions for sign-up procedure, breakout locations, and assignment for system-wide action planning.	Deliver System-Wide Action Planning assignment on cue.
	(20) Break (and sign-up for system-wide action planning groups).	Return from break in system-wide action planning groups and begin working.

TIME	CONTENT	PROCESS
9:45 (120)	**System-Wide Action Planning** *Assignment:* Select a facilitator and recorder: • Read, sort, and analyze the input you have received from the total group; • Write a preferred future statement based on your own beliefs and the "Post-it" themes; • Focus on the preferred future you just developed: — What are all of the things happening right now in the organization that will help you move toward your preferred future; — What are all of the things happening right now that will make it more difficult to achieve your preferred future; • Now, brainstorm a list of ideas you have about what actions we could take in the next six months to really accelerate our progress on this part of our strategy;	

TIME	CONTENT	PROCESS

- As a group, agree on the two or three most important actions to recommend to the total group;
- Create a flip chart showing your preferred future and recommended actions, who should do it and when for the total group to read and vote on. Leave a six-inch margin on the left side of your actions for the voting.

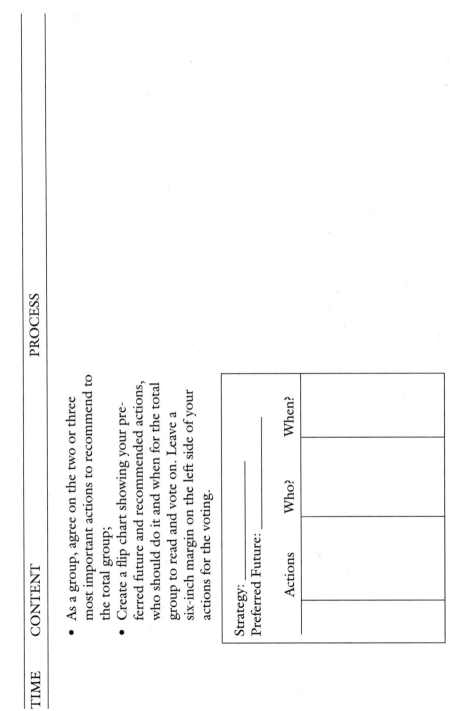

Strategy: _____
Preferred Future: _____

Actions	Who?	When?

TIME	CONTENT	PROCESS
	Remind participants that they need to post their recommendations in the main room under the appropriate header and be seated in their original max-mix table by 11:45.	
11:45 (60)	Circulate, Read, Vote, and Eat **Lunch.**	Give voting instructions. Hand out stars and dots on cue.
		Recruit reporters for each part of the strategy and coach them on how to tally votes.
		Distribute Back Home Planning assignment and break-out locations to in-boxes.
		Return to back home group seating after lunch—refer to seating list posted on door and in participant packets.
12:45 (20)	Report on Voting by area of strategy.	Logistics ready with mikes around the room to get reports.

TIME	CONTENT	PROCESS
1:05 (40)	**Back Home Teamwork** (05) Introduce assignment • Take a few minutes to yourself and think about what you have learned about good teamwork during the past three days from your max-mix and system-wide action planning groups. • Now, reflect on how your back home group has worked together in the past, and identify one thing you would like to change about how you work together in the future. (05) Individual time to think about answers. (30) Group Work (sharing experiences and making commitments).	Verbal instructions

TIME	CONTENT	PROCESS
1:45 (80)	**Back Home Planning** (05) Introduce assignment	Consultant up front.
		Refer to handout in in-box.
	• Choose a facilitator, recorder, and reporter;	
	• Discuss what you have heard during the past three days that particularly affects your work group;	
	• Agree on what you will do differently in the future to contribute to success of your new strategic direction;	
	• Plan for how you will bring your co-workers who were not able to attend this event on board when you get back to work.	
	(75) Group Work	
3:05 (15)	Break	
3:20 (40)	Back Home Group Report Outs (2 min. each x 20 groups)	Logistics ready with mikes and to collect reports as they are completed.

TIME	CONTENT	PROCESS
4:00 (10)	**Wrap-Up** • Progress I have seen us make in this event; • The work we still have to do; • Thank the logistics and design teams.	Leader up front.
4:10 (15)	**Evaluation** • What were the most significant outcomes of these three days for you; • On a scale of one to ten, how confident are you that we will carry out our commitments to each other: 1——2——3——4——5——6——7——8——9——10 Not a Snowball's Chance. . . Watch Our Dust! • Why did you mark it where you did?	Evaluations handed out on cue. Leadership and design teams invited to stay and read evaluations.
5:00 pm	**Close**	Extra time built in as a cushion in case groups need more time to work.

REFERENCES

Ackoff, R. L. "The Corporate Rain Dance." In *The Wharton Magazine*, pp. 36-41, p. 38. Philadelphia: The Wharton School, 1977.

Argyris, C. "Double Loop Learning in Organizations." *Harvard Business Review*, pp. 115-125. Boston: President and Fellows of Harvard College, 1977.

Beckhard, R. and Harris, R. *Organizational Transitions*. Reading, MA: Addison-Wesley, 1987.

Bridges, W. "Managing Organizational Transitions." In *Organization Dynamics*, pp. 24-33. New York: American Management Association.

Burns, J.M. *Leadership*. New York: Harper & Row, 1978.

Carlzon, J. *Moments of Truth*. New York: Harper & Row, 1987.

Dannemiller, K. D. "Team Building at a Macro Level, or 'Ben Gay' for Arthritic Organizations." In *Team Building: Blueprints for Productivity and Satisfaction*, edited by W. B. Reddy with K. Jamison, Alexandria, VA: NTL Institute for Applied Behavioral Sciences, 1988.

Davis, S. M. *Future Perfect*. Reading, MA: Addison-Wesley, 1987.

Drucker, P. F. *Management: Tasks, Responsibilities, Practices*, New York: Harper & Row, 1974.

Jusela, G.E. "Meeting the Global Competitive Challenge: Building Systems that Learn on a Large Scale." In *Goodwill Games Citizen Initiatives Conference Proceedings*, Seattle, WA: Goodwill Games Citizen Initiatives Conference on Planned Change, 1990.

Lippitt, R. "Future Before You Plan." In *The NTL Managers' Handbook*, edited by R. A. Ritvo and A. G. Sargent, p. 7, Arlington, VA: NTL Institute, 1983.

Marrow, A. J. *The Practical Theorist*. New York: Basic Books, 1969.

Peck, M. S. *The Different Drum: Community Making and Peace*, p. 17. New York: Simon & Schuster, 1987.

Taylor, F. W. *The Principles of Scientific Management*. New York: Harper & Row, 1915.

Waterman, R. H., Jr., p. 90. *The Renewal Factor*. New York: Bantam, 1987.

Weber, M. *The Theory of Social and Economic Organization* (translated by A.M. Henderson and T. Parsons). T. Parsons (ed.), New York: Free Press, 1947.

INDEX

Robert W. Jacobs is a senior consultant and partner in Dannemiller Tyson Associates, a consulting firm with extensive experience in working with organizations around the world to bring about rapid, significant, and lasting change.

His life and work have been fueled by a natural curiosity about how organizations and the people in them can change most effectively. He also has a penchant for innovation and a deeply held desire to make a positive contribution to the world. His consulting practice creates a focal point where these three paths merge into one. This book represents a major milestone on his personal journey into each and all of these arenas.

He has consulted to a wide variety of Fortune 500 companies, educational institutions, government, and non-profit agencies and communities. He has collaborated with CEOs, front-line workers, and everybody in between.

Jacobs's publications include several articles describing real time strategic change and its conceptual underpinnings, and detailed case studies of its application. He has also made numerous presentations at professional conferences and other gatherings on accelerated whole-system change.

He and his wife, Cheryl, live in Chelsea, Michigan with their daughter, Alison; son, Aaron; and four-legged writing companions, Sandy and Madison.